THE NEW MODERN TIMES

FACTORS RESHAPING
THE WORLD OF WORK

Edited by
David B. Bills

STATE UNIVERSITY OF NEW YORK PRESS

Published by
State University of New York Press, Albany

For information, address State University of New York
Press, State University Plaza, Albany, N.Y., 12246

Production by Diane Ganeles
Marketing by Dana Yanulavich

Library of Congress Cataloging-in-Publication Data

The new modern times: factors reshaping the world of work / edited by
    David B. Bills.
        p.   cm.
    Includes bibliographical references and index.
    ISBN 0-7914-2227-5. — ISBN 0-7914-2228-3 (pbk.)
    1. Work—Social aspects—United States. 2. Industrial sociology-
-United States. 3. Technological innovations—United States.
4. Labor supply—United States. 5. Social change—United States.
HD6957.U6N48 1995
306.3′6′0973—dc20   94-1044
                                                                CIP

10 9 8 7 6 5 4 3 2 1

This book is dedicated to my parents,
Everett and Phyllis Bills,
who know more about the world of work
than I ever will.

Contents

Acknowledgments

The origins of this volume go back farther than I care to remember. I am very grateful to the people who hung in there with me to finally get it out the door. Many of them showed more patience than I might have had the roles been reversed. Many of them also missed deadlines of their own, but I have always appreciated the good cheer and collegiality of everyone who has had a hand in this volume.

The Center for Advanced Studies at the University of Iowa, under the capable and protective leadership of Jay Semel, allowed me time away from various academic tasks to work on this volume. My colleagues in the Division of Planning, Policy, and Leadership Studies—Bill Duffy, Chet Rzonca, Ray Muston, and Brad Sagen— have participated with me in an ongoing discussion of how the workplace is changing. I also want to acknowledge Ginny Lambert's help in shaping my thinking about the world of work. Thanks to everyone.

Adam Smith and Emile Durkheim taught us much about the division of labor. I've learned that part of this means having graduate students who are good at things at which I am not. Two of my students, Anne Zalenski and Mary Ellen Wacker, have a lot of skills that I lack, and I am grateful for their contributions to this book.

My editor at the State University of New York Press, Clay Morgan, has shown an unusual appreciation for the special difficulties of organizing an edited volume. I thank Robert Asher for putting me in touch with him.

All the thanks and love I can offer to my wife Valerie for her support of both this particular effort and every other aspect of my working and non-working life. A theme of this volume is how we reconcile our time at work and away from work. She makes it easy for me.

Introduction

David B. Bills

Any serious history or sociology of work in the United States must show that prevailing forms of work and employment have never remained static for long. Our transition from agriculture to manufacturing to services, our opening of the labor force to include women and our closing of it to exclude children, the waxing and waning of collective efforts to change the terms and rewards of work, and the continuing implementation of technology in all areas of work are well known and comprehensively documented. An understanding of work demands an analysis of work and social change.

Still, there is a broadly sensed if perhaps poorly conceived understanding that the world of work is now changing in too rapid a fashion to be accommodated by the "normal" functioning of social institutions. The pace of this change over the past decade is difficult to deny. Plunkert (1990, 3) has pointed out that the "1980s began with two recessions in three years and then posted the longest peacetime expansion on record." Ritzer (1989, 244), characterizing the current situation as a "permanently new economy," has observed that "economic change is accelerating at such a dizzying pace."

Both the popular media and scholarly discourse dwell upon a range of institutional transformations, technological developments, and demographic changes believed to be profoundly altering the ways we do business and make a living. The tone of this societal conversation varies, ranging from the rapid-fire optimism of

1

Naisbitt's *Megatrends* (1984) to the sober warnings of Wassily Leontief (1982) or Harley Shaiken (1984). There is dissent about how the world of work is changing, and even some doubt that the changes are as consequential as is typically supposed (Levitan 1984). Still, many observers would share the judgment of historian Stephen Meyer (elaborated upon in his contribution to this volume) that we may be crossing some sort of an historical threshold in the workplace, or as Piore and Sabel (1984) would have it, a second industrial divide.

The three themes noted above—institutions, technology, and demographics—to varying degrees inform each of the essays in this volume. The authors are concerned with analyzing how these factors are changing the nature and pace of work, and how they are in turn being transformed by emerging work arrangements. The essays address changes in such institutions as labor unions, communities, and families. Some are interested in both the specific characteristics of newly developing technologies and the problematic nature of their implementation. Others recognize the simple yet fundamental importance of numbers of people, and how the flow of people can affect work relationships. The important point is that these authors understand work and employment as embedded in a larger structural and institutional setting. Their writings direct our attention towards not only the realignments in institutions, technology, and demographics but towards their persistence as well.

These essays do not begin with the assumption that work is undergoing cataclysmic change, as many popular prophets of the workplace would have it. Rather, each is based on an assessment of the best available evidence, as informed by the concepts and theories of the author's discipline. While many of the contributors do attempt some speculation (and all offer considerable interpretation), the volume is designed to be based on empirical data and a sound research footing.

There is a certain hubris in trying to document changes in "the" world of work. There were, after all, some 120 million gainfully employed Americans at the end of 1990, organized in a complex division of labor beyond what even Adam Smith might have envisioned. As Licht (1988, 20) has observed:

A survey of the workplace in the 20th century should begin with a discussion of its diversity. Americans work in a variety of settings from the home to mills and stores. Large-scale worksites, such as the multistoried office building, the hospital complex, and the sprawling plant, dominate the landscape, but small to medium size enterprises persist and proliferate, finding niches in our protean and layered market, receiving small-batch orders on contract from larger core sector firms. An array of services and products are produced in these various environments.

While one volume cannot capture this full diversity, it can help to bring some perspective to it. This volume is organized into three parts. The first part offers some historical perspective on the changing world of work. A theme drawing these chapters together is the causes and consequences of changing demands for worker skills and the attendant processes of "skill disruption"—deskilling, upgrading, and reskilling. Historian Stephen Meyer reviews the history of industrialization and the impact of technological change in a number of American industries. Meyer's chapter is important both for the conclusions it draws on the social consequences of technological and industrial innovation and for its detailed attention to research that still needs to be conducted in this area.

Robert Asher brings even more historical specificity to the debate through a careful appraisal of how technological change has affected the working lives of an assortment of Connecticut workers. Asher argues strenuously against the idea that technological evolution is inexorable. He emphasizes that it can be resisted as easily as embraced, and that its implementation is at bottom a social decision.

Kenneth Spenner brings a sociological perspective to this set of questions. He painstakingly and critically sifts through three decades of evidence on skill change. Spenner concludes that "the dominant feature of aggregate study evidence is uncertainty." To recognize uncertainty and contingency, though, is not to say that we know little, as Spenner elucidates the influence of managerial discretion, markets, and organizational culture on technological change and skill requirements.

A final essay in this part by Chet Rzonca, Douglas Gustafson, and Sandra Boutelle, concentrates on the role of vocational education in the acquisition and utilization of skills. Adopting more of a "problem-solving" than "science-building" approach, the authors carefully explain the history and purpose of vocational education, and provide a valuable overview of several contemporary initiatives. Their chapter is a welcome response to often poorly conceived attacks on vocational education.

The second part of the volume turns to contemporary transformations in the world of work. The chapters by Teixeira and

Mishel and DiTomaso and Friedman provide forceful critiques of the influential *Workforce 2000* report (Johnston and Packer 1987). Teixeira and Mishel offer a skeptical appraisal of the ongoing debate on the alleged skill crisis in the American economy. While recognizing the needs for policies that enhance worker skills, they conclude that the real shortage is one of managerial skills. They note that efforts to reorganize the workplace—the demand side—are more important than supply side measures as a means to facilitate competitiveness.

DiTomaso and Friedman offer a sustained assault on the quality of data analysis and interpretation presented by the authors of *Workforce 2000*. They maintain that the report makes fundamental errors in its labor force projections, presents these projections in a misleading way, and as a result provides a poor guide for policy decisions.

Donald Mayall addresses a particular instance of the changing nature of the social contract between labor and management, the use of temporary employees. Mayall details the use of "temps" in a number of industries, paying particular attention to the rationale for their use and the motivations of employees who seek such employment. While perhaps less troubled by the growing use of temps than some observers, Mayall does recognize the potentially disruptive effects of a workforce with a weakened attachment to the workplace.

A wide-ranging essay by Sue Rosser looks at the emerging role of women and people of color in American science and technology. After drawing attention to the changing workplace demographics of American society, Rosser looks in some depth at the implications of these trends for science and technology education. She argues that the very practice of science might change (for the better) as American institutions open up to new members.

Two final essays help chart the way for future theory and research on the emerging world of work. Randy Hodson brings the worker back into the debate on transformations in corporate and industrial structure. Arguing that researchers have for too long treated working people as "passive objects of structural constraints," Hodson brings together an enormously diverse literature in an attempt to reinvigorate our understanding of the workplace.

Arne Kalleberg and Richard Rockwell discuss the possibilities of resolving many questions previously largely unresearchable because of data deficiencies through the design and development of innovative new data bases. They outline an ambitious but reasonable program of research that would permit the assessment of questions that up to now have eluded us.

The trends analyzed in this volume go to the heart of contemporary American society, and how we understand and respond to them will largely determine the kinds of work lives we will lead in the future. For all practical purposes, all of us at some point hold or hope to hold jobs, or we depend on someone who does. While the issues raised and the concerns expressed in this volume are in large part questions of values and priorities, they are also trends that are amenable to rigorous empirical examination. Serious debate of these matters must rely upon carefully planned and executed research programs. The authors in this volume all combine skilled "fact finding" with a willingness to explain and interpret these facts.

WHAT TRENDS ARE CHANGING THE SHAPE OF WORK AND EMPLOYMENT?

Before turning to these essays, it will be useful to elaborate on some of the factors that are transforming the nature of work and employment. I will construe "the nature of work and employment" quite broadly, without claiming to be comprehensive. Seven broad sets of factors seem to be of considerable explanatory power in understanding the transformation of work.[1] These are the enduring impacts of the 1980s recession and the Reaganomic response; the ongoing trend towards a service society; demographic changes; the internationalization of the economy; the new regionalism; emerging, primarily computer-based, technology; and a redefinition of the postwar labor-management relationship. Clearly, these distinctions are analytical only; empirically, these factors interact in any number of ways that require continued sorting out by analysts of the workplace.

THE 1980s' RECESSIONS AND THE REAGANOMIC RESPONSE: PERMANENT LOSSES OR TEMPORARY ECONOMIC ADJUSTMENTS?

For many Americans, the late 1970s and early 1980s was the bitterest economic period since the Great Depression. While glibly drawn parallels with the 1930s are of little value, a reading of the sociological and historical literature of the Depression years suggests that many of the factors operating then do have parallels in the last great recession (McElvaine 1984). If the scope of the change was less in the early eighties than in the thirties, the nature of the effects of economic dislocation on communities, families, and regions was often similar.

The recession of the early eighties hit the poor harder than the affluent (Levy 1988). Despite often sympathetic concern in the business literature about corporate efforts to trim managerial "fat" by the wholesale elimination of middle management positions, the fact remains that groups toward the bottom of the income distribution were more susceptible to unemployment and wage cuts than were those more well-off. Research on the disruptive effects of plant shutdowns, newly obsolete job skills, and efforts to retrain displaced workers became a minor industry in the eighties (Kohlberg 1983; Bluestone and Harrison 1982; Summers 1984). Unquestionably much of this dialogue has an ideological tinge, yet the enormous effects of the economic slump of the early eighties on patterns of employment cannot be denied.

Neither can the effects of changes in social policy be denied. Working people in the early eighties were subject not only to lower wages and more frequent layoffs than at any time in the post-war era, but cuts in transfer payments (principally unemployment compensation) reversed several provisions of the social contract that had emerged since The New Deal. In fact, the proportion of unemployed workers receiving benefits was lower in 1985 than at any time since the beginning of the program in 1935. Similarly, the ability or willingness of states to alleviate poverty with income transfers varied widely in the eighties (Plotnick 1989).

Analysts of various persuasions seem to agree that, at least in the short run, Reaganomic social policy, like Reaganomic economic policy, had a negative effect on the poor while aiding the more affluent, with more modest effects on middle-income groups (Levy and Michel 1983; Congressional Budget Office 1984). The effects of the recession and social welfare and economic development policies seem more enduring as increasingly unmanageable budget deficits on the federal level and ever-tighter resources at state and local levels characterize the post-Reagan years. Harrington (1984) contends that the recovery of the late eighties will in the long run exacerbate class polarization, widening the gap between the haves and have-nots. Harrington's position is that the recovery was based on disciplining labor to accept lower wages, which will in turn dampen consumer demand and choke off the prospects for a more lasting prosperity. As Herz (1990) reminds us, job displacement continues to occur even during periods of recovery. Similarly, several analysts maintain that both federal and local development policies of the eighties were fundamentally inegalitarian (see the papers in Sawers and Tabbs 1984). Others, however, argue that such policies represent little more than a temporary "belt tightening" that will lay the foundation for real economic growth. This will, in turn, contribute to an improved standard of living for all Americans. McKenzie (1988) provides a particularly pointed critique of both direct and indirect efforts by government to interfere with the flexibility of open labor markets, objecting to a set of policies that "relies more on centralized federal controls and less on decentralized market incentives for determining how and where jobs are destroyed, how and where jobs are created" (1988, 17). McKenzie holds that government policies toward labor tend to be disguised restrictions on the mobility of both labor and capital in that "the firm would become the social agent of the state, supplanting many government-run welfare offices" (1988, 17). He believes that American competitiveness is contingent on letting the market run its course.

THE SERVICE SOCIETY: TOWARDS TWO AMERICAS?

Probably the most important ongoing structural change in the American economy is the movement towards a service society and the corresponding relative declines in manufacturing. More people are now employed in service occupations and industries, however defined, than in any other sector of the economy. This trend has been taking place for decades. Some ninety percent of the new jobs added to the economy in the 1970s were in the service and trade sectors, nearly half in just four industries (health, business services, finance, and eating and drinking places). This continued through the eighties, which "witnessed the shifting of another six percent of employment from the goods-producing to the service-producing sector" (Plunkert 1990, 3).

We need to ask, though, both what these new jobs are like and what has happened to existing jobs. As Rosenthal (1989) points out, what makes a job "good" may not be self-evident, but it does involve more than wages.[2] There has been a great deal of debate on the sorts of jobs the "American Job Machine" (McKenzie 1988) has been creating (Loveman and Tilly 1988).

The trend towards a service society is important both because of its effects on the nature of jobs and because of its effects on the distribution of rewards. The first trend speaks to what has become a perennial sociological question—whether we are moving towards Bell's knowledge-based and meritocratic Post-Industrial Society of increasingly autonomous and skilled workers (Bell 1973) or towards Marx's vision of a proletarianized and de-skilled society, best described by Braverman's *Labor and Monopoly Capital* (1974; see also Wood 1982). The former vision at least suggests the possibility that work for many of us might be a liberating experience; the latter holds that, barring substantial changes in property and production relations, a future of dehumanizing and alienating work is more likely. Both images may be overdrawn, yet each suggests a not altogether implausible future.

Determining how the nature of jobs is changing is a matter for empirical investigation. Still, there is a growing sense that much of the conceptual apparatus used to think about these trends has become deficient in important ways. Ritzer (1989, 245), in reaction to the Post-Industrial Society model, calls for a new perspective that "is more general, more forgiving, allows for a much wider set of both differences and continuities with previous economic circumstances, and recognizes the continuing nature of economic change rather than a static new economic reality." Abbott (1989) challenges as outmoded the way that sociologists think about occupations and the division of labor, while Reich (1991) maintains that the distinction between service and manufacturing industries is no longer useful.

Changes in the nature and pace of work will be one set of consequences of the continual development of the service society. Another will be the distribution of rewards. Forecasts of the coming effects of industrial transformation on the distribution of income have reached no consensus, and analysts are not even in accord on what the trends have been. Out of these analyses has emerged a debate raising the possibility of the United States becoming an increasingly unequal, even "two-tier," society.

The debate on trends in the American income distribution has been a curious one. Many of the most forceful opening vollies were fired by journalists (Steinberg 1983; Kuttner 1983, 1984; Samuelson 1983), setting off a burgeoning but often confusing literature. Only recently has a clearer picture of trends in American income inequality begun to emerge. Much of the problem has been that analysts have often failed to distinguish between several analytically distinct issues. For instance, changes in the tails of the income distribution (i.e., proliferations or disappearances of especially low-paying or high-paying jobs) need bear little relationship to trends in the middle (the allegedly declining middle-class). Similarly, choices between a wide array of seemingly straightforward considerations (for example, whether to sample individuals or households, whether to examine wage and salary or total income, what baseline years to use) are more than technical decisions. They are rather contentious conceptual decisions that can profoundly affect the interpretation of trends in inequality (Horrigan and Haugen 1988, 4).

What does seem clear is that American incomes are less equal than they once were, although the nature of these shifts is complex. Horrigan and Haugen (1988, 9), for instance, present evidence that the middle-class has declined in number, but note that "most of the decline in the families in the middle has gone to the upper-class, not the lower." Littman (1989, 17), however, has shown that even if there are proportionately fewer poor families now, they "are no better off in the 1980s than they were in the 1960s and 1970s." Still others maintain that, "these findings appear to justify fears about 'deindustrialization': The employment shifts from manufacturing to services have made the distribution of earnings in this country more unequal, particularly between 1960 and 1970. However, a more pervasive finding is that inequality has increased within almost all sectors, especially in those with well-trained or highly educated workers" (Grubb and Wilson 1989, 9).[3]

Levy (1988) offers the most comprehensive analysis of trends in the American income distribution. He makes the important point that while growing American income inequality has been real and significant, the more important story has been the relative stagnation of incomes over the past two decades. Equally important, Levy shows that the causes of these trends are complex, including at the least changes in the industrial structure of the economy, geographic differences in income, labor force composition and occupations, and family and household structure and the welfare state (1988, 9). His analysis is a useful demonstration that unicausal accounts of distributional trends are of little value (see also Blackburn 1990).

DEMOGRAPHIC CHANGES:
POPULATION PRESSURES AND PROSPECTS

Basic demographic processes have much to do with shifting patterns of employment, wages, and labor force participation. Unfortunately, isolating demographic effects from those of other social forces is extremely difficult. Probably all participants in the debate over work and employment would concede that the demographics do matter, while disagreeing on the magnitude of such effects. To return to the example of the apparent polarization of incomes, strikingly divergent positions have been presented on one side by Thurow (1984) ("the baby boom theory does not explain what needs to be explained"), and on the other by Linden (1984) ("The reason for this [crowding into lower income brackets] is to be found largely in demographic and social change").

A crucial demographic trend has been the baby boom of 1946-1964 and the subsequent baby bust. By profoundly altering the American age structure for the past four decades and for the foreseeable future as well, this boom and bust phenomenon continues to transform the world of work through a pattern of labor shortages and surpluses (Flaim 1990). Largely as a simple result of the numbers, the youth unemployment problem of a few years ago already has started to give way to the "promotion squeeze" of the nineties (Patton 1981).

Trends in unemployment and wage rates are in part outcomes of demographic processes (Flaim 1990; Easterlin 1987; Smith and Welsh 1981). We are increasingly coming to realize the enduring effects on people's working lives of the size and composition of the birth cohort to which they belong. From an economic standpoint, as Smith and Welsh (1981) have observed, the 1970s were very simply "no time to be young."

Baby boomers are now aging, and presumably beginning to move beyond the relatively low-wage jobs typically held by young workers. It is possible that the aging of baby boomers and their anticipated movement into better positions will reduce unemployment rates and, conceivably, income inequality. Beyond this, though, we have little indication of what to expect from what is probably a permanently aging workforce (Cooperman 1983; Herz and Rones 1989). In the long run, we can anticipate a strain on the Social Security system and private retirement and pension systems (and eventually cemeteries) as baby boomers begin retiring in the not too distant future. In the short run, the issue might become the balance between the presumably enhanced work skills and human capital of experienced baby boom workers and the possible loss of innovativeness that young cohorts (now much smaller) typically bring with them to the workplace.

As important as the baby boom is the rapid and ongoing movement of women into the labor force. The specific features of this trend are well known, and need not be recounted here (Hartmann et al. 1986). It is enough to point out that it is now the norm for women to be employed. Plunkert (1990, 3) notes that in the eighties, "women's participation in the labor force increased from 51 to 57 percent." Not only has women's participation in the labor force grown, but so has their attachment to it, as Shank (1988, 3) observes that, "women today work more hours per week and more weeks per year than they did 10 or 20 years ago." Such trends may slow, but they will surely persist. Levitan (1984) believes that three of every five new entrants into the labor market over the next decade will be women.

This increased participation has not led to equality. The ratio of women's to men's wages for full-time, year-round work has increased modestly at best (Hartmann et al. 1986), despite some recent signs of improvement (Horrigan and Markey 1990). A high proportion of the new jobs held by women are characterized by low wages and lack of opportunity (belonging to the economists' "secondary labor market"). Gender-based wage inequality persists even within apparently homogeneous job categories (Bielby and Baron 1986), and there is little evidence that jobs have become appreciably less sex-typed.

To many, once-accepted accounts by economists of the gender gap in earnings have become increasingly unpersuasive. Likewise, arguments that adduce "culture" or "attitudes" as explanations seem to have lost force. Current scholarship is demonstrating that the processes underlying gender-based inequalities are constantly being disrupted and recreated. Reskin and Roos and their colleagues (1990) have presented a number of case studies describing how changes in social and economic arrangements (for example, the transformed work of insurance adjustors) can influence gender inequality.

The racial and ethnic composition of the labor force is also changing. Hispanics, for instance, accounted for nearly a fifth of the labor force growth between 1980 and 1987 (Cattan 1988), while Blacks and Asian-Americans also contributed disproportionately to the supply of new workers. Again, though, we have not approached equality. The earnings of college-educated black men continue to lag behind those of comparably educated whites (although this is less true for women [Meisenheimer 1990]), and patterns of hiring discrimination and underemployment persist.

Another vital demographic trend affecting patterns of work and employment is immigration. There is little reason to expect the flow of immigrants to the United States to ebb any time soon. Whatever the overall stringency of American labor markets, unskilled entry-level workers are likely to become scarcer as baby bust cohorts continue to enter the labor market. Further, the economic prospects of the nations from which we receive most migrants show little promise of being able to absorb their own unskilled workers. Even in the unlikely (and perhaps undesirable) event of forceful legislation, immigration to the U.S. (for political as well as economic reasons) is going to grow.

Meyer's contribution to this volume is a useful reminder of another period in American history (roughly 1910-1920) characterized by public concern over the effect of immigration on labor markets. Employers have always sought low-wage, unskilled workers, even while remaining suspicious of their cultural differences. The question posed by Meyer about that period remains relevant to this one: "Did the fact of unskilled immigrant labor force the adoption of mechanized industrial processes or did the existence of unskilled jobs facilitate the migration of large numbers of people to the United States?"

Most of all, perhaps, we need to be reminded that demography is not destiny and that projections of the economic future are risky. This simple fact is often misunderstood. Two of the essays in this volume, by DiTomaso and Friedman and Teixeira and Mishel, provide critical appraisals of the influential *Workforce 2000* report (Johnston and Packer 1987), probably the most frequently cited recent policy statement on the future of work in America. Both sets of authors advise considerable caution towards the more extravagant claims of *Workforce 2000*, and both suggest a greater tolerance for ambiguity in any pronouncements about the unfolding of work and employment in the United States.

THE INTERNATIONALIZATION OF THE ECONOMY:
THE EMERGING AMERICAN ROLE

A recurrent theme in both scholarly writings and the popular press over the past few years is that the United States is more and more simply a player rather than the unchallenged leader in an increasingly interconnected world economy. To some extent this is true—even before the advent of OPEC and its effect on world oil prices many American markets had begun to erode and there has been a substantial redistribution of economic power around the globe (Kennedy 1987; Thurow 1992). Still, much of the contemporary debate lacks an historical focus. A world economy has existed for centuries, and Chandler's *The Visible Hand* (1977) has documented the early entry of many American firms into overseas markets. While recent developments (primarily increasingly sophisticated telecommunications and the more rapid flow of capital across borders) have certainly heightened our sense of being enmeshed in a global system, this is not something that crept up on us overnight.

Analysts are divided about the effects on American work and employment of the increasing internationalization of the economy. One crucial issue is the exportation of American jobs overseas. Clearly, many industries have lost jobs. This is particularly true of micro-electronics and textiles, where American wage scales are uncompetitive in world markets. Still, it is unclear if the loss of these low-paying jobs represents a net loss of employment for the United States or rather a shift into more productive industries. Samuelson (1983) believes that "Foreign trade has generally aided employment in well-paid industries, such as computers, and hurt employment in poorly paid industries, such as clothing." Lawrence (1983) basically concurs, arguing that world trade benefitted U.S. employment in the 1970s but negatively affected it in the 1980s. More recently, Singleton (1990) shows that much of the 1987-88 rebound in manufacturing employment was based in export-related industries, while Warf (1990) describes the job creation possibilities of foreign investment in the United States. Still others (e.g., Bluestone and Harrison 1982) point to substantial job loss in U.S. communities brought about by managerial decisions to export production. The collapse of many foreign markets and the deterioration of many foreign economies have had similar effects.

Much of the evidence brought to bear on this discussion follows political lines. Liberal analysts point to worker dislocations, numerous and disruptive plant closings, and permanently high unemployment rates. More conservative observers highlight temporary readjustments in the labor market that can be addressed through appropriate retraining and relocation assistance. Most, however, will agree with Zysman and Tyson (1983, 51) that "The real political challenge to the formulation of effective industrial policy is reconciling the demands of those dislocated by international trade with the necessity of continued industrial development."

What seems clear is that we need to move toward new models of the role of the United States in the world economy. A provocative analysis by Reich (1990) claims that the importance of corporate ownership and control has given way to workforce skills as the key to international competitiveness. At the least, we need to recast our concepts away from a preoccupation with nations and towards more global aggregations.

THE NEW REGIONALISM: THE NEW CORPORATE LANDSCAPE[4]

Shifts in the occupational structures of broad regions of the United States, even in the relatively condensed period between 1970 and 1990, have been substantial. Wheeler (1990, 435) summarizes these well:

> the dominance of the service sector in the creation of new jobs, especially in the suburbs; the importance of large metropolitan areas with well-developed localization economies in job creation in the services; the significance of Sunbelt metropolises in service employment growth; and the key role of small firms in job creation.

Hansen (1979, 11) characterizes the 1970s as a period in which, "manufacturing activity has been shifting from the Northeast and North Central regions of the country to the South and West." In general, Sunbelt occupational structures were upgraded in the 1970s, while Snowbelt occupational structures were not. These trends continued throughout the 1980s, with California assuming an increasingly important role in corporate growth (Wheeler 1990), albeit a role that has even more recently experienced difficulties. As Doeringer et al. (1987, 8) have observed, "industries in specific states and localities often prosper or decline in ways that deviate significantly from the corresponding national trends."

Simple "Sunbelt/Snowbelt" models, however, are no longer adequate (if they ever were) to describe these shifts. The United States is very simply an unevenly developed economy. While it is not certain whether migration leads to economic development or whether economic development leads to migration (Doeringer et al. 1987), the importance of these regional shifts should not be downplayed. Indeed, there remain throughout the United States not only markedly different patterns of work and employment, but surprisingly large variations in even basic demographic character (Morrill 1990). Hansen (1979) points out that the Sunbelt should not be viewed simplistically, and that while "the South recently made significant strides in human resource development . . . the region ranks worst in terms of any objective measure of health, poverty and education." The Northeast, despite its economic losses of the early eighties, remains the economic center of the nation, and there are signs that both it and the Middle Atlantic states have checked and possibly even reversed the flight of capital and population to warmer climates. Midwestern agricultural and industrial states have not done so. The slump of the domestic energy industry has also stalled the growth of such eighties boom towns as Houston.

As important as large-scale regional shifts are shifts from some kinds of cities and towns to others. The dominant trend in the seventies, of course, was from large metropolitan areas to small cities and rural areas, a process that has had severe consequences for many central cities (Kasarda 1983).

Regional shifts of employers and economic activities within the United States contribute to new patterns of work and employment. As attractive and well-paying jobs moved South and West, growing numbers of unskilled (or those with newly obsolete skills) and marginalized workers were either left behind or made typically futile efforts to pursue jobs in regions that are now themselves economically distressed.

There is evidence that economic inequality between states and regions grew in the 1980s, as measured by both the distribution of incomes (Amos 1988, 1989) and unemployment rates (Devens 1988). Further, Connaughton and Madsen (1986) demonstrate a very uneven economic recovery across states in the late eighties, as the states hardest hit by the recession typically had the weakest recoveries. All of this is in some contrast to the apparent convergence between states in the sixties and seventies. Grubb and Wilson (1989, 8) report a "declining significance of region in the distribution of wage and salary income" between 1960 and 1980, but their conclusion that "regional patterns can be ignored in the analysis of national inequality" is probably premature.

In their contribution to this volume, Rzonca, Gustafson, and Boutelle show differences in how states have responded to transformed economic conditions through the use of what may become an increasingly important policy option—the provision of vocational education. The authors provide a much-needed discussion of the historical and social context of vocational education, highlighting the multiple roles these programs can play in economic revitalization. Their analysis reminds us of the humanistic aspect of educational reform efforts, and emphasizes that attention to only the technical side of skill provision is inadequate to the demands of the emerging economy.

Locational transformations will continue during the nineties, as will regional redistributions of wealth, capital, and jobs. A survey conducted by the Interstate Conference of Employment Security Agencies (reported in the September 1990 *Monthly Labor Review*) projects substantial differences between states and regions in the availability of both young and experienced workers, economic growth rates, and sectoral change.

The continued industrial transformation—or collapse—of many urban areas is attracting renewed concern. While some cities have begun to rebuild their central business districts that only a few years ago some wrote off as hopeless (St. Louis and Cincinnati being good examples), conditions in many central cities have continued to deteriorate. Without question, such trends have disproportionately affected minorities, and observers such as Wilson (1987) have documented an increased polarization within the black population. That is, the growth of a black middle-class, no longer located in predominantly black neighborhoods, has coincided with an increasingly entrenched unskilled and, according to some, unemployable, underclass (Auletta 1983; Lemann 1986).

Regional reallocations of resources are important, and entail pain for both regions losing dollars and people and for those on the receiving end. At the same time, they are nothing new. Recall Schumpeter's classic portrayal of capitalism as "creative destruction." The policy concern, made apparent as early as the Carter Administration, is whether we want to direct our attention to places or to people. We face choices between redeveloping declining regions, perhaps at the cost of industrial efficiency, or finding ways to facilitate the movement of displaced workers into more productive industries and regions, perhaps at the costs of allowing some communities to further decline and uprooting people and families from these communities.

TECHNOLOGICAL CHANGES:
THE SOCIAL EMBEDDEDNESS OF TECHNOLOGICAL SYSTEMS

Theory and research on the effects of technological change on the nature of work and employment has exploded in the past decade. Probably all parties to the debate on the future of work agree that the pace and character of technological change will have impacts on the pace and character of work. Just as clearly these are impacts that we do not yet fully understand.

At the most basic level, we need a great deal of research on the relationships between technological change and both job loss and job growth. In particular, we need to carefully distinguish between different technologies, different jobs, and different managerial practices. Although Samuelson (1983) is entirely correct when he points out that "although automation may eliminate jobs, it does not necessarily reduce total employment," this answer does not go far enough. As the Panel on Technology and Women's Employment points out, "the job-creating aspects of new technologies are more difficult to predict than the job-displacing aspects are to observe" (Hartmann et al. 1986, 63). The Panel goes on to note, citing technology expert Nathan Rosenberg and labor expert Eli Ginzberg, that the resolution of such questions is important not only for the concerns of social science, but for those of public policy and private industry as well (see also Hartmann et al. 1986, 13).

Technological change advances unevenly, both within and across occupations and industries. What often appears as job loss may be in fact job transferral (Mark 1987). Put simply, we still lack a clear understanding of what technology does to levels of employment.

Often lost in the debate, however, is the recognition that "technology" or "automation" in and of itself does not affect worker skills or employment. Rather, the specific form in which people choose to implement the technology is what matters. Indeed, the organization of work is a crucial aspect of workplace technology. This raises a more troubling set of questions than those typically posed by industrial engineers or proponents of job redesign. Opposing the "technologically deterministic approach," Noble maintains that we need to examine "how technical possibilities have been delimited by social constraints," and concludes that "when technological development is seen as politics, as it should be, then the very notion of progress becomes ambiguous" (Noble 1984, xii-xiii).

Some analysts, however, suggest that technological determinism might not be altogether misguided. That is, some forms of technology may be inherently disruptive of peoples' work lives. In Robert Asher's contribution to this volume, he approvingly cites Meissner's observation that "the intrinsic characteristics of production machinery are the prime determinants of the kinds of skills workers will use." Meyer's essay is consistent with the spirit of this observation. Further, Feldberg and Glenn (1983) have observed the perhaps inevitable temptation of management to monitor some kinds of work and workers with sophisticated new technologies.

Automation of factories and offices not only displaces jobs and workers, affecting both the middle-class and the working poor. It also alters the character of other work at the same site (Hounshell 1984). Patterns of deskilling in some jobs along with skill upgrading in others have occurred in ways that show great overall but little net change. Kenneth Spenner's meticulous survey presented in his chapter in this volume demonstrates the range of skill requirement options made possible by technology, while historians Steven Meyer and Robert Asher each caution against simplistic statements on the relationship between technological change and work. Meyer makes the important point that "Americans have forestalled and forgotten an important debate since the 1920s—the relationship between technology and unemployment." He suggests that an important threshold has since been crossed, and that "the possible applications of the much more flexible and adaptable computer and robot along an extensive front in homes, offices, shops, and factories once again calls for a reopening of that social debate."

In fact, some scholarship has cast doubt on the thesis that technology necessarily deskills workers. Hirschhorn's *Beyond Mechanization* (1984) makes a strong case that, to the contrary, much post-industrial work will require more autonomy, diagnostic ability, and even creativity. While it is unclear how representative Hirschhorn's flexible and skilled post-industrial workers are of all production workers (and he is aware of the problem of worker displacement), his analysis does point to the need to factor informal and institutional elements into the design of technological systems. Work by Sabel (1982; Piore and Sabel 1984), Adler (1986), and Chaykowski and Slotsve (1992) develops similar themes.

LABOR-MANAGEMENT RELATIONS: A NEW SOCIAL CONTRACT?

One legacy of the New Deal and post-war prosperity was a truce, however uneasy at times, between management and industrial labor. By taking wages out of competition, formalizing job duties, and institutionalizing nascent conflict, labor and management forged a social contract that persisted well into the 1970s.

Some important evidence on the breakdown of the labor-management truce has been garnered by Sleemi (1990), who reports that even in the relatively healthy economy of 1989, management negotiators were able to retain many of the new industrial relations labor-cost reduction strategies developed in the recession years. This included such contractual features as back-loading, lump-sum payments, and COLA restrictions. For analysts such as Weiler (1983) and Freeman and Medoff (1984), such trends are not accidental, but represent concerted and systematic efforts to dismantle the power of labor.

Again, we need to separate enduring from temporary change. Kochan and Piore (1984) believe that the industrial relations system that has characterized the half-century since the New Deal has in fact been fundamentally changed. They maintain that each of the key characteristics of this system are being challenged.[5] Freedman broadly concurs, attributing altered union-management relations to "competition—from abroad, from deregulation, and from nonunion companies" (1988, p. 35). She adds that "This is not a cyclical pattern of alternating ascendancy between labor unions and management."

Others are less willing to characterize these changes as particularly enduring or consequential. Dunlop (1988) holds that most of the changes of the 1980s will prove to be transitory. He cites in particular two-tier contracts, lump-sum payments, and COLA restrictions. For Dunlop (who surprisingly says nothing about increased foreign competition), the relationship between labor and management is unlikely to shift significantly towards either hostility or cooperation.

If the labor-management social contract is breaking down, however, it is unclear what is replacing it. Despite professed commitment to partnership and cooperation (Foulkes 1980), it is difficult to believe that the inherent antagonism between labor and management is going to vanish (Levitan and Johnson 1984). Indeed, corporations have little trouble in simultaneously pursuing policies of job enlargement and downsizing. If anything, the tensions between the democratic workplace and the efficient one have only begun to be sorted out.

In his contribution to this volume, Mayall provides a reasonably sympathetic account of one particular change in labor-management relations—the growth of the temporary work industry. While Mayall sees advantages to temporary work for both workers and their bosses, this development clearly represents a different conception of labor force attachment than earlier models. It may in fact represent an example of growing managerial efforts to "decollectivize" work.

These seven factors do not exhaust the determinants of changes in the world of work, nor do they operate independently. They do, however, give some idea of the scope of the problem at hand. The following essays go a long way in identifying and explaining what we can expect from the new modern times.

NOTES

1. Other categorizations are, of course, possible. See Ritzer (1989) and Hage (1989).

2. Rosenthal (1989, 4) suggests that we also consider job duties and working conditions, job satisfaction, period of work, job status, and job security.

3. Note that Grubb and Wilson's analysis only goes to 1970.

4. This subheading is taken from Wheeler (1990).

5. These characteristics are 1) the pragmatic acceptance by employers of unions and collective bargaining, 2) "job control unions," which "entail[s] highly articulated and sharply delimited jobs assigned to a particular worker and surrounded by complexes of specific rules, customs, and precedents concerning how the work is to be done and the obligation of the workers to the employer," 3) the underconsumptionist view that union wages could grow along with the expansion of markets and the growth of productivity, and 4) labor's progressive role within the political system (Kochan and Piore 1984, 179).

REFERENCES

Abbott, Andrew. 1989. "The New Occupational Structure: What Are the Questions?" *Work and Occupations* 16:273-291.

Adler, Paul. 1986. "New Technologies, New Skills." *California Management Review* 29:9-28.

Amos, Orley M. Jr. 1988. "Unbalanced Regional Growth and Regional Income Inequality in the Latter Stages of Development." *Regional Science and Urban Economics* 18:549-566.

———. 1989. "An Inquiry into the Causes of Increasing Regional Income Inequality in the United States." *Review of Regional Studies* 19:1-12

Auletta, Ken. 1983. *The Underclass*. New York: Vintage.

Bell, Daniel. 1973. *The Coming of Post-Industrial Society*. New York: Basic.

Bielby, William T. and James N. Baron. 1986. "Sex Segregation Within Occupations." *American Economic Review (Papers and Proceedings)* 76:43-47.

Blackburn, McKinley L. 1990. "What Can Explain the Increase in Earnings Inequality Among Males?" *Industrial Relations* 29:41-456.

Bluestone, Barry and Bennett Harrison. 1982. *The Deindustrialization of America: Plant Closings, Community Abandonment, and the Dismantling of Basic Industry*. New York: Basic.

Braverman, Harry. 1974. *Labor and Monopoly Capital: The Degradation of Work in the Twentieth Century*. New York: Monthly Review Press.

Cattan, Peter. 1988. "The Growing Presence of Hispanics in the U.S. Work Force." *Monthly Labor Review* 111 (8):9-14.

Chandler, Alfred D. Jr. 1977. *The Visible Hand: The Managerial Revolution in American Business*. Cambridge, Mass.: Belknap Press.

Chaykowski, Richard P. and George A. Slotsve. 1992. "The Impact of Plant Modernization on Organizational Work Practices." *Industrial Relations* 31:309-329.

Congressional Budget Office. 1984. Study of effects of budget and tax changes on the nation's poor, cited in *New York Times*, April 4.

Connaughton, John E. and Ronald A. Madsen. 1986. "Recession and Recovery: A State and Regional Analysis." *Review of Regional Studies* 16:1-10.

Cooperman, Lois F. 1983. *Adjusting to an Older Work Force*. New York: Van Nostrand Reinhold.

Devens, Richard M. 1988. "A Movable Beast: Regional Employment Patterns." *Monthly Labor Review* 111 (4):60-62.

Doeringer, Peter B., David G. Terkla and Gregory C. Topakian. 1987. *Invisible Factors in Local Economic Development*. New York: Oxford University Press.

Dunlop, John T. 1988. "Have the 1980s Changed U.S. Industrial Relations?" *Monthly Labor Review* 111 (5):29-34.

Easterlin, Richard A. 1987. *Birth and Fortune: The Impact of Numbers on Personal Welfare*. Chicago: University of Chicago Press.

Feldberg, Roslyn L. and Evelyn N. Glenn. 1983. "Technology and Work Degradation: Effects of Office Automation on Women Clerical Workers." In Joan Rothschild (Ed.), *Machina ex Dea: Feminist Perspectives on Technology*. New York: Pergamon Press, chapter 4.

Flaim, Paul O. 1990. "Population Changes, the Baby Boom, and Unemployment." *Monthly Labor Review* 113 (8):3-10.

Foulkes, Fred K. 1980. *Personnel Policies in Large Nonunion Companies*. Englewood Cliffs, New Jersey: Prentice-Hall.

Freedman, Audrey. 1988. "How the 1980s Have Changed Industrial Relations." *Monthly Labor Review* 111 (5):35-38.

Freeman, Richard B. and James L. Medoff. 1984. *What Do Unions Do?* New York: Basic.

Grubb, W. Norton and Robert H. Wilson. 1989. "Sources of Increasing Inequality in Wages and Salaries, 1960-80." *Monthly Labor Review* 112 (4):3-13.

Hage, Jerald. 1989. "The Sociology of Traditional Economic Problems: Product Markets and Labor Markets." *Work and Occupations* 16:416-445.

Hansen, Niles. 1979. "The New International Division of Labor and Manufacturing Decentralization in the United States." *Review of Regional Studies* 9:1-11.

Harrington, Michael. 1984. *The New American Poverty*. New York: Holt, Rinehart, and Winston.

Hartmann, Heidi I., Robert E. Kraut, and Louise A. Tilly (Eds.). 1986. *Computer Chips and Paper Clips: Technology and Women's Employment*. Washington, D.C.: National Academy Press.

Herz, Diane E. 1990. "Worker Displacement in a Period of Rapid Job Expansion, 1983-1987." *Monthly Labor Review* 113 (5):21-33.

Herz, Diane E. and Philip L. Rones. 1989. "Institutional Barriers to Employment of Older Workers." *Monthly Labor Review* 112 (4):14-21.

Hirschhorn, Larry. 1984. *Beyond Mechanization: Work and Technology in a Post-industrial Age*. Cambridge, Mass.: MIT Press.

Horrigan, Michael W. and Steven E. Haugen. 1988. "The Declining Middle-Class Thesis: A Sensitivity Analysis." *Monthly Labor Review* 111 (5):3-13.

Horrigan, Michael W. and James P. Markey. 1990. "Recent Gains in Women's Earnings: Better Pay or Longer Hours?" *Monthly Labor Review* 113 (7):11-17.

Hounshell, David A. 1984. *From the American System to Mass Production: The Development of Manufacturing Technology in the United States.* Baltimore: Johns Hopkins University Press.

Johnston, William B. and Arnold E. Packer. 1987. *Workforce 2000: Work and Workers for the 21st Century.* Indianapolis, IN: Hudson Institute.

Kasarda, John D. 1983. "Entry-Level Jobs, Mobility, and Urban Minority Unemployment." *Urban Affairs Quarterly* 19:21-40.

Kennedy, Paul M. 1987. *The Rise and Fall of the Great Powers: Economic Change and Military Conflict from 1500 to 2000.* New York: Random House.

Kochan, Thomas A. and Michael J. Piore. 1984. "Will the New Industrial Relations Last? Implications for the American Labor Movement." *Annals* (May) 473:177-189.

Kohlberg, William H. 1983. *The Dislocated Worker: Preparing America's Workforce for New Jobs.* Washington, D.C.: Seven Locks Press.

Kuttner, Bob. 1983. "The Declining Middle." *Atlantic* (July):60-72.

——— . 1984. "Jobs." *Dissent* 31:30-41.

Lawrence, Robert Z. 1983. *Can America Compete?* Washington D.C.: Brookings.

Lemann, Nicholas. 1986. "The Origins of the Underclass, two parts." *Atlantic* (June):31-55, (July):54-68.

Leontief, Wassily W. 1982. "The Distribution of Work and Income." *Scientific American* 247:188-204.

Levitan, Sar A. 1984. "The Changing Workplace." *Society* 21:41-48.

Levitan, Sar A. and Clifford M. Johnson. 1984. "The Changing Workplace." *The Annals* 473 (May):116-127.

Levy, Frank. 1988. *Dollars and Dreams: The Changing American Income Distribution.* New York: Norton.

Levy, Frank and Richard C. Michel. 1983. "The Way We'll be in 1984: Recent Changes in the Level and Distribution of Disposable Income." Washington, D.C.: The Urban Institute.

Licht, Walter. 1988. "How the Workplace Has Changed in 75 Years." *Monthly Labor Review* 111 (2):19-25.

Linden, Fabian. 1984. "Linden on Thurow." *New York Times*, March 4.

Littman, Mark S. 1989. "Poverty in the 1980s: Are the Poor Getting Poorer?" *Monthly Labor Review* 112 (6):13-18.

Loveman, Gary W. and Chris Tilly. 1988. "Good Jobs or Bad Jobs: What Does the Evidence Say?" *New England Economic Review* (Jan-Feb):46-65.

McElvaine, Robert S. 1984. *The Great Depression: America, 1929-1941.* New York: Times Books.

McKenzie, Richard B. 1988. *The American Job Machine.* New York: Universe Books.

Mark, Jerome A. 1987. "Technological Change and Employment: Some Results from BLS Research." *Monthly Labor Review* 110 (4):26-29.

Meisenheimer, Joseph R. II. 1990. "Black College Graduates in the Labor Market, 1979 and 1989." *Monthly Labor Review* 113 (11):3-12.

Morrill, Richard L. 1990. "Regional Demographic Structure of the United States." *Population Geographer* 42:38-53.

Naisbitt, John. 1984. *Megatrends.* New York: Warner Books.

Noble, David E. 1984. *Forces of Production: A Social History of Industrial Automation.* New York: Oxford University Press.

Patton, Arch. 1981. "The Coming Promotion Slowdown." *Harvard Business Review* (March/April) 46:50-52,56.

Piore, Michael J. and Charles F. Sabel. 1984. *The Second Industrial Divide: Possibilities for Prosperity.* New York: Basic.

Plotnik, Robert D. 1989. "Do States Reduce Poverty Through Transfer of Income?" *Monthly Labor Review* 112 (7):21-26.

Plunkert, Lois M. 1990. "Job Growth and Industry Shifts in the 1980s." *Monthly Labor Review* 113 (9):3-16.

Reich, Robert B. 1990. "Who Is Us?" *Harvard Business Review* 68:53-64.

———. 1991. "The REAL Economy." *Atlantic* (February):35-52.

Reskin, Barbara F. and Patricia A. Roos. 1990. *Job Queues, Gender Queues: Explaining Women's Inroads into Male Occupations.* Philadelphia: Temple University Press.

Ritzer, George. 1989. "The Permanently New Economy: The Case for Reviving Economic Sociology." *Work and Occupations* 16:243-272.

Rosenthal, Neal H. 1989. "More than Wages at Issue in Job Quality Debate." *Monthly Labor Review* 112 (12):4-8.

Sabel, Charles F. 1982. *Work and Politics: The Division of Labor in Industry.* Cambridge, England: Cambridge University Press.

Samuelson, Robert J. 1983. "Middle Class Media Myth." *National Journal,* December 31:2673-2678.

Sawers, Larry and William K. Tabb. 1984. *Sunbelt/Snowbelt: Urban Development and Regional Restructuring.* New York: Oxford University Press.

Shaiken, Harley. 1984. *Work Transformed: Automation and Labor in the Computer Age.* New York: Holt, Rinehart, and Winston.

Shank, Susan E. 1988. "Women and the Labor Market: The Link Grows Stronger." *Monthly Labor Review* 111 (3):3-8.

Singleton, Christopher J. 1990. "The 1987-88 Surge in Exports and the Rise in Factory Jobs." *Monthly Labor Review* 113 (5):42-48.

Sleemi, Fehmida. 1990. "Higher Settlements in 1989 End Innovative Decade." *Monthly Labor Review* 113 (5):3-10.

Smith, James P. and Finis Welsh. 1981. "No Time to Be Young: The Economic Prospects for Large Cohorts in the United States." *Population and Development Review* 7:71-83.

Steinberg, Bruce. 1983. "The Mass Market is Splitting Apart." *Fortune,* November 28.

Summers, Gene F. (Ed.). 1984. "Deindustrialization: Restructuring the Economy." Special Issue, *Annals of the American Academy of Political and Social Science* (September):475.

Thurow, Lester B. 1984. "The Disappearance of the Middle Class." *New York Times,* February 5.

Thurow, Lester B. 1992. *Head to Head: The Coming Economic Battle Among Japan, Europe, and America.* New York: Morrow.

Warf, Barney. 1990. "US Employment in Foreign-Owned High Technology Firms." *Professional Geographer* 42:421-432.

Weiler, Paul. 1983. "Promises to Keep: Securing Worker Rights to Self-Organization Under the NLRA." *Harvard Law Review* 96:1769-1827.

Wheeler, James O. 1990. "The New Corporate Landscape: America's Fastest Growing Private Companies." *Professional Geographer* 42:433-444.

Wilson, William J. 1987. *The Truly Disadvantaged: The Inner City, the Underclass, and Public Policy.* Chicago: University of Chicago Press.

Wood, Stephen (Ed.). 1982. *The Degradation of Work: Skill, Deskilling and the Labour Process.* London: Hutchinson.

Zysman, John and Laura Tyson. 1983. *American Industry in International Competition: Government Policies and Corporate Strategies.* Ithaca: Cornell University Press.

I

Historical Perspectives

1

Technology and Work:
A Social and Historical Overview
of U.S. Industrialization

Stephen Meyer

Over the past twenty-five years or so, the issue of technological change attracted an increasing amount of attention from historians. This new research of social and labor historians, business historians, and historians of technology provides the opportunity for a substantive analysis of the social history of industrialization and of the social impact of technological change in the United States. Much of this work focuses on the history of the labor process, occupational and class structure, management practices, and work traditions. The object of this essay is to offer a brief social and historical overview of the more important historical literature on problems of technology and work. A more general objective is the amalgamation of these sometimes diverse fields and the examination of the technical background to the development of American industrial capitalism.

This overview begins with a survey of differing patterns of American industrialization in the shoe, textile, railroad, metal-working, iron-and steel-making, and automobile industries. It specifically examines the recent historical work to uncover the relationship between technology and work in industrializing America. By no means a thorough or comprehensive survey, it touches on the main trends in the development of the division of labor, work reorganization, mechanization, and continuous flow processes in American industry. Additionally, it raises several larger issues and patterns about the relationships among technology, work, and society within the context of American industrialization.

From the earliest years of the American republic, the boot and shoe industry demonstrates a pattern of work transformation through the division of labor. Through most of the eighteenth century, shoemaking was a highly skilled craft with little or no division of labor. The refined craft of shoemaking involved a long apprenticeship for the acquisition of journeyman status. Master craftsmen, journeymen, and apprentices all worked in the small ten-footer (a shop named for its dimensions) and produced their product on special order for a very localized market. For the most part, skilled craftsmen performed all the principle divisions of the trade—cutting the leather, binding together the pieces for the upper part of the shoe, and bottoming, or attaching the sole to the bound upper. In time, however, merchant capitalists gradually transformed this handicraft through the reorganization of work processes without significant mechanization of work. The combination of merchant capital and artisanal skills resulted in the first steps toward work reorganization in the shoe industry. Merchants who had access to broader markets and who possessed the capital laid the groundwork for the reorganization and centralization of shop production. They rearranged the shoemaking craft, establishing a "proto-industrial" system which marked a transition from older artisanal to more modern industrial forms of production. In the new system, highly skilled male workers cut the leather, less skilled men and women bound the uppers in their homes in the surrounding countryside, and more skilled journeymen bottomed the shoes in their small shops. This pattern followed the simple division of labor of the skilled shoemaker's trade (Faler 1981; Dawley 1979; Mulligan 1986; Laurie 1980).

By the 1830s, the larger manufacturers further reorganized production and established the central shop, a larger and centralized building for the manufacture of shoes. Although more and more workers gradually moved into the central shop which soon took on the appearance of a large, modern factory, the domestic, or putting out system, persisted in order to provide a flexible workforce for the expansion and contraction of the shoe market. Skilled craftsmen cut the leather in the central shop and then sent the pieces for uppers out to the men and women on farms in the countryside, to proletarianized journeymen, or to new unskilled urban migrants for binding. The bound uppers returned to the central shop for the more skilled work of bottoming. Gradually, the central shop began to employ more and more cutters and bottomers, growing to fifty or more workers in a single location. By the 1850s, the first genuine shoe factories emerged with cutters, binders, and bottomers employed in a single industrial setting. This process facilitated the employers' control over the quality of the product and the discipline of the workforce. At this time, the larger firms developed and began to use machines for shoe manufacture. Beginning in the 1850s and taking hold in the 1860s with the introduction of the McKay stitcher, a full-fledged factory system evolved featuring both the division of work and the mechanization of work tasks. Finally, in the 1860s and 1870s, leather-cutting machines eased the labor of the skilled cutters (Faler 1981; Dawley 1979).

For the shoe manufacturer, the impetus for work reorganization rested on the need to control supplies of the product, the quality and quantity of work, and the activities and behavior of the workforce. As industrialization advanced in other sectors of the American economy, this control over the labor process, the labor force, and the labor market proved an essential feature of American industrial capitalism. To this end, the division and subdivision of labor gradually transformed highly skilled trades into routinized factory work. In the mid-nineteenth century, the number of subdivisions of the shoemakers' trade included approximately forty distinct tasks; at the end of the century, this had increased to about one hundred. Once they reorganized and simplified work processes, the shoe manufacturers could readily develop and apply new machinery to the less complicated work tasks.

The American textile industry reveals a quite different pattern of industrialization. In this instance, mechanization played a direct role in the rise of the modern factory system. Moreover, although the production of cloth involved discrete and varied skills, it was not organized around a highly developed craft tradition. Originally domestic labor, the production of cloth involved women in carding and spinning the raw material and men and women in weaving the cloth. They used simple machines—spinning wheels and hand looms, which dated back to at least medieval Europe. Furthermore, the emergence of an American textile industry illustrates the transfer of a "high" technology from industrialized Great Britain to the more underdeveloped and economically backward United States (Jeremy 1981; Dublin 1979 and 1981; Wallace 1978; Kulik, Parks, and Penn 1982; Prude 1983; Haraven 1982; Haraven and Langenbach 1978).

From its beginnings in the late eighteenth century, this classic example of American industrialization also combined artisanal skills and merchant capital. It began with Samuel Slater's near mythical migration to the United States in the early 1790s. A skilled mechanic, apprenticed with the British Arkwright and Strutt textile machine manufacturing firm, Slater migrated to New York with his toolbox in his hands and visions of textile machines in his mind. After his arrival, he connected with William Almy and Moses Brown, two Rhode Island merchants. Under contract with the two merchants, Slater reinvented the British carding and spinning machines. In time, Slater-inspired spinning mills dotted the rivers and streams of the New England countryside. These mills, recognizable from their similar features—the small size of the firms, the small amounts of capital from local investors, the concentration on carding and spinning operations, the employment of entire families at the workforce, and the emergence of a rural cottage industry for weaving—were collectively known as the "Rhode Island" system (Dublin 1979; Kulik, Parks, and Penn 1982).

Around 1814, a similar combination of craft skills and merchant capital established another pattern for the textile industry. In this case, a Boston merchant and financier, Francis Cabot Lowell, who had visited British textile towns and firms, recognized the industrial potential of combining the carding, spinning, and weaving operations in a single factory. Along with Paul Moody, another skilled mechanic, Lowell reinvented the power loom from his memories of British machines. Subsequently, he accumulated additional financial resources from other Boston investors and acquired water rights along the Merrimac River from the Massachusetts legislature. Thinking on a grander scale, he created large factories and towns first at Waltham in 1815 and later at Lowell in 1821 (Dublin 1979).

The factories of the "Waltham" or "Lowell" system shared common features and represented an entirely different form and scale of American textile production. First, they integrated all phases of production and assured greater technical control over the workforce. Second, they were much larger and much more capital intensive enterprises which employed from 200 to 1,000 workers. Third, they focused on the production of cheaper cloths for a much wider mass market. Fourth, resident agents managed and supervised the mills for absent owners who lived in Boston. Finally, they utilized young women from New England farms for most machine operations. The latter was a consequence of the traditional shortage of labor and the much lower cost of female labor (Dublin 1979).

Women, thus, were the first genuine American working-class in large factories. Compared to women's other possible job opportunities, the Lowell factory operatives were relatively well-paid. Since these young women usually worked for short periods in their transition from adolescence to marriage, the main problem was the assurance of a continuous supply of young women from the "virtuous" New England farms. Given the contemporary social debates about the ills of the British factory system and the Puritan morality of the New England farmsteads, the fundamental task was to convince fathers to send their daughters off to the new factory towns. Consequently, the Lowell system instituted what one contemporary labelled the "moral police" which consisted of a complex network of overseers in the mills, boarding-housekeepers in residences, and female workers themselves to watch for lapses in behavior and conduct (Dublin 1979).

Unlike the shoe-making, cloth-making was technologically advanced. By the 1830s, the complex textile machines increased in the sophistication and perfection of their movements and operations. In the Lowell mills, a gendered technical division of labor emerged. The men were either the supervisors or the most skilled workers—the agents, overseers, second hands, machine repairmen, and carding machine operators. Women were the machine tenders for the spinning and weaving operations. The textile machines were essentially automatic. When threads broke, the machines stopped. The principle tasks of female machine operatives were to load and unload the machines and to repair broken threads and restart the automatic equipment. The nature of the work and workforce influenced the social organization of the workplace. Since the work often involved some idle time between problems, women socialized, trained the new spare hands, and shared work with their shopmates (Dublin 1979; Wallace 1978).

Interestingly, two quite different patterns of textile industrialization emerged—one urban and another rural. Although the image of large factories associated with the Lowell system has profoundly shaped our impressions of the early American industrial system, both patterns evolved simultaneously through the first half of the nineteenth century. On the one hand, large factory towns, such as Lowell or Waltham in Massachusetts and Nashua and Manchester in New Hampshire, were often financed with Boston capital, concentrated along the larger rivers, and employed large numbers of native-born American women. On the other hand, small mill villages, similar to the original Slater system, evolved in southern New England, along the Brandywine river in Delaware, and to some extent in the South. These rural enterprises were characterized by their smaller scale, their concentration on only one or two operations, their employment of whole families, and their small village paternalism (Wallace 1978; Kulik, Parks, and Penn 1982; Prude 1983).

Throughout the nineteenth century, a third pattern of American industrialization evolved in metal-working shops, plants, and factories. This pattern involved gradual industrialization through both work reorganization and mechanization. Since the metal-working firms produced the machines so crucial to American industrialization, their technological advances were fundamental for the continued progress of the American industrial revolution. This key area of technical innovation established what British manufacturers and engineers labeled the "American System of Manufactures" and laid the foundation for American industrial prominence in the twentieth century. Originating in the small arms industry, this distinctive American system rested on a set of industrial practices which emphasized mechanization, the standardization and interchangeability of parts, the substitution of unskilled for skilled labor, and high-volume production (Hounshell 1984; Smith 1977; Mayr and Post 1981).

In this instance, the U. S. government subsidized the experimentation and innovation of numerous small arms manufacturers and craftsmen. Since the U. S. Army believed that interchangeable parts were essential no matter how high the cost, the American System of Manufactures evolved in the small arms industry, first in the shops of governmental armories and later in small private armories. Despite the Eli Whitney legend about the achievement of standardized and interchangeable parts as early as 1800, John R. Hall, a skilled mechanic under contract at the Harpers Ferry Armory, actually accomplished the manufacture of rifles with standardized and interchangeable parts in the 1820s. From this time to the early twentieth century, these novel manufacturing techniques diffused through the metal-working industry from shop to shop and industry to industry. A small and mobile fraternity of skilled mechanics carried the new practices from government to private armories and then from the small arms workshops to the agricultural tool and implement, sewing machine, office equipment, bicycle, and finally the automobile shops, plants, and factories (Hounshell 1984; Hounshell 1981; Smith 1981).

The fundamental technical problems in small arms manufacture were associated with the nature of the product, its raw materials, and the difficulty of working metal. At the beginning of the nineteenth century, American fears of being drawn into the global conflict between Great Britain and France generated considerable interest in the efficient manufacture of small arms. The initial efforts at work reorganization resulted in a primitive division of labor of the armorer's craft for making rifles—stockers, forgemen and barrel-makers, and filers, grinders and polishers, and assemblers for the complex firing mechanism. The manufacture of the dozen or so small parts for the firing mechanism presented the greatest problems. Without machines for their production, they required the highest skills for their manufacture. Moreover, their assembly into the finished firing mechanism also necessitated the skilled and time-consuming labor of filers and fitters who put together each unique mechanism (Hounshell 1984; Smith 1981).

Through the influence of Whitney (who first inspired the ideal of standardization and interchangeability) and Simeon North and Thomas Blanchard (who invented the early metal-working and wood-working machines to produce rifle parts), John R. Hall established a shop for the production of his breechloader rifles in the Harpers Ferry Armory. He successfully achieved the production of 1,000 standardized and interchangeable breechloaders in 1824. His success rested on borrowed ideas from Blanchard and North for new machines, his own skilled design and construction of machinery, his use of templates and fixtures for filing and machining operations, and particularly his rigid system of gauging and inspecting parts (Hounshell 1984).

From the 1820s through the 1840s, Hall's theories and practices spread through the governmental and private armories through the migration of skilled armorers, metal workers, and machinists from shop to shop. In 1851, the products of American metal shops and plants first received recognition at the first major international industrial fair—the Crystal Palace Exposition in London. Subsequently, a British commission toured American industrial firms and discovered what they labelled the American System of Manufactures. These practices were adapted to numerous other American industries which allowed them to establish their systems of high volume production (Hounshell 1984; Mayr and Post 1981).

The evolution of the American System of Manufactures had considerable impact on how skilled metal tradesmen performed their work. The process of mechanization initially eased and facilitated the metal workers' labor. Through a process which mechanical engineers called the "transfer of skill," new machine tools performed the complex and arduous tasks of giving form and shape to metal parts. By the end of the nineteenth century, the principal classes of machine tools—drills, lathes, milling machines, planters, and grinders—had acquired their basic form. And, although the elimination of laborious and tedious hand work did result in some skill dilution, the operation of the new machines and the expansion of the new metal-working industries created whole new categories of skilled work, in particular machinists. At the time, the new machinists' work still contained large amounts of skill, discretion, and autonomy. Only after the emergence of continuous flow production did the skilled metal trades suffer significant and substantial skill dilution (Hounshell 1984; Woodbury 1972; Montgomery 1979; Meyer 1981).

In the mid-nineteenth century, the development of a national railroad network was central to the American industrial experience. The steam locomotive became the metaphor for the early American industrial revolution. The mechanization of transport established the first large corporations and linked manufacturers and producers with both sources of materials and widening markets of consumers. It blurred distinctions among the city, the town, and the country. From the late 1840s through the early 1870s, the railroad industry underwent a period of continuous growth and significant organizational innovation. Through the creation of the first extensive and large corporate organizations, the railroad managers created the first modern forms of corporate organization and administration (Chandler 1977).

In the railroad industry, American workers intensely experienced the new forms of corporate organization and control. The extensive rail networks required modern management methods to insure control of the widely-dispersed workforce. Additional reasons supporting new methods of worker control included the problems of safety, scheduling, competition, and multiple tasks and skills. For railroad workers, modern management meant "working to rule," or more precisely following the detailed instructions of corporate rule books. Although work rules had existed in the past, never before had they been so detailed and so restrictive. In general, the railroad rule books established authority structures, standards of worker behavior, and precise norms and procedures for work. Slowly, the railroad management methods diffused to other large American firms (Licht 1983 and 1986; Stromquist 1987).

In the iron and steel industry, the idea of continuous flow production arose as a basic tenet for high-volume production. Through the nineteenth century, the successful integration or connection of all industrial processes was a principal limitation to genuine mass production. The early textile industry represented an important ideal where a single raw material—cotton—moved through the successive mechanized phases of the manufacturing process. In the second half of the nineteenth century, inherently chemical industries, such as iron and steel, petroleum, brewing, and others, began to develop along the principles of continuous flow due to the molten or liquid nature of their industrial processes. The notion of continuous flow production proved central for the development of modern American industrial practice in the twentieth century (Chandler 1977).

Before its technical and organizational transformation, the iron and steel industry was conducted in small scattered industrial enterprises. These small firms divided into three basic branches—ore refining, iron and steel making, and iron and steel products. Until the 1860s, the decentralized iron and steel furnaces employed relatively small work crews numbering from 50 to 200 workers. As in the metal-working industries where inside contracting also prevailed, often highly skilled workers hired, supervised, and controlled their own work groups whose members possessed varying degrees and levels of skill. The manufacture of steel involved the highly skilled craft of puddling, which stirred carbon and combined oxygen into a molten mass of iron. Around the 1860s, the use of new Bessemer converters started to eliminate the skilled puddlers and to increase greatly the volume of production (Chandler 1977; Brody 1969 and 1965).

Around the same time, the nature of steel making concentrated attention on the efficient and economic use of heat for the separate processes of ore refining, steel making, and product making. The high cost of reheating iron and steel resulted in the horizontal integration of the metal making industry along the lines of continuous flow from furnaces to converters to roller and product mills. In the 1870s and 1880s, large and integrated steel mills made their appearance in the United States. The Carnegie Edgar Thompson Works near Homestead, Pennsylvania, was a typical prototype of the new modern steel mills. The use of railroads, mechanized methods of materials handling, and coordinated phases of production established integrated and synchronized work processes and work groups. Alfred Chandler used the concept of "through put," a notion centered on the speed of the flow of materials through different industrial processes, as a means to explain the continuous flow innovation in the iron and steel industry (Brody 1969; Chandler 1977).

New management practices also became increasingly important in the modernized iron and steel corporations. Through cost
accounting, the steel magnates determined the productivity of workers through the different divisions of the iron and steel mills.
Moreover, while unions managed to eliminate the inside contract
system where skilled workers hired and supervised their work crews,
the gradual emergence of a brutal drive system allowed plant managers and supervisors to prod their less skilled immigrant workers to
greater and greater levels of output. With modernization and mechanization, the number of highly skilled craftsmen declined until
only a small core of skilled workers remained. By the turn of the
century, the large open-shop firms destroyed a vibrant and vital steel
workers union. For skilled workers, these firms offered elaborate
and paternalistic plans of welfare capitalism which attached these
prized workers to the large steel corporations. At the same time, the
reorganized industry now employed a huge number of unskilled
Southern and Eastern European immigrant workers who received
low wages and who were left to fend for themselves during hard
times (Brody 1969; Eggert 1981; Stone 1974).

In America's twentieth-century "industry of industries," the
automobile industry, all of the significant nineteenth-century
trends—the division of labor, mechanization, refined management
techniques, and high-volume and continuous-flow production—
came together. In the new automobile industry, these trends coa-
lesced, rapidly transformed industrial and work processes, and created the modern system of mass production. In fact, because of their
extension to the automobile industry, the basic principles of the
American System of Manufactures could be universalized with the
general emergence of mass production industries from the 1920s
through the present. The automobile industry pattern was the rapid
and extensive division of labor which both resulted in considerable
skill dilution and what has been called the "degradation of work"
(Meyer 1981; Lichtenstein and Meyer, 1989; Nevins 1954; Hounshell
1984; Gartman 1986; Peterson 1987; Edsforth 1987; Braverman 1974).

The Ford Motor Company was the classic example of the rise of
modern mass production. Along with Taylorism, Fordism has come
to signify the routinized, monotonous, and repetitive work of the
modern industrial world. The image of Ford resonates throughout
modern culture—for example, the classic image of modern factory
work with Charlie Chaplin in *Modern Times* or the dating of time in
Aldous Huxley's futuristic novel, *Brave New World*, as "the year of

our Ford." In the first decades of this century, Ford proved to the world that he indeed had a better idea for the manufacture of automobiles.

Between 1908 and 1914, that better idea was captured in four interrelated principles which derived from nineteenth-century industrial technology and manufacturing practice. First, Ford insisted on a standard design for his product—he boasted that the customer could have any color so long as it was black. The Model T, Ford's "motorcar for the great multitude," was his standardized product. Ford produced this simple and standardized product, believing that smaller profit margins on a larger volume of production would lead to much greater profits. Ultimately, this design and marketing strategy had profound implications for industrial practice (Meyer 1981).

With an unchanging product, considerable time and money could be invested in two of the other principles—the design of work tasks, Taylorism, and the design of machines throughout his new Highland Park plant. Around the time that Ford developed the Model T, the ideas of Frederick W. Taylor gained considerable currency among mechanical and industrial engineers in the Detroit area. With continuous runs of the same product, Taylorism, which included the task idea, the minute division and subdivision of labor, and the separation of conception from execution, became both possible and profitable. Moreover, from the 1900s on, the design of machines also commanded considerable attention from mechanical engineers and machine-tool builders. During this period, a cluster of technical innovations made the new metal-working tools more automatic, more rigid, and more adaptable to high-volume production with unskilled workers. The use of jigs and fixtures and of uniquely designed machines created special and single purpose machines to produce and reproduce large runs of the same part over and over again (Nelson, 1980; Meyer 1981).

Finally, with the construction of the Highland Park plant in 1910, Ford engineers and managers paid considerable attention to the design and flow of materials through the world's most modern factory. In their minds, the fundamental concept was "progressive production." It began not in assembly operations, but in the machine shops which processed metal parts. Initially, the new single-purpose machines were arranged according to the flow of the work on metal castings. This resulted in considerable savings from the reduced costs for the transportation of materials through the shop, the more efficient use of floor space, and the greater control over the pace of workers. The huge savings initiated a quest for "progressive" assembly, beginning in the magneto department in 1913 and culminating in the final assembly line in early 1914 (Meyer 1981).

Despite the remarkable technical achievements of Highland Park, the Ford Motor Company faced considerable labor problems due to the changed social organization of work. First, the redesigned and reorganized production and assembly jobs resulted in the significant dilution of skills for the new job classifications in the plant. It marked the beginning of the genuinely mechanized, routinized, and monotonous work creating the social problems of "work and its discontents" in the modern industrial age. Second, it resulted in a transformed social structure of work. Prior to the Ford revolution, Detroit metal workers fell into three general classes of skill and work—highly skilled mechanics, partially skilled specialists, and unskilled laborers. Each constituted about one-third of the total workforce. At the Ford Highland Park plant in 1917, 55 to 60 percent of the workforce were employed in unskilled machine tending and assembly jobs. This profoundly altered the social relations of the Ford shops. Third, the redesigned and reorganized work processes established new forms of technical control embedded in the new machines and work processes. The new automated machines only required loading and unloading and set the pace of work. The assemblers performed their minute and subdivided tasks over and over again. The synchronized, coordinated, and sequential arrangement of the work also determined the speed and pace to complete all work. Only the financial incentive of the $5 Day and the social controls of the Ford Sociological Department brought the new technical system up to production levels of the engineers' expectations (Meyer 1981).

Fully developed in a brief timeframe, the Ford ideas spread quite rapidly through the Detroit automobile firms in the 1910s. Through the 1920s, Fordization became a national and even international movement for plant modernization and improvement. In the United States, other consumer goods industries adopted the Fordist mass production methods. In other capitalist, fascist, and socialist economies, Ford had his disciples and adherents for the transformation of the workplace. In the mid 1920s, Alfred Sloan, who as head of General Motors introduced the concepts of different styles and different models to the automobile industry, contributed to the modification of the original Fordist ideas. In fact, Sloan introduced the notion of flexible mass production, a mass production system which accounted for changes in product design. Nonetheless, Sloan retained the inner-core of Ford's basic ideas. The Sloanist production system relied on "semi-specialized machines which required skilled "set-up" workers to adjust machines for production changes and unskilled production workers for their operation (Meyer 1989; Hounshell, 1984).

In the mid-1950s, automation, another major innovation in automotive production technology, refashioned the labor process and the distribution of worker skills on the shop floor. An extension of Fordist principles, automated production received government funding during World War II and surfaced in the Ford Cleveland plant in the post-war years. It was a significant advance in the mechanization of machining operations. Unlike earlier technical changes in production technology, automation raised the needed skills of production workers. Highly skilled machine setters and operators monitored production and repaired breakdowns. In this instance, skilled workers became direct production workers and the number of unskilled workers virtually disappeared from automotive machining shops. Moreover, automation initially represented a departure from the Sloanist principle of flexible mass production. At first, automation relied on large costly and inflexible equipment which combined machining operations. In recent decades, shop-floor computers and industrial robots have made automated industrial systems more flexible (Meyer 1989; Noble 1984 and 1979).

From a social historical perspective, the examination of technology and work raises important questions about the relationships among technology, work, and modern industrial society. Unlike conventional social science research, history offers the vital perspective of social and technological change over time and enables an analysis of the long-term trends of social, economic, and technological change. To be sure, this brief historical overview cannot provide the needed detailed and comprehensive account of the richness of the new labor and social histories which touch on the history of technology and work. Nonetheless, the new histories prompt a number of observations on the social consequences of technical and industrial innovation.

First, too little is known about the changing distribution of people and positions in the American occupational structure. A pressing need exists for longitudinal studies which map out the evolving social contours of American society. Despite the considerable attention paid to historical social mobility studies, too little is known about the changing social composition of the American class structure. This would require an historical and sociological analysis of the actual jobs or positions and the social characteristics of the people who fill these positions. In recent years, Herbert Gutman, Margo Anderson, and David Montgomery have provided a glimpse into the complex process whereby waves of immigrants move into the bottom rungs of American society and push their predecessors upward through the occupational structure. In this instance, while patterns of social migration and mobility alter the social and cultural make-up of the people, technical change at the workplace continuously transforms the occupational positions which they fill. Much more needs to be known about the dynamics of this complex process (Gutman 1977; Anderson 1980 and 1988; Montgomery 1987).

On a related topic, David Gordon, Richard Edwards, and Michael Reich recently raised the idea of labor market segmentation as an important feature of the American economy, especially since around 1920. Despite their important periodization and synthesis of American industrial development, the historical record reveals that the American working-class has always been segmented. Through the nineteenth-century, the principal division was between the highly skilled mechanic and the unskilled laborer who often fetched and carried (literally a human beast of burden) for the skilled craftsman. By the end of the century, new industrial techniques created the less skilled specialist who performed a fragment of the all-around mechanic's work. Around 1900, census officials came up with a "semi-skilled" category to label these workers. With the transformation of work in the automobile industry in the 1920s, they applied this label to the deskilled and unskilled jobs of production workers in the automobile and other new mass production industries (Gordon, Edwards, and Reich 1982).

Second, since E. P. Thompson's pathbreaking analysis of the role of culture for the making of the British working-class, American social and labor historians have paid considerable attention to the cultural dimension of the transition from preindustrial to industrial society and to the adaptation of new workers to the new industrial order. Whether journeymen shoemakers, New England mill girls, master armorers, Southern and Eastern European immigrants in the steel mills, or new production workers in the automobile plants, the internal or transoceanic rural to urban migrations entailed a difficult transition to the modern industrial ethos and values. In the eyes of American factory owners and managers, all workers needed to accommodate to a "new industrial morality," a "moral police," a timeclock, a drive system, or a sociological department (Thompson 1967; Gutman 1977; Dublin 1979; Faler 1981; Meyer 1981).

In the recent past, American labor and social historians have followed Thompson's lead and have more thoroughly investigated the social and cultural dimensions of workers' lives. Often, they have moved beyond the direct impact of technical change and explored the more subtle and indirect ways in which it has shaped worker consciousness. For example, Montgomery has essentially examined workers' culture of the shop floor and has delineated a worker ethos for dealing with technological change. Roy Rosenzweig has penetrated further into the cultural sphere to show how the struggle over the use of leisure time involved the shaping of worker attitudes toward the shop and factory. Moreover, Neil Harris, Warren Susman, T. J. Jackson Lears and Richard Wrightman Fox, and Lizabeth Cohen have all explored the culture of consumption with suggestive implications about the character of popular and worker consciousness in America (Montgomery 1979 and 1987; Rosenzweig 1983; Harris 1981; Susman 1984; Fox and Lears 1983; Cohen 1990).

Third, American historians of industrialization have paid increasing attention to the question of management or worker control of the workplace. Montgomery first raised this in his examination of skilled and autonomous craftsmen in the late nineteenth-century. Moreover, Daniel Nelson's examination of a new factory system between 1880 and 1920 suggests that the rise of large-scale corporations in the late nineteenth-century also required the assertion of management controls over the "foreman's empire" as well as the terrain of the skilled worker. Howell Harris has shown that the central issue of management rights was an important strategy to contain the assertion of union power at the workplace in the post-World War II period. Meyer has explored the emergence of militant industrial unionism as a forceful means to restrict managerial prerogatives on the shop floor. Indeed, the struggle over structures of control over work and industrial processes has been an essential feature of the American working-class experience (Montgomery 1979; Nelson 1975; Harris 1982; Meyer 1992).

Fourth, in the past decade, the issues of race and gender have literally exploded as areas of investigation among American labor and social historians. The technical restructuring of work has brought large numbers of African-American and women workers into the workforce through the twentieth-century. Several African-American labor historians have greatly enriched our sense of the social contours of race and the racial division of labor. Joe Trotter has explored the making of the Black proletariat in the Appalachian coalfields in the early twentieth-century. Earl Lewis has examined the black working-class in twentieth-century Richmond. Both offer detailed analyses of the interplay of race, social class, and power in the workplace and in the community. Robin Kelley has examined the social and cultural forms of black resistance to the segregated South (Trotter, 1990; Kelley, 1993; Lewis, 1991).

Even more extensive has been the recent work of women labor and social historians, exploring the world of women's work in the factory, shop, office, and home. Mary Blewett has added the women's perspective to the much studied shoe industry. Jacqueline Hall and associates have significantly contributed to our understanding of work, family, and community in the twentieth-century southern textile industry. Susan Porter Benson and Marjorie Davies have extended the analysis of Taylorized work reorganization to women in the service economy of department stores and offices. Historical sociologist Ruth Milkman has surveyed the relationships of industrial structures, union programs, and management policies to the sexual division of labor in the electrical and automobile industries. Ruth Schwartz Cowan has examined how technological change in the home differentially affected the domestic tasks of men and women. Finally, Ava Baron has called for a new gendered labor history which delineates the gendered features of both men's and women's work. (Blewett 1988; Hall, et al. 1987; Benson 1986; Davies 1982; Milkman 1987; Cowan 1983; Baron 1991).

Fifth, many of the new labor histories imply a social analysis of technology and work which reaches into the realms of worker organization and worker protest. Indeed, technological change at the workplace seems to induce worker organization and widespread worker protest. Although a time lag of from ten to twenty years may exist, the technically dynamic sectors of the industrial economy seem to induce phases of worker activism. For example, the shoe industry reorganized in the 1820s and mechanized in the 1860s and exploded in the Great Shoe Strike of 1861. The textile industry mechanized in the 1810s and 1820s and realized extensive worker organization and activism in the 1830s and 1840s. The railroads were centers of managerial innovation in the 1850s and 1860s and experienced repeated extensive and explosive worker protests in the 1870s, 1880s, and 1890s. The iron and steel industry underwent technical and organizational change in the 1870s and 1880s and exploded in the 1890s and again in the 1910s and later in the 1930s. In the metal trades, a continuous process of mechanical and organizational innovation disrupted the traditional arrangements of work and skills causing continuous strikes in the first decades of the twentieth-century. And, the development of the mass production industries in the 1910s and 1920s brought about the social explosion of the Congress of Industrial Organizations in the 1930s.

To be sure, the connection between innovation and worker protest was neither direct nor immediate. Nonetheless, a phase of technological change consistently preceded a phase of worker activism and protest. Sometimes the strength of management created a demoralizing legacy of defeat and inhibited the success of organization or protest. But, often after another lag or other innovations, the worker efforts at organization and protest reappeared. Despite the considerable attention paid to issues of work and technology and to worker organization and worker protest, few have fully explored the broader patterns of the relationship between technological change and worker activism.

Finally, Americans have forestalled and forgotten an important social debate since the 1920s—the relationship between technology and unemployment. Beginning in the 1920s and continuing into the early 1930s, the "machine civilization" debate attracted the attention of social commentators, theorists and critics. To a certain extent, this debate now takes the form of an historical debate over the causes of the Great Depression in the 1930s, specifically in theories of overproduction and underconsumption. As a consequence of extensive mechanization, the nation's output rose by about fifty percent with a nearly stable workforce in the 1920s. Nonetheless, the social, economic, and political crisis of the economic catastrophe commanded the attention of policy makers. In the next decade, World War II sidetracked the social debate. But, the debate reemerged in the post-war period as a consequence of the automation of the Ford engine plant in the 1950s. The "prophets of doom" were denounced for their "automation hysteria," since the hard, costly, and inflexible mechanical automation did not readily adapt to the new conditions of production. Now, however, the possible applications of the much more flexible and adaptable computer and programmable robot along an extensive front in homes, offices, shops, and factories once again call for a reopening and continuation of that social debate that first appeared over fifty years ago.

REFERENCES

Anderson-Conk, M. 1980. *The United States Census and Labor Force Change: A History of Occupational Statistics, 1870-1940.* Ann Arbor: UMI Research Press.

Anderson, M. 1988. *The American Census: A Social History*. New Haven: Yale University Press.

Baron, A. 1991. "Gender and Labor History: Learning from the Past, Looking into the Future." In *Work Engendered: Toward a New History of American Labor*. Ithaca: Cornell University Press.

Benson, S. P. 1986. *Counter Cultures: Saleswomen, Managers, and Customers in American Department Stores, 1890-1940*. Urbana: University of Illinois Press.

Blewett, M. H. 1988. *Men, Women, and Work: Class, Gender, and Protest in the New England Shoe Industry, 1780-1910*. Urbana: University of Illinois Press.

Braverman, H. 1974. *Labor and Monopoly Capital: The Degradation of Work in the Twentieth Century*. New York: Monthly Review Press.

Brody, D. 1965. *Labor in Crisis: The Steel Strike of 1919*. Philadelphia: J. B. Lippencott Company.

——. 1969. *Steelworkers in America: The Nonunion Era*. New York: Harper and Row.

Chandler, A. D. 1977. *The Visible Hand: The Managerial Revolution in American Business*. Cambridge, Mass.: Harvard University Press.

Cohen, L. 1990. *Making a New Deal: Industrial Workers in Chicago, 1919-1939*. New York: Cambridge University Press.

Cowan, R. S. 1983. *More Work for Mother: The Ironies of Household Technology from the Open Hearth to the Microwave*. New York: Basic Books.

Davies, M. W. 1982. *Women's Place is at the Typewriter: Office Work and Office Workers, 1870-1930*. Philadelphia: Temple University Press.

Dawley, A. 1979. *Class and Community: The Industrial Revolution in Lynn*. Cambridge, Mass.: Harvard University Press.

Dublin, T. 1979. *Women at Work: The Transformation of Work and Community in Lowell, Massachusetts, 1826-1860*. New York: Columbia University Press.

——. 1981. *Farm to Factory: Women's Letters, 1830-1860*. New York: Columbia University Press.

Edsforth, R. 1987. *Class Conflict and Cultural Consensus: The Making of a Mass Consumer Society in Flint, Michigan*. New Brunswick: Rutgers University Press.

Eggert, G. G. 1981. *Steel Masters and Labor Reform, 1886-1923*. Pittsburgh: University of Pittsburgh Press.

Faler, P. G. 1981. *Mechanics and Manufacturers in the Early Industrial Revolution: Lynn, Massachusetts, 1780-1860*. Albany: State University of New York Press.

Fox, R. W. and T. J. J. Lears, eds. 1983. *The Culture of Consumption: Critical Essays in American History, 1880-1980*. New York: Pantheon Books.

Gartman, D. 1986. *Auto Slavery: The Labor Process in the American Automobile Industry*. New Brunswick: Rutgers University Press.

Gordon, D., R. Edwards, and M. Reich. 1982. *Segmented Work, Divided Workers: The Historical Transformation of Labor in the United States*. New York: Basic Books.

Gutman, H. 1977. *Work, Culture, and Society in Industrializing America*. New York: Vintage.

Hall, J. D., et al. 1987. *Like a Family: The Making of a Southern Mill World*. Chapel Hill: University of North Carolina Press.

Haraven, T. K. 1982. *Family Time and Industrial Time: The Relationship Between Family and Work in a New England Industrial Community*. New York: Cambridge University Press.

Haraven, T. K., and R. Langenbach. 1978. *Amoskeague: Life and Work in a New England Industrial Community*. New York: Pantheon Books.

Harris, H. 1982. *The Right to Manage: Industrial Relations Policies of American Business in the 1940s*. Madison: University of Wisconsin Press.

Harris, N. 1981. "The Drama of Consumer Desire." In Mayr and Post (Eds.), *Yankee Enterprise*. Washington, D. C.: Smithsonian Institution Press, 189-216.

Hounshell, D. A. 1981. "The System: Theory and Practice." In Mayr and Post (Eds.), *Yankee Enterprise*. Washington, D. C.: Smithsonian Institution Press, 127-52.

———. 1984. *From the American System to Mass Production, 1800-1932: The Development of Manufacturing Technology in the United States*. Baltimore: Johns Hopkins University Press.

Jeremy, D. J. 1981. *Trans-Atlantic Industrial Revolution: The Diffusion of Textile Technologies Between Britain and America, 1790-1930s*. Cambridge, Mass.: Massachusetts Institute of Technology Press.

Kelley, R. D. G. 1993. "'We Are Not What We Seem:' Rethinking Black Working-Class Opposition in the Jim Crow South." *American Historical Review*, 80:75-112.

Kulik, G., R. Parks, and T. Z. Penn, eds. 1982. *The New England Mill Village, 1790-1860*. Cambridge, Mass.: Massachusetts Institute of Technology Press.

Laurie, B. 1980. *Working People of Philadelphia, 1800-1850*. Philadelphia: Temple University Press.

Lewis, E. 1991. *In Their Own Interests: Race, Class, and Power in Twentieth Century Norfolk, Virginia*. Berkeley: University of California Press.

Licht, W. 1983. *Working for the Railroad: The Organization of Work in the Nineteenth-Century*. Princeton: Princeton University Press.

———. 1986. "The Case of Nineteenth-Century American Railroad Workers. In Stephenson C. and R. Asher (Eds.), *Life and Labor: Dimensions of American Working-Class History*. Albany: State University of New York Press.

Lichtenstein, N. and S. Meyer. 1989. *On the Line: Essays in the History of Auto Work*. Urbana: University of Illinois Press.

Mayr, O. and R. C. Post, eds. 1981. *Yankee Enterprise: The Rise of the American System of Manufacturers*. Washington, D. C.: Smithsonian Institution Press.

Meyer, S. 1981. *The Five Dollar Day: Labor Management and Social Control in the Ford Motor Company, 1908-1921*. Albany: State University of New York Press.

———. 1988. "The Persistence of Fordism: Workers and Technology in the Automobile Industry, 1900-1960." In Lichtenstein and Meyer (Eds.), *On the Line: Essays in the History of Auto Work*. Urbana: University of Illinois Press.

———. 1989. *On the Line: Essays in the History of Auto Work*. Urbana: University of Illinois Press.

———. 1992. *'Stalin Over Wisconsin': The Making and Unmaking of Militant Unionism, 1900-1950*. New Brunswick: Rutgers University Press.

Milkman, R. 1987. *Gender at Work: The Dynamics of Job Segregation by Sex during World War II*. Urbana: University of Illinois Press.

Montgomery, D. 1979. *Workers Control in America: Studies in the History of Work, Technology, and Labor Struggles*. New York: Cambridge University Press.

———. 1987. *The Fall of the House of Labor: The Workplace, the State, and American Labor Activism*. New York: Cambridge University Press.

Mulligan, W. H. 1986. "From Artisan to Proletarian: The Family and Vocational Education of Shoemakers in the Handicraft Era." In Stephenson, C. and R. Asher (Eds.), *Life and Labor: Dimensions of American Working-Class History*. Albany: State University of New York Press.

Nelson, D. 1975. *Managers and Workers: Origins of the New Factory System in the United States, 1880-1920*. Madison: University of Wisconsin Press.

———. 1980. *Frederick W. Taylor and the Rise of Scientific Management*. Madison: University of Wisconsin Press.

Nevins, A. 1954. *Ford: The Man, the Times, the Company*. New York: Charles Scribner's Sons.

Noble, D. F. 1979. "Social Choice in Machine Design: The Case of Automatically Controlled Machine Tools." In Zimbalist, A. (Ed.), *Case Studies in the Labor Process*. New York: Monthly Review Press.

———. 1984. *Forces of Production: A Social History of Industrial Automation*. New York: Knopf.

Peterson, J. S. 1987. *The Automobile Industry: A Social History, 1900-1933*. Albany: State University of New York Press.

Prude, J. 1983. *The Coming of Industrial Order: Town and Factory Life in Rural Massachusetts, 1810-1860*. New York: Cambridge University Press.

Rosenzweig, R. 1983. *Eight Hours for What We Will: Workers and Leisure in an Industrial City, 1870-1920*. New York: Cambridge University Press.

Smith, M. R. 1977. *Harpers Ferry Armory and the New Technology: The Challenge of Change*. Ithaca, N.Y.: Cornell University Press.

———. 1981. "Military Entrepreneurship." In Mayr and Post (Eds.), *Yankee Enterprise*. Washington, D. C.: Smithsonian Institution Press, 60-102.

Stone, K. 1974. "The Origins of Job Structures in the Steel Industry." *Review of Radical Political Economics* 6:113-73.

Stromquist, S. 1987. *A Generation of Boomers: The Pattern of Railroad Labor Conflict in Nineteenth-Century America*. Urbana: University of Illinois Press.

Susman, W. I. 1984. *Culture as History: The Transformation of American Society in the Twentieth-Century*. New York: Pantheon Books.

Thompson, E. P. 1967. "Time, Work-discipline, and Industrial Capitalism. *Past and Present* 38:56-97.

Trotter, J. W. 1990. *Coal, Class, and Color: Blacks in Southern West Virginia, 1915-32.* Urbana: University of Illinois Press.

Wallace, A. F. C. 1978. *Rockdale: The Growth of an American Village during the Industrial Revolution.* New York: W. W. Norton Company.

Woodbury, R. S. 1972. *Studies in the History of Machine Tools.* Cambridge, Mass.: Massachusetts Institute of Technology Press.

2

Work Skill in Historical Perspective

Robert Asher

Homo sapiens is nature's most innovative technologist. But until the Industrial Revolution, humans developed new technologies at a relatively glacial pace. During the last two hundred years, the pace of human technological change has accelerated dramatically. Today the transformation of work is proceeding with unprecedented rapidity. As human technologies changed, the working experiences of humans were transformed, altering the skills used, the pace of work, the rewards received by the producer, and the social and physical environment in which work is done.

In this chapter I will analyze the character of changes in work skills in the United States in the years since the Civil War, focusing on the work of non-professional and non-managerial workers in manufacturing and in the service sector. My field work in Connecticut factories and offices and the investigations of other historians and journalists will be used to provide examples of the reactions of men and women to the way their work has been transformed during the last half century. I will consider the negative and positive aspects of this uneven, often polarized transformation.

In 1889, David A. Wells, one of America's most widely read economists, published *Recent Economic Changes*, a book that considered at length the emergence of mechanized production technologies and the impact they had on working people. Wells believed that new machinery was essential to progress. Like so many of his contemporaries who were awed by the sublime power of modern industrial technology, Wells admired the way machinery was "summoned into existence" by the "seemingly weird power of genius." Unlike many of his less analytical contemporaries, Wells went beyond the reification of technology to consider the social factors involved in the way technology developed and the impact it had on workers.

Wells understood that militant worker defense of their prerogatives often led employers to seek out technologies that would make labor more tractable by undermining the relative monopoly of skills that augmented worker bargaining power. As Wells put it, "the first remedial idea of every employer whose labor is discontented being to devise and use a tool in place of a man." Wells also understood that skill dilution and the elimination of specific occupations caused by the introduction of new work technologies created hardships for workers. "All transitions," he wrote, "even those to a better stage,are inevitably accompanied by human suffering." Such "growing pains" were unavoidable. Laws, wrote the classical economist, could not "arrest such transitions" to a better world that would bring "an almost immeasurable degree of increased good to mankind in general" (Wells, 127).

Without question, Wells described accurately the operation of a profit-driven, competitive capitalist economy in which planning and coordination existed only at the firm level. Little has changed since Wells wrote. Today, the force of international competition in product markets, combined with production technologies that can be diffused more easily than ever before, produces a searing work discipline that has intensified the pace of labor and alters work skills in ways that are often dehumanizing (Thompson 1983; Harastzi 1977).

Throughout the last two centuries, an intensified division of labor reduced the degree of autonomy exercised previously by most workers, a power which had given them some manner of control over the pace of work, the length of work periods, the location of work and the actual techniques of work. New machinery and the restructuring of work by managers frequently has downgraded the physical skills and use of experiential knowledge employed by producers.

Any analysis of the process of skill reduction since the onset of the Industrial Revolution is complicated by the difficulty of comparing agricultural work with manufacturing activity. Many of the first factory workers were women and men who were raised in agricultural settings and first performed in their homes the kind of work—e.g., spinning, weaving and shoe making—that they would do in non-mechanized and then mechanized factories. Factory work generally required a more intense division of labor and entailed a much more rigid work discipline, determined largely by the factory owner. Within many nineteenth century factories, there was a great deal of non-mechanized labor—involving transporting materials, delivering messages, inspection, and record keeping. Was such work any less skilled than similar—and generally low skilled—functions performed on a farm or in a small family-owned shop? And how are we to compare the skill levels of many factory machine tenders, who were usually classified as semi-skilled workers, with much of the agricultural labor that was performed in barns, fields, gardens, and kitchens? It would be fair to suggest that there was more variety in the low and semi-skilled work performed on a farm and more autonomy, especially for individual proprietors, but also for hired hands. I believe most agricultural work should be considered to be on a par with the kind of "semi-skilled" work that does involve the use of significant amounts of discretion and accumulated knowledge, a point cogently demonstrated by the work of Kenneth Kusterer (1978).

Mechanization of cotton and wool spinning began in the United States in the last quarter of the eighteenth century. By the 1820s integrated factories that combined mechanized thread production and weaving were rapidly spreading throughout New England. While the loom fixers who repaired and adjusted textile machinery were artisans skilled in woodworking and metal forming, the bulk of the machine tenders were young women who undoubtedly had been exposed to hand carding, spinning and weaving in the households where they were raised. The extant materials on the reactions of these women to shifting from hand work to machine tending suggest that their strong negative reactions focused on the noise and physical danger in machine work, the fatigue produced by the combination of long hours of work and increases in the speed of the textile machinery, the number of machines each operative was required to tend, and inequities in the discipline imposed by overseers. These women did not view thread-making and weaving as life-long occupations that embodied traditions, and skills, whose erosion by machine production would create a threat to their identity (Robinson 1898; Dublin 1979).

Throughout the ante-bellum period, large numbers of the immigrant English, Irish and German handloom weavers, concentrated in large cities (e.g., Philadelphia and New York), and continued to practice their traditional skills, while complaining about the intense work-pace necessary to make a living in a market flooded with the output of other hand weavers and low-priced, machine-made cloth. Unfortunately, there is no information on the number (or reactions) of hand weavers who eventually ended up working in textile factories as machine operatives (Laurie and Schmitz 1981).

Shoemaking was another artisanal trade that shifted from home to factory production and was mechanized, step by step, during the nineteenth century. Shoe artisans protested bitterly about the loss of income and independence that came with these developments. One bootmaker interviewed by investigators of the Massachusetts Bureau of Labor Statistics in 1870 commented that shoemaking machinery had "rendered skilled labor of less value." Another concurred, but added that skilled labor was not yet "entirely valueless." A man of unknown background who worked as a shoe inspector in a factory commented that machinery had "rendered work more tedious and monotonous" (Massachusetts Bureau of Labor Statistics, 176). Skilled lasters, whose craft was the last part of the shoemaking process to be mechanized, unionized and struggled in the 1890s to delay the introduction of lasting machinery that threatened to eliminate totally their specialized skills. Historians do not know whether many hand lasters operated the lasting machines that were common throughout the shoe industry by the first decade of the twentieth century (Yellowitz 1977).

The best material on worker reaction to skill destruction in the nineteenth century comes from machinists. There is a certain irony here, in that metal machining was a skilled trade that was created, *de novo* in the late eighteenth and early nineteenth centuries. From the inception of widespread metal machining—to produce firearms, textile machinery, and steam engines—a significant division of labor was present. Very simple, single-purpose metal cutting machinery was tended by low paid operatives and by apprentices, who were working their way up to more complicated equipment. But until the late 1860s, it appears that the number of jobs calling for the work of skilled, all-around machinists was actually increasing. By the 1880s skilled machinists began to complain, for the first time, that their talents were under assault—not by new machinery but because of the advent of more specialization in the production process. John Morrison, a twenty-three year old machinist who worked in New York City, told the U. S. Senate Committee on Labor and Capital in 1883 that

. . . the trade has been subdivided and those subdivisions have been again subdivided, so that a man never learns the machinist's trade now. Ten years ago he learned, not the whole of the trade, but a fair portion of it. . . . wherever there is one particular kind of machinery built, every man learns his particular part and is kept steadily at that and knows no other part . . . It has a very demoralizing effect upon the mind throughout (U.S. Congress 1885, I 755-756).

Skilled workers clearly did not enjoy seeing the range of applicability for their skills being restricted. Some believed that there would be natural limits to the subdivision of labor. James M. McIntosh, a Scottish-born engraver who made sketches for the plates used to print designs on textiles, told the Senate Committee that he did not think that the division of labor would "go any farther . . . It is found that a man who is only acquainted with one item of a branch is not a productive workman . . . he will by and by have to step over the border of his experience and do something that will be productive in another line. That has been carried as far as possible in England . . ." However, when asked whether there would be a halt to technological unemployment resulting from new labor-saving machinery McIntosh was more ambivalent: "I don't know, I am sure, what to say about that," he replied (U.S. Congress 1885: II, 161).

As industrialization and technological change continued during the next fifty years, many traditional forms of hand production were entirely eliminated (glass bottle blowing is perhaps the most dramatic example), some forms of machine production became more simplified and other types of machine production became more complicated. In 1934, Harry Jerome conducted a pioneering investigation of the impact of mechanization on skill. Responses to questionnaires mailed to 101 factories indicated that labor-saving machinery introduced since 1920 had reduced the number of skilled workers in 25 percent of the cases reported, eliminated semi-skilled workers 43 percent of the time and led to declines in common labor in 32 percent of the cases. Another sampling taken by Jerome (which he did not describe in adequate detail) suggested that when *skill* was *reduced* by mechanization, most (80 percent) of the jobs downskilled or eliminated were skilled labor positions. In his most precise study, Jerome found that

of 39 labor-saving changes in handling equipment and methods for which our informants stated the grade of labor before and after the change, 3 lowered the grade required, 24 made no substantial

change and 12 raised the skill requirements for all or part of the
crew, chiefly by substituting semi-skilled workers for unskilled . . .
On the other hand, in 45 . . . [cases] . . . affecting . . . processing operations . . . the number of common laborers was reduced from 36 to
6, semi-skilled from 698 to 331, and skilled from 231 to 8 (Jerome,
402).

Jerome pointed to four types of mechanization: innovations in
materials handling that did not alter the actual processing operation; changes in materials handling that allowed a standardization of
production processes that altered both the number of people
employed and the skills they used; changes in processing that
directly displaced hand skills with machinery; and changes in
machine production that increased the quality and quantity of output and either upgraded or downgraded the skills needed by machine
operatives and repair people. In his qualitative analysis Jerome identified both skill dilution and skill enhancement. His account of the
latter process is particularly instructive. Jerome noted that when
displaced manual methods of production involved low skill labor,
mechanization had led to an upgrading of work skills:

For example, the warp tying-in machine, used in cotton weaving,
enables a skilled machine operator, with an assistant, to do work
formerly requiring 12 to 18 tying-in girls. Their work required considerable adeptness and experience, but not a degree of skill comparable with that required of the machine operator.

Jerome also noted that mechanization did require some additional
skilled workers to produce and repair production machinery. He did
not discuss an important aspect of this phenomenon: the evolution
of some types of production machinery from relatively simple equipment controlled by semi-skilled operatives to extremely complex
machinery that required highly skilled operatives.

I first encountered this phenomenon in interviews with workers at a modern glass-bottle factory in Connecticut. A retired veteran
machine repairman, who had worked in the midwest and had trav-
elled throughout the country with his factory managers to study
production techniques, explained that since the 1920s "automat-
ics", as they were called, had become much more complicated and
called for a higher grade of labor among the operators. In the early
1970s, continued technological changes—the introduction of new
Independent Section (IS) machines, eliminated some traditional skills
but required the addition of others. For example, it had once been

essential for machine operators to use visual observation to estimate the temperature of the molten glass that was fed into the
machines by air suction:

> Everything was by the eye . . . I could look up at a glob of glass
> and tell you within five degrees how hot or how cold it was . . . We
> had to govern the heat in our feeders. We had three sections. The
> one end out there would be the hottest end so we'd cool that off a
> little bit, start cooling the glass down until we got it down to where
> we wanted it for the heat, and we had to do that all by hand.

While electronic feedback devices allowed automation of this aspect
of the machinery, the higher speed of operation and the greater number of molds on the IS machines made their operation more challenging. A skilled IS machine operative explained:

> an ordinary person doesn't realize that there can be approximately
> three hundred things wrong with a bottle . . . You make an adjust-
> ment and you fix it . . . You have to feel your way on all of your ail-
> ments on a bottle . . . Man, it's a tough job sometimes, to get them
> [the machines] going.

Moreover, cost-efficient production required many major adjustments in the IS machines to be made while the machine is still running. "Somebody's got to stand there and throw the glass out on
that particular section and you've got to reach in and grab the blanks
or the molds while the machine is still going" (Asher 1983: 40-41).

A somewhat similar pattern emerged in Connecticut's brass
industry. Casters had once been an elite group of workers, whose
hand skills and monopolized experiential knowledge of casting gave
them tremendous freedom of action on the job and the power to
take short vacations (especially during the summer) when they felt
they needed a respite from work (Brecher 1982; Bucki 1980). Between
1910 and 1917 Connecticut's largest brass manufacturers introduced
oil fired and electric furnaces that allowed relatively inexperienced
workers to be used as furnace operators. Skilled casters, who resented
this degradation of their labor, refused to work on the new furnaces
and sought employment in smaller factories that still used traditional equipment. A man who learned casting in the 1920s on traditional, coal-fired furnaces and then saw them replaced by state of the
art equipment commented that the new equipment required "no
skill at all. You are an operator. The skill goes to the laboratory"
(Brecher 1982, 65-130). As time passed, both casting furnaces and

annealing furnaces became larger and more complicated to operate. Edward Labacz remembered the open hearth annealing furnaces of the 1930s and 1940s and recounted the transition in 1950 to newer models:

> We had to load the pans with metal . . . When we pulled it out, it was hot metal. We had to take long prongs and push it [the metal] out of the way. We didn't have jitneys like you have now. Now it's easier. You just load the table; it goes in the door . . . it comes out cooled. There's no more handling of hot metal . . . We had three men on a furnace; now we've got one man doing the same job.

But the job of the remaining operator on the highly mechanized furnace was more complicated: "It takes more skill to run the equipment; you have to be knowledgeable if something is not cycling properly." The newer furnaces were atmospheric furnaces that did not use oxygen. The operator had to adjust the gas mixture in the furnaces and constantly check for leaks. "And you walk around and check it to make sure the water pressure is not dropping . . . You have to be careful how you load it too." Consequently, the labor grade on the newer furnaces introduced in the 1950s was raised from a three to a seven. "You couldn't put just anybody on it," recalled Labacz (Interview, March 3, 1983). In the nineteenth century, when hand-operated printing presses were increasingly being replaced by high-speed, steam-powered machinery, there was significant labor displacement of skilled hand-printers. As the Typographical Association of New York lamented, "many who had spent from five to seven years of the flower of their lives acquiring a knowledge of their profession, were left without employment, or were obliged to resort to some business with which they were unacquainted . . ." The Columbia Typographical Society of Washington, D.C. hoped to use its bargaining power to preserve hand skills by "making such alterations to the price of presswork and the introduction of rollers and roller boys as will enable employers to have their work done as cheap, better and with greater certainty, by hand, than by the use of steam or power presses, while at the same time pressmen will be able to make as good wages, if not better than under the present system." Such strategies rarely were effective in the long run. The steam press displaced hand-printing. But as the nineteenth century wore on, steam presses became more complex to operate. An 1893 article in the union journal, *American Pressman*, explained that the idea that there is "little brainwork needed in running a web press" was erroneous: "These monsters have to be watched as closely as a baby; and watched, too, with a sharp eye to one's own personal safety as much as to the proper conduct of the press and paper." In 1949 the head of the International Printing Pressmen's Union commented that contemporary printing presses were "good machines" that required "good men" as operators. "It is a mistake to allow a machine which costs thousands of dollars to be managed by an incompetent pressman . . .The superior performance of the qualified workman fairly justifies his higher wages . . ." (Baker 1957). On the other hand, during a tour of the pressroom of the *Hartford Courant*, which had recently (1982) installed fully automated presses, several pressmen told me that despite their good pay, they felt the most recent technological changes had taken the "art" out of their jobs because they no longer loaded large paper rolls and manually adjusted the presses.

In the 1960s Floyd Mann and Richard Hoffman reported on the differences between work in a new, automated electric power plant and work in an older plant owned by the same company. Unfortunately, these investigators did not question workers who had shifted from semi-automatic to automatic machinery about the actual effects of the change on their work skills. But the investigators provided data on the distribution of wages in each plant that clearly indicated that a significant polarization had taken place in the automated plant. Workers earning $105 and over per week constituted 31 percent of the workforce in the automated plant and only 11 percent in the older plant. Workers earning under $85 per week were 44 percent of the labor force in the new plant and 29 percent in the older one. These data suggest that *on average* there were more skilled jobs, and more low skilled jobs in the automated plant. An interview I had with a boiler operator in the power plant of the Pratt and Whitney Aircraft Company in Middletown, CT provides concrete details about the upskilling process that accompanies *some* forms of automation. Fred Drosehn described the installation of automated controls on the boilers, exhausters and compressors in the plant. Consolidation of control functions on one master board had displaced some labor. Actual direct observation of burners to be sure that they were lit and running properly had been eliminated, as had the need to be next to each burner to start it up. Drosehn preferred the net effect of these changes, describing the new jobs as "more demanding. You had more things to watch than you did before, but everything was right in front of you in one place" (Drosehn interview).

Paper making machinery required skilled operators, from the development of the first machines in the ante-bellum period to the present. Papermakers had to constantly adjust their equipment as it was running, a job that required both knowledge and agility, which was essential in the nineteenth century mills to avoid being caught in rows of revolving knives (McGaw 1977). I interviewed a veteran paper machine operator who had spent thirty years (1947-1977) operating machines that produced specialty paper products. Working with a helper, the operator set-up and ran his machine *and* used a knife to cut heavy-duty particle board as it came off the rollers of the paper machine. This job was one of the few hand-labor craft positions left in the paper industry in the 1960s. Cutting was physically demanding (only tall, strong men were chosen) because of the thickness of the particle board, the speed of the machine and the dampness of the mills, all of which made arthritis a common problem that forced the retirement of many bowmen by their middle forties. "It's an art in itself, a talent cutting this board," recounted a younger papermaker. Asked about his experience with machinery (introduced in 1962) that automated the cutting process and added more pulp-refining vats to the machine, the veteran described the complex of changes associated with the new equipment: he no longer worked with a helper, he had increased responsibilities for the pulp refining vats and he did not have to cut paper coming off the revolving drums of the machine. On balance, the total work load increased, as did his pay. Equally important, he viewed favorably the elimination of the physical skill of paper cutting positively because it prolonged his working life: "A person our age, they couldn't be on the paper machine the way it was thirty years ago. We wouldn't have had the strength or anything."

The preceding examples of upskilling should *not* be interpreted as an argument that the degree of skill, worker control over the content of their jobs and the relative earning power of most of today's skilled machine tenders are comparable to those of the traditional artisan. These examples indicate that during the last two hundred years, the ongoing process of mechanization has displaced and downskilled large numbers of highly skilled artisans and then selectively and gradually, for a limited minority of workers, expanded the mental skills (and occasionally the physical skills) used on the job.

As the work of Kenneth I. Spenner (1983 and in this volume) and Patrick C. Walker (1983) suggests, there is an appalling lack of reliable information on the overall balance of changes in work skills since 1945. The precision of analyses of skill levels that rely on the

DOT classification of occupations is very suspect. No data bases exist to allow even the crudest quantification of changes in worker autonomy. While Bluestone and Harrison (1982) report that workers who are displaced by new technologies and have to leave the company in which they were employed experience, on average, a 15 percent decline in income if and when they find new jobs, they are not able to offer a precise analysis of the actual changes in job skills such workers encounter. (But any attempt at this kind of analysis will be complicated, especially because many of the workers displaced from jobs in transportation and manufacturing have found and will continue to find new employment in service jobs that have only recently been analyzed (by proponents of comparable worth payment schemes) in ways that allow meaningful comparisons with blue collar work.

The continued rationalization of labor, by the restructuring of work (with and without the introduction of new machinery) is, as Harry Braverman (1974) and Paul Thompson (1983) maintain, a function of the drive of capitalist (and socialist) managers for greater efficiency (to earn higher profits and to free-up resources for producing more material goods). *Forces of Production*, David Noble's study (1984) of technological change and labor relations in metal machining, suggests that technological imperatives and a desire to both eliminate and weaken the job-control and bargaining power of skilled machinists motivated the push for automated production technologies by managers of aerospace firms and Air Force officials (who fund a great deal of the research on automation).

Many workers who shift from manufacturing to service jobs are undoubtedly transferring from jobs that have been downskilled (or eliminated) to jobs in another production sector (the service sector) that have also seen the autonomy of the worker circumscribed and work skills diluted by new technologies and by changes in work organization. *There were innumerable relatively uncreative, unskilled and semi-skilled jobs in both manufacturing and service occupations before the advent of the potent electronic technologies that have transformed so much work in the years since World War II and especially since the mid-1960s.* This crucial point must be factored into any analysis of the reaction of working people to small decreases or increases in the level and variety of job skills. As the following analysis will demonstrate, workers whose jobs were already relatively routine before new technologies reduced the skills involved *often did not mind the changes, especially if repetitive or strenuous physical operations were eliminated.* This is not to say that such "low" and "semi-skilled" jobs did not require workers to exercise important cognitive faculties, both to monitor production quality and to adjust and repair quickly malfunctioning equipment (Kusterer 1978).

Although space limitations have restricted the focus of this essay to the reactions of workers to changes in job skills, the historical reaction of workers to technological change has never focused on this aspect to the exclusion of others. For workers, who regularly had to cope with intermittent employment, long working hours, an intense work pace dictated by competition in handicraft markets and by machinery in many factories, and the ravages of occupational injuries and diseases, technological change was viewed as a general threat to jobs, incomes and skills. Thus, printers faced with the threat of job-displacement embodied in the linotype machine, rarely discussed whether or not work on this new technology was more skilled than hand typesetting. Their union focused first on obtaining guarantees that hand printers would be employed on linotype machines and secondarily on reducing the length of the working day and controlling output to preserve jobs and protect printers who were now machine operators against the great increase in stress that accompanied the faster pace of machine typesetting.

Similarly, at the end of the nineteenth century, pottery workers in the Eastern factories in the United States resisted machine production for a short time but eventually succumbed when faced by the threat of losing all their jobs to mechanized producers in the midwest. John A. O'Neill, a leader of the National Brotherhood of Operative Potters told the United States Industrial Commission in 1901, "We saw the competition that was rapidly arising . . . and urged the adoption of the improved machinery . . . and the modernizing of factories . . ." (United States Industrial Commission XIV 652, 654). Skilled steelworkers organized in the Amalgamated Association of Iron, Steel and Tin Workers never tried to prevent directly the introduction of mechanized rolling mills that eliminated the need for most of the physical skills of rollers but still required operators with a broad base of experiential knowledge. Attempts to preserve jobs through featherbedding were successful in the short run but ended after the effective bargaining power of the Amalgamated was broken (in 1892) in the Pittsburgh district plants of the Carnegie Company (Cotnoir 1984). In the 1890s and early twentieth century unionized coal miners were able to slow the diffusion of coal cutting machinery by negotiating pay scales that reduced employer profits on machine mining in mines that did not have thick seams. While the UMWA could not prevent the skill dilution that accompanied machine mining, union pay scales did give machine operators a rough parity of income with the more skilled hand pick-miners (U.S. Commissioner of Labor 1904).

American workers understood that even the strongest trade unions were virtually powerless to prevent business owners from purchasing production technologies that reduced skills and eliminated entire occupational classifications. British workers, by contrast, were much more successful in delaying many types of mechanization. Only direct control of industry by workers, which was favored by those who leaned towards state socialism or worker-owned cooperatives, would give workers the power necessary to control the selection of production technologies. As sociologist Martin Meissner demonstrated so capably, the intrinsic characteristics of production machinery are the prime determinants of the kinds of skills workers will use on the job (Meissner 1969).

In the past, even socialist trade union leaders were often silent about the deskilling that accompanied mechanization or found themselves caught up in contradictory analysis. In the 1920s, Sidney Hillman, leader of the Amalgamated Clothing Workers of America, persuaded his union to adopt a policy of cooperating with management in union shops to rationalize clothing production through time-study of work and by accepting more efficient equipment. (For additional examples of unions helping management to introduce new technologies to prevent jobs from migrating to competing factories, see Slichter, Healy and Liverwash 1960, 357). Market competition (with non-union shops) made job preservation the prime objective of the ACWA. Quality of work life issues had to take a back seat to the quest to preserve work itself (Fraser 1983, 1984).

Consider also the views of a lower-level union leader, Antonino Crivello, of the Boot and Shoe Workers Union, as he responded in the late 1930s to union members who wanted "all special machines" thrown out of union shops. Crivello acknowledged the views of anthropologists like Ernest A. Hooton who warned the American Society of Mechanical Engineers in 1937 about the diffusion of "mechanical contrivances which eliminate the necessity of thought, judgment and skill in the user," pragmatic and ideological considerations effects of machinery, but he thought it wrong to oppose mechanization and "to declare ourselves against scientific advancement." After all, he said, "This is the machine age." It was also an era of competitive capitalism. His union tried, as Crivello put it, "to minimize the evil effects [of machinery] . . . [on] our members."

But the union could not "be unilateral . . . in this." Crivello hinted that there was another solution, but he demurred broaching it directly: "I am not going to dwell on the political aspect of this question. The economic problem [of unemployment] concerns us primarily at present" (Crivello, Box 1).

During World War I, many groups of militant workers—including members of the ACWA—raised the issue of worker control of industry. Although they discussed structural mechanisms for worker management of production, proponents of worker-control did not spell out the explicit meaning of such control for the maintenance of job skills. In the late 1930s and during WW II, organized workers in the mass production industries—and especially assembly-line workers—used their power on the shop and plant level to slow down production rates. These workers made no attempt to influence directly the kinds of production technologies that would be used and the manner in which the division of labor with existing technologies would be structured (Montgomery 1979; Lichtenstein 1982; Harris 1982).

During WW II socialists within the United Steelworkers raised the issue of worker management. In *The Dynamics of Industrial Democracy* Clint Golden and Harold Ruttenberg (1942) justified co-management on the grounds that "Management's assumption of sole responsibility for productive efficiency actually prevents the attainment of maximum output." The whole thrust of their argument suggests that skill preservation through the control of technological innovation and the division of labor were not seen as high priorities (or were not considered feasible in a competitive world marketplace) even by many radicals. Walter Reuther's 1942 statement of his position on wartime production explicitly eschewed direct worker control as he argued that greater efficiency in war production would be achieved by expanding labor representation on the principal war production agencies of the federal government (*New York Times*, December 13, 1942). As Nelson Lichtenstein and Howell J. Harris have demonstrated, the War Labor Board's policy makers took strong action to curb wildcat strikes and job actions, many of which were challenges to management prerogatives in setting payment scales and rates of output on machinery converted from civilian to war production (Lichtenstein 1982; Harris 1982).

In 1945 and 1946 management in many mass production industries (especially the automobile industry) launched a vigorous counter-offensive against the gains some unions had made in achieving a modest degree of control over production standards and machine rates in the late 1930s and during WW II. Management won the battle and forced union leaders and the rank and file to accept "management rights" contract clauses that renounced union claims to any direct authority over the kinds of production technologies that would be used. American unions were pressured, for the most part, into a reactive position (Harris 1982).

Since 1945, as new technologies have been introduced, unions have tried to protect the interests of workers by negotiating pay rates and job classifications that maintained earnings and kept jobs in the hands of members of the existing bargaining units. Since 1982 even the strongest "protections" against technological change that *some* unionized workers have been able to negotiate have not prevented the deskilling of the work of the workers whose jobs have been saved. Rather, UAW, IUE-UE-IBEW and IAM contracts provide some weak limits on management's right to use labor-saving technology to lay off workers, limit layoffs caused by outsourcing by restricting outsourcing itself, provide funds for retraining workers who lose their jobs when entire factories are closed as a consequence of new production technologies, and provide for short term maintenance of income for workers who are forced into lower skill, lower-paying jobs by technological change.

My interviews with workers at the West Haven, Connecticut plant of the Armstrong Rubber Company were particularly instructive about the way unions have been powerless to challenge the introduction of deskilling technology and the speed-up. These rubber workers could only obtain one concession from management when it introduced new work technologies: maintenance of earnings. Since 1950, the New Haven tire builders encountered three new generations of machinery. Each change in technology reduced the physical effort and removed some of the manual dexterity skilled tire-builders needed. The intensity of labor increased with each change in technology. "The pace does get harder, because you're pushing yourself harder because the ticket [the base rate] got harder," explained one tire builder. This man briefly switched jobs and became a tire inspector. He remembered the "peace of mind" that he had as an inspector because "I knew I didn't have to keep up with that pace." But he returned to tire building because the pay was higher. The local union's (United Rubber Workers) time study specialist indicated the fatalism of the workers about the tradeoff between manual effort and speed—as long as take home pay remained constant:

> That was their big bitch—commensurate earnings—if you changed the rate [per tire, and hence the speed]. They didn't care if you

changed the rate. We didn't care as long as the guys were able to make the same money they were making prior to the change in the rate.

Militant struggle was necessary to secure this objective. The tire builders used production slowdowns, plant-wide strikes and, after 1970, departmental walkouts to maintain their take home pay. They lacked the bargaining power to influence the way the new production technologies affected the quality of their work life (Asher 1983, 51).

Printers in some big cities—and especially New York—were actually able to delay the introduction of the first generation of *relatively* primitive automated typesetting equipment. But eventually linotype operators succumbed to the computerized, cold-typesetting process, and obtained the right to income security and, if they chose, jobs on the new equipment. An excellent sociological study of New York printers revealed that personality orientations determined the manner in which printers reacted to the technology that eliminated their refined mental and physical skills. Instrumentalists, who saw a job as a job, a way of earning a living, were either positive or neutral about the deskilling process. Traditionalists, who viewed their work as a craft and whose personal identity was closely linked to the pride they had in their work, disliked intensely the change thrust upon them (Rogers and Friedman 1980). In Connecticut, in the 1970s, many printers lost their jobs and livelihood outright. Among the printers who were still employed—in varying capacities, including page paste-up—a small minority were fortunate enough to obtain the more varied and complex jobs of typesetting for advertisements. These men enjoyed their new jobs. They griped when they were occasionally asked to do straight copy typesetting, but as one phototypesetter put it, "you thank the Lord you're setting them" instead of being unemployed (Asher 1983, 48).

A graphics artist who had transferred to computer designing after thirty-five years of hand drawing was in a position similar to this photo typesetter—her job had been downskilled, but she still used a large part of her knowledge in her work with the new production technology. She appreciated the fact that she still had a job that was relatively creative, but she knew things had once been better:

There's a different sort of fulfillment. The computer is not as demanding. You can get more done. It's challenging, but it's not a self-fulfilling thing. It's my job—its what I have to do to make a living . . . But the other way of doing the kind of work I do is more self-satisfying than the computer (Asher 1983, 59).

The effects on worker skills and autonomy of computer controlled machine tools has been subjected to particularly intensive analysis by historians and field researchers. Historian David Noble's (1984) research indicates that the developers of numerically controlled (N/C) machine tools were well-aware of the constricting effect such technologies would have on the work skills, autonomy and bargaining power of machinists. The Air Force explicitly sought (and still seeks) to reduce the influence that blue collar workers can bring to bear on defense production. Consequently, the Defense Department financed research and development of N/C machine tools and guaranteed their use by reimbursing defense contractors for the higher production costs arising from the imperfections of the first generation of N/C machine tools. It is clear that the pace of deskilling of work on N/C machine tools lagged far behind the timetable that business and government proponents of technological deskilling desired. Production with N/C machine tools continued, through the early 1960s, to require skilled all-around machinists in far greater numbers than had been anticipated.

Noble presents a detailed account of the disputes between unionized machinists (I.U.E. Local 201) and the management of General Electric's Lynn, Massachusetts jet-engine plant over the way work on N/C lathes was organized and compensated. In 1963, plant officials decided that rates on new N/C machines should be set at labor grade R-17, two levels under the R-19 classification of lathe operators. Militant veteran machinists disputed this classification and led shop-level (October 1964) and plant-wide (January 1965) strikes before GE agreed to the R-19 classification. GE also tried to get the IUE to waive seniority bidding on the N/C jobs, which union veterans interpreted as a device to staff N/C machines with carefully selected employees who would not raise issues of control (especially the right to program) and pay on the N/C machines, which GE hoped would eventually (as more production experience was gained and as machine capabilities were expanded) be operable by less experienced, lower paid workers (Noble 1984, 270-290).

In his field interviews and observations, Harley Shaiken, a machinist who is now an academic specialist, found that most employers did not want to use skilled workers on N/C metalworking equipment. In many U.A.W. plants, Shaiken found that management was hamstrung in its efforts to use younger, less experienced workers on N/C equipment by contractual seniority requirements. Consequently, managements often tried to manipulate job classification schemes and found the only way they could keep veteran employees from working on N/C machines was to upgrade job (and pay) classifications (Shaiken 1984, 93-95, 113).

By the early 1980s, N/C machine tools were much more reliable, more automated (they often changed tools and fed parts into fixtures) and operated at faster speeds than their predecessors. Small batch production on N/C machine tools often still required skilled workers, since frequently changed machining programs had to be debugged by knowledgeable workers. The veteran machinists who worked on such machines, and had the authority to reprogram when they discovered faults, enjoyed this work. One such machinist, who worked for the Emhart Company, cutting parts for automatic glass bottle blowing machines, told me that there were times when he missed some of the "fancy, intricate threading" he had done on traditional machine tools. But he admired the technical capabilities of the N/C machines:

> Oh, no. Never back to the manual things. This is wonderful. To be able to take a machine like that with all its intricate components and to make it do your bidding, this is the ultimate. It makes you feel good (Asher 1983, 35).

Several elderly machinists who operated N/C equipment told me that although they missed the hands-on experience of controlling the metal cutting operations on traditional machine tools, the reduced physical and mental effort on N/C operation had prolonged their working careers and reduced the fatigue they experienced. One veteran, who recounted that the "day went by faster" on traditional machine tools since there was more physical activity required of the operator, said that N/C equipment was "better for my eyes" and that switching to N/C machines was like becoming "a designated hitter for the Red Sox. You add to your career." And as I talked on the floor of a Connecticut job shop with a machinist who had learned his trade in Poland after World War II, the man pointed across the aisle to a youthful operator of a N/C multi-purpose milling center and commented, contemptuously, that the youngster would "die on it" without learning how to do complex hand work. Yet the machinist grudgingly admitted that N/C machines would allow him to prolong his career "when I'm a lot older" (Asher 1983, 29).

By the early 1980s, many companies, both large and small, used relatively inexperienced workers on many N/C machines. A job shop owner told Harley Shaiken that for many types of work, one N/C machine operated by a worker with one or two years of experience could replace an all around machinist with fifteen years of experience (Shaiken 1984, 113). Even these inexperienced workers, however, want to have more opportunity than they are often given to learn programming skills and to be able to take the initiative in correcting errors in programs written by specialized programmers who often lack the experiential knowledge of even relative newcomers who actually work with the equipment. One such worker, at the Pratt and Whitney Aircraft Company's East Hartford plant, pointed to the alienating effect of his work on N/C machines:

> People have pride in their work, but at the same time the company, by breaking things down into the simplest steps, and keeping you on the same routine jobs, leads to a lot of frustration . . . People feel like they're being cheated out of something (Asher 1983, 32).

The continued technological improvement in N/C machines and their rapid diffusion in the 1980s throughout factories in the United States and the rest of the industrial world has frequently led to layoffs of skilled machinists and other less skilled metalworkers. In large, modern factories, the percentage of skilled workers in all trades has fallen off significantly (Sabel 1982). This trend was first adumbrated in the mid-1950s by James A. Bright. Bright's analysis, which has been validated, went against the grain of prevailing opinion, including that held by union leaders, that "automation" would create more skilled jobs for most workers (Bright 1958; Walker 1983).

The use of new technologies to improve production efficiency and reduce the number (and militancy) of skilled workers, has been aptly summarized by Charles Sabel:

> once management begins to apply Fordist principles [i.e., increasing efficiency by using labor-saving machinery and a more advanced division of labor] in even a halting way, it quickly discovers the advantages of extending their application by further attacking the craftsmen's autonomy.

Sabel argues that even when management cannot dilute the skills needed for production with sophisticated machinery as quickly as it wants to, skilled workers "live a perpetual cliff-hanger" (p. 169). I believe that the most highly skilled workers are particularly aware of the possibilities of technological deskilling and technological unemployment because they *directly experience the manner in which their skills are used by management to develop and debug the technologies that will eventually be operated by less skilled workers.*

In 1968, a local manager at the GE Lynn plant decided to experiment with the kind of organization of N/C production that proponents of co-management would have endorsed. A *small* experimental group of thirteen operators manning five N/C lathes was given authority to program their machines, inspect their work and schedule production runs without the supervision of foremen and without any requirements to punch a time clock. These machinists were given a 10% pay bonus, presumably as a recognition of the extra managerial skills they were being asked to master and perform. The machinists involved in this experiment were fearful that it was a temporary ploy to pick their brains. But they forged ahead. Problems developed, however, as both foremen and other front-line supervisors at the factory felt their jobs were threatened by the autonomy given to the machinists. Some production planners openly refused to cooperate with the experimental machinists. Corporate officers at national headquarters grew uneasy about the plan, because of the freedom to structure worktime the machinists enjoyed and because of their bonus pay. The manager who initiated the pilot program was transferred to another plant. For reasons that Noble was not able to pinpoint, the experiment began without any attempt being made to measure pre-experimental productivity. Without a baseline, assessment of the cost-saving effect of the experiment was difficult (Noble, 271-313).

The machinists involved in the experiment came to enjoy the new structure of work and claimed that it saved the company money. There is some evidence to show that while actual output per lathe operator did not increase under the pilot program, the company saved on the *managerial* functions performed by the machinists. When the program was discontinued in 1972, General Electric brought three new managerial workers into the production area. Noble's entire account suggests that GE's top management ended the experiment because of its reluctance to share managerial authority with workers. This was part of a consistent pattern at GE. In the early 1980s, when inexpensive microprocessors became available, N/C machinists could have been taught, at very little expense, to do machine programming. But GE did not want to give its unionized workers this kind of power. GE has pushed ahead with elaborate automated production systems (Integrated Computer Aided

Manufacturing) that replace most machinists with machine tenders who load and unload banks of 4-5 machines (Noble, 271-333).

Technological change also has important effects on the work of "semi-skilled" metalworkers, people who do not have the high level of skills as all-around machinists and tool and die makers but who have exercised significant amounts of discretion and used important, albeit specialized, knowledge to increase the efficiency of their work. At the West Hartford plant of the Colt Firearms company, I interviewed a veteran drill press operator who made small parts on his drill press and took a great deal of pride in his low scrap (defective parts) rate. Installation of a new drill press (1979) reduced the number of spindles from six to four but increased machining speed to obtain a 100% increase in total output. The increased strain and the higher scrap rate of the new job troubled the press operator: "I used to love my job, but now I fight every day and it just breaks my heart" (Asher 1983, 23). On the other hand, a worker at a lower skill level, who had hand-fed blanks for metal buttons into a stamping machine, welcomed automation (1965) because it eliminated a very low skill, highly repetitive job. Tending three automated button stamping machines was "not as boring, because you're walking around, checking more things than if you just sit there and feed it over and over and over again" (Asher 1983, 31). Small watch parts makers at Timex welcomed mechanization of their machinery, since the physical exhaustion of their foot and leg muscles (that operated non-hydraulic foot controls for their drills or punches) had been a serious problem. But when fully automated machinery was introduced, the workers complained about the mental stress that accompanied their visual monitoring of banks of high-speed machines (Asher 1983, 60-64). There is, unfortunately, a dearth of controlled studies of the effects on workers of the tradeoff that automation often creates as it reduces physical stress while expanding responsibility for monitoring an increased volume of output, a change that has led to considerable mental stress.

When technological change removes *small* amounts of skill from relatively low skill jobs, many workers appreciate the trade-off between the loss of their mental (or physical) skills and the convenience and speed that are usually gained. Computer-linked teller machines were welcomed by every bank teller I interviewed for precisely this reason. Similarly, supermarket cashiers were generally pleased with optical scanners that read bar codes on packages and automatically entered prices on the cash register. The greater speed of the scanners helped to reduce the tension of customers, especially when there were long lines. Cashiers appreciated this improvement in their working environment, although they made it clear that their jobs were and continued to be boring (Asher 1983, 84-85). It should be noted that the workers interviewed about this type of tradeoff had not been pressured to increase work speeds to a point that they regarded as onerous. The following analysis of the computerization of telephone operators' work will illustrate the effect of such a speed-up on workers.

Interviews with electronics technicians who repair office equipment suggest that these tradesmen, who need two years of intensive study after high school to qualify for their jobs, do not mind the introduction of modular components or diagnostic computers that remove *some* of the skill from their job. But an electronics technician who worked at Hamilton Standard, debugging computers that monitored the flow of fuel on jet aircraft, indicated that in the last ten years new equipment and increased job specialization had made his work, on average, more repetitive and less skilled: "It's more boring and not so much of a challenge any longer . . . the way the machines are coming in, it's push a button, there's the results." On occasion, a problem developed that was more challenging than his previous work had been: "That aspect isn't too bad . . . But then, again, you're stuck on one item. And I find that drawing the shaft . . ." (Asher 1983, 67-68).

The preceding discussion has focused on the reaction of workers to changes in physical and mental work skills. The subject of worker autonomy deserves some attention, especially since some social scientists argue that on-the-job autonomy is the single most important predictor of people's degree of satisfaction with their work. As suggested earlier, one of the most fundamental changes wrought by the Industrial Revolution has been the shift of workers from agricultural work in which they had a large amount of autonomy in the performance of day-to-day work routines to supervised service and industrial work, in which business owners dictated many of the terms of work—length of the working day, work pace, production standards—to hired labor. In the nineteenth and early twentieth centuries, as sociologist Dan Clawson and historian David Montgomery have demonstrated, many skilled factory workers retained much more autonomy than had hitherto been assumed (Clawson 1980; Montgomery 1979). The development of modern science and industrial engineering facilitated the gradual transfer of power over production to business managements. By the 1920s this process was considerably advanced, and many unions had actually collaborated with management in the use of machinery and time-study procedures that reduced the autonomy of workers. The advent of computer-guided materials processing and computerized information processing was accompanied by increased levels of computer monitoring of workers. This monitoring encompasses more precise measurement of output than was previously possible and also involves the creation of a record of how a worker actually spends every minute of the working day. These developments have produced substantial stress for workers, especially since managements often *overestimate* the increase in production that new technologies make possible and because many business managers are especially prone to underestimating the rise in stress that is caused by new technologies that lead to a marked increase in the number of machines a worker has to monitor or to the amount of information a worker has to process.

An interview with a worker who had spent thirteen years in a Connecticut insurance company, ending up as a supervisor of a small unit (four workers), illustrates the increase in stress induced by machine-facilitated work reconstitution. Initially, each data-entry clerk specialized in processing only one type of claim. In 1985 new desktop computers were introduced and the clerks' jobs were redesigned to increase the variety of claims they handled. The degree of skill needed for actual claim handling was not increased. The workers were troubled by the new form their jobs had taken because their work routines, which were now closely monitored by their computers, no longer had any slack time. Without the small five or ten minute "breathers" that they had formerly been able to take, the insurance workers found that their jobs produced unbearable tension. Many resigned or requested transfers. Others were simply not able to meet the new production standards and were fired, which they found especially humiliating since they assumed that people they knew considered insurance work to be "easy" work that anyone could do (Asher, confidential interview, October 2, 1985).

Telephone operators who had been able to exercise *some* control over their work pace before the advent of computerized consoles, described work on the Traffic Service Position system introduced in the mid 1970s as "brain battering" because more calls had to be handled per hour, which eliminated the opportunity for brief exchanges with callers that had made their work less tedious, and because operators totally lost their control over the pace of work. They could no longer take a breather, *when they wanted to* by simply not plugging in to answer incoming requests for service. Now as soon as one customer had been disconnected, the computer routed another call into the operator's headset. To avoid this uninterrupted demand for service, an operator had to disconnect her or his head set. The computer recorded this act, which was a violation of company policy that had to be explained to a supervisor (Asher 1983, 75-80).

In 1984 pollster Daniel Yankelovich issued a widely publicized report, *Putting the Work Ethic to Work*, that included questions about the impact of technological change on people's work experiences. Responses indicated that only 22 percent of those polled experienced increased monotony as a consequence of technological change and 74 percent said new technologies made their work less routine and more interesting. Unfortunately, as is so common with such surveys, no attempt was made to ask refined questions that would shed light on the types of changes in work technology the respondents actually encountered. Meaningful analysis must distinguish between small changes, like improvements in the tensile strength and durability of materials being processed, the addition of digital readouts to machine tools (which all the machinists I interviewed thought were a very helpful innovation), or more user-friendly programming for routine information processing, and qualitatively different major changes in work technology that involve substantial or drastic alterations in the way work is done.

Given the lack of precision in most cross-sectional studies of changes in work skill, it is very difficult to provide hard data on the changes that have taken place during the last forty years of rapid technological advancement. There is absolutely no question, however, that millions of workers have had to endure the trauma of technological unemployment, hardships created by declines in income and the frustrations caused by reductions in work skill that have varied in extent from minor downskilling to the elimination of entire categories of skill. It is also evident that hand skills are rapidly eroding in most service and manufacturing occupations. My impression is that worker autonomy is also being undermined. However, we must be careful to avoid exaggerating the number of truly high-autonomy jobs that have existed in the post-World War II epoch. Nevertheless, since people at work value any degree of autonomy that they have, however small, it follows that even small intrusions on worker autonomy are not welcomed and produce a decline in work satisfaction.

The combination of profit-oriented, hierarchical control of work and work technology, combined with the existence of growing levels of international economic competition, does not bode well

for most workers presently or in the future. Significantly, the existing accounts of worker-owned factories in the United States suggest
that while increased worker economic power over management has
led to more consultation with production workers, to more respect
shown by managers to workers and to more workers exercising managerial functions (accompanied by a decline in the ratio of managers
to workers), competitive market pressures have forced worker-owned
companies to use the same skill-diluting technologies that are used
by purely capitalist enterprises providing the same products and services (*Changing Work* 1985; Yourie 1983).

In varying degrees technology is reducing skills and constricting
worker autonomy in most production (of goods and services) jobs
and in many middle and lower management jobs. On the other hand,
most upper-level managers and scientists and engineers, physicians,
registered nurses, mental health professionals and other professionals have found that advances in production and communications
technologies, combined with the growth of the total amount of
knowledge needed to do their jobs effectively, has required more
extensive and more continuous training to acquire new skills and
new knowledge bases. (It should be noted that the rate of growth of
such highly skilled work positions, as a proportion of all available
jobs, has slowed down considerably since 1970 (Walker 1983). The
most reliable recent estimate of overall skill changes in the
American work place suggests that between 1960 and 1978 for middle level skill jobs, 19 percent of total jobs were eliminated or transformed modestly so that a 7 percent increase appeared in the next to
the highest (rank 60-80) bracket of the work skill continuum, while
a 16 percent increase appeared in the tenth ranked 35-45 (on a scale of
1 to 100). The percentages of jobs in the top 20 percent and the bottom 35 percent of the skill continuum did not change appreciably
(Walker, 270). (Of course, these data do not measure the creation or
elimination of skill in specific jobs in any of these categories.)

The large number of changes in actual jobs create serious economic and psychological problems for many working people, especially those whose skills have been drastically curtailed at the mid-
point or end of their working lives. As Walker himself is quick to
point out, there are many biases—and most probably biases that
underestimate downskilling—in the data he uses (105-108).
Moreover, Walker's most recent series is from 1978, which is, in
my view, the first peak of a continually rising curve of job-skill erosion and job elimination. (These trends became especially acute in
the early 1970s.) In the absence of more sensible Census Bureau def-

initions of occupations it will be very difficult to study quantitatively the ongoing trends in skill distribution on a national scale. Mainstream politicians unwilling to consider the kinds of drastic changes that would halt the negative consequences of technological change cannot be expected to have any enthusiasm for spending the large sums of money that are needed to collect the accurate data that would help Americans understand the complex pattern of changing work skills in our society.

The trend towards job skill dilution and job skill polarization is not inherent in the process of technological evolution. Rather, decisions about which work technologies to adopt and the way worker skills are utilized are made almost exclusively by business and governmental elites who control the ownership and development of technology. Elite decisions about work technology are strongly influenced by the existence of competitive market pressures, including international power-bloc rivalries. Altering the current direction of change in the character of work will be very difficult because two radical changes would have to transpire. First, workers and consumers would have to acquire much more power over economic and technological decisions. Second, the pernicious influence of competitive imperatives on the social relations of work and on work technologies would have to be muted by a quantum leap in the level of trust and cooperation between peoples of different nations. The prospects for these developments are not encouraging.

REFERENCES

Asher, Robert. 1983. *Connecticut Workers and Technological Change.* Storrs, CT: Center for Oral History.

Baker, Constance M. 1957. *Printers and Technology: A History of the International Printing Pressmen and Assistants' Union.* New York: Columbia University Press.

Bluestone, Barry and Bennett Harrison. 1982. *The Deindustrialization of America: Plant Closings, Community Abandonment, and the Dismantling of Basic Industry.* New York: Basic Books.

Braverman, Harry. 1984. *Labor and Monopoly Capital: The Degradation of Work in the Twentieth Century.* New York: Monthly Review Press.

Brecher, Jeremy, Jerry Lombardi, and Jan Stackhouse. 1982. *Brass Valley: The Story of Working People's Lives and Struggles in an American Industrial Region.* Philadelphia: Temple University Press.

Bright, James. 1958. *Automation and Management*. Cambridge: Harvard Graduate School of Business Administration.

Bucki, Cecelia. 1980. *Metal, Minds and Machines: Waterbury at Work*. Waterbury: Mattatuck Historical Society.

Changing Work. 1985, spring/summer.

Clawson, Dan. 1980. *Bureaucracy and the Labor Process*. New York: Monthly Review Press.

Cotnoir, Ernest. 1984. "The Homestead Strike of 1892." Unpublished honors thesis, Robert Asher, director, University of Connecticut.

Crivello, Antonino Papers, Immigration History and Research Center, University of Minnesota.

Drosehn, Fred. 1983. "Connecticut Workers and A Half Century of Technological Change Project". Interview by author. Historical and Manuscripts Division, Homer Babbidge Library, University of Connecticut, Storrs.

Dublin, Thomas. 1979. *Women at Work: The Transformation of Work and Community in Lowell, Massachusetts, 1826-1860*. New York: Columbia University Press. Fieldnotes in possession of author.

Fraser, Steven. 1983. "Dress Rehearsal for the New Deal: Shop-Floor Insurgents, Political Elites, and Industrial Democracy in the Amalgamated Clothing Workers." In Michael H. Frisch and Daniel J. Walkowitz (Eds.), *Working Class America: Essays on Labor, Community, and American Society*. Urbana: University of Illinois Press.

———. 1984. "From the New Unionism to the New Deal." *Labor History* 25 (summer):404-430.

Golden, Clinton and Harold Ruttenberg. 1942. *Dynamics of Industrial Democracy*. New York: Harper.

Harastzi, Miklos. 1977. A *Worker in a Worker's State*. New York: Universe Books.

Harris, Howell J. 1982. *The Right to Manage: Industrial Relations Policies of American Business in the 1940s*. Madison: University of Wisconsin Press.

Interview. March 3, 1983, tape in possession of author.

Jerome, Harry. 1934. *Mechanization in Industry*. New York: National Bureau of Economic Research.

Kusterer, Ken C. 1978. *Know-How on the Job: The Important Working Knowledge of "Unskilled" Workers*. Boulder: Westview Press.

Laurie, Bruce and Mark Shmitz. 1981. "Manufacture and Productivity: The Making of an Industrial Base, Philadelphia, 1850-1880." In Theodore Hershberg, (Ed.), *Philadelphia: Work, Space, Family and Group Experience in the 19th Century*. New York: Oxford University Press.

Lichtenstein, Nelson. 1982. *Labor's War At Home: The CIO in World War II*. New York: Cambridge University Press.

Mann, Floyd. 1960. *Automation and the Worker: A Study of Social Change in Power Plants*. New York: Holt.

Massachusetts Bureau of Labor Statistics. 1870. Annual Report.

McGaw, Judith A. 1977. "The Sources and Impact of Mechanization: The Berkshire County, Massachusetts Paper Industry, 1801-1855." Unpublished doctoral dissertation, New York University.

Meissner, Martin. 1969. *Technology and the Worker: Technical Demands and Social Processes in Industry*. San Francisco: Chandler Pub. Co.

Montgomery, David. 1979. *Workers' Control in America: Studies in the History of Work, Technology, and Labor Struggles*. New York: Cambridge University Press.

New York Times. December 13, 1942. Section VII, p. 8.

Noble, David F. 1984. *Forces of Production: A Social History of Industrial Automation*. New York: Alfred A. Knopf.

Robinson, Harriet H. 1898. *Loom and Spindle: Or, Life Among the Early Mill Girls*. New York: Crowell.

Rogers, Theresa F. and Natalie S. Friedman. 1980. *Printers Face Automation: The Impact of Technology on Work and Retirement Among Skilled Craftsmen*. Lexington, MA: Lexington Books.

Sabel, Charles F. 1982. *Work and Politics: The Division of Labor in Industry*. New York: Cambridge University Press.

Shaiken, Harley. 1984. *Work Transformed: Automation and Labor in the Computer Age*. New York: Holt, Rinehart and Winston.

Slichter, Sumner H., James J. Healy, and Robert E. Liverwash. 1960. *The Impact of Collective Bargaining on Management*. Washington, D.C.: Brookings Institution.

Spenner, Kenneth I. 1983. "Deciphering Prometheus: Temporal Change in the Skill Level of Work." *American Sociological Review* 48:824-837.

Thompson, Paul. 1983. *The Nature of Work: An Introduction to Debates on the Nature of the Labour Process*. London: The Macmillan Press.

U.S. Industrial Commission. 1901. *Report of the Industrial Commission on the Relations and Conditions of Capital and Labor Employed in Manufactures and General Business*, XIV. Washington: Government Printing Office.

U.S. Commissioner of Labor. 1904. *Regulation and Restriction of Output. Eleventh Special Report of the Commissioner of Labor*. Washington: Government Printing Office.

U.S. Congress. 1885. Senate Committee on Education and Labor. Report upon the Relations Between Labor and Capital, and Testimony Taken by the Committee. Washington: Government Printing Office.

Walker, Patrick C. 1983. "The Distribution of Skill and the Division of Labor, 1950-1978." Unpublished doctoral dissertation, University of Massachusetts.

Wells, David A. 1889. *Recent Economic Changes*. New York: D. Appleton.

Yankelovich, Daniel and John Immerwehr. 1984. *Putting the Work Ethic to Work*. New York: Public Agenda Foundation.

Yellowitz, Irwin. 1977. *Industrialization and the American Labor Movement*. Port Washington, N.Y.: Kennikat Press.

Yourie, Ralph. 1983. Field notes on interviews at Hyatt-Clark Company, in possession of author.

3

Technological Change, Skill Requirements, and Education: The Case for Uncertainty

Kenneth I. Spenner

Several centuries of controversy surround the relationship between technology and work. In the United States, national panels and commissions have periodically considered the role of technology in the economy and society, with one of first commissions on the topic dating back at least to the Great Depression (National Resources Committee 1937).

Given the larger debate, this review concentrates on three questions. First, what do past studies tell us about how technological change alters the skill requirements of work? Second, how does past knowledge apply to the near-term future? Finally, what are the policy implications for education and training?

My thesis is straightforward: Uncertainty dominates the answer to each of the questions. Past research contains considerable gaps in quality and coverage such that judgments about how technological change affects work contain substantial uncertainty. Much of what we do know suggests an uncertain, complicated and contradictory relationship between technological change and the skill requirements of work. Technology has substantial effects on the composition and content of work in the economy, but these effects vary for different dimensions of skill, for different jobs, occupations, industries, and firms, and for different technologies. The effects involve complicated mixtures of offsetting compositional and content changes, of skill upgrading and downgrading. Most important, the effects of technological change on the skill requirements of work are set in a larger context of market forces, managerial prerogatives (in implementing technologies), and organizational cultures, all of which condition the effects of technological change. The forces of managers, markets and organizational cultures are sufficient to reverse the effects of a technology on skill upgrading or downgrading. Major arguments about a different technological future also involve uncertainty, in the validity of the argument and in the intrinsic nature of the proposed relationships. Finally, public and private policies for education and training must attend to the uncertainties. To be avoided are education and training policies that assume a single, simple, or unitary effect of technological change on the number or quality of jobs.

The first section offers a selective review and critique of past studies. The second section considers arguments about a different future, and the final section considers education and training policy in the face of uncertainty. Throughout, I use a broad definition of *technology*, one that includes new materials and machines as well as new ways of organizing production, people, and ideas. Thus, technology includes "hard" products and things along with process and organization, although the large portion of available research on technological change and skill requirements of work studies various forms of mechanization and computerization, a serious limitation of current evidence.

PAST STUDIES: REVIEW AND CRITIQUE

Major Theoretical Positions

Three central positions inform the debate on how technological change alters the number and quality of jobs: the **upgrading, downgrading,** and **mixed- change** or **conditional** positions. The arguments and evidence span different disciplines, models, and types of evidence. The industrialization thesis and the central premises of neoclassical economic theory form the basis for the **upgrading** position (Kerr, Dunlop, Harbison, and Myers 1964; Bell 1973; Standing 1984). In simplified form, the argument says that the division of labor in the economy evolves along the lines of greater differentiation and efficiency. Technological changes increase productivity, lower costs, and expand markets, in the process requiring a broader variety of skills and higher average skills from the labor force. In some versions of the thesis, the post-industrial economy increasingly relies on highly automated and high-technology work environments that require new forms of skill: responsibility for monitoring, making adjustments, visualizing the whole of the production process, and responding to emergency situations (Crossman 1960). Such arguments have been made for continuous process and chemical manufacturing (Blauner 1964), petroleum refining (Gallie 1978), applications of robotics in metal-working industries (Miller 1983), automated banking operations (Adler 1983), and virtually any industry that uses advanced mechanization (Hirschhorn 1984).

Downgrading arguments focus on the deterioration in the quality of work because of changes in the nature of the labor process. For example, according to Braverman's (1974) thesis, technology has been a key instrument for fractionating and deskilling jobs. Management uses devices such as scientific management, numerical control, automation and the redesign of jobs to separate the planning and conception features of work from the execution features of work. The eventual result is a polarized labor force: a growing mass of unskilled and semi-skilled jobs and workers at the bottom and an elite of managers and professionals at the top. Braverman includes operatives, sales workers, clerical workers, and even some professions such as engineering and computer programming in the deskilling process (for further examples, see Kraft 1977; Scott 1982; Shaiken 1984).

Other versions of the downgrading position point to **proletarianization**, a process in which skill downgrading occurs through the elimination of non-working-class positions and the creation of working-class locations (Wright and Singelmann 1982), or differential growth of high versus low skill occupations and industries (Ginzberg 1982; Levin and Rumberger 1983; Rumberger 1984; Rumberger and Levin 1985; Singelmann and Tienda 1985). These latter arguments do not rest on actual changes in the nature of work but depend on differential growth for sectors of the economy to produce skill polarization and net downgrading.

Economists have identified a final type of downgrading argument that focuses on larger economic and social processes to which technology contributes and of which deskilling is a consequence (Bluestone and Harrison 1982). Structural unemployment that issues from technological change forms a part of this larger process. When displaced and structurally unemployed workers return to work—if at all—it is at a lower skill level, especially for workers who remain in the same community (Ferman 1983; Office of Technology Assessment 1986). Deskilling is a secondary consequence of deindustrialization.

A final position in the larger debate, the **mixed-change** or **conditional** position, is more a characterization of the empirical evidence than a well-developed theory. According to this position, the effects of technological change or changes in the labor process are mixed and offsetting (Jaffe and Froomkin 1968). Alternately, the effects depend on level of automation (Bright 1966)—upgrading in the early stages, downgrading in the later stages—or depend on the organization milieu (Davis and Taylor 1976; Webster 1986), the way management chooses to implement the change (Adler 1983), other features of the work environment (Vallas 1988), or larger demographic and economic forces (McLaughlin 1983). The outcome is little net change in skill requirements of work (Horowitz and Herrnstadt 1966; Spenner 1979) or offsetting trends in the composition of the occupational structure as some sectors and jobs experience upgrading and others downgrading (Spenner 1982; 1983; 1985).

In summary, the arguments are diverse. The above synopses illustrate rather than offer complete review. The critique that follows takes the theoretical positions as given.

Critique[1]

Societal, Sector and Occupational Variations; Aggregate and Case Studies. The economy of a society contains an overall skill level at any point in time that reflects both the mixture of jobs and the distribution of people to jobs. Aggregate studies average skill changes across a large number of occupations or industries, looking for shifts in the overall level. It is roughly the case that aggregate studies have been more the domain of the upgrading tradition and have provided more of the support for skill upgrading (Mueller et al. 1969; Rumberger 1981).

A major study conducted for the National Commission on Technology, Automation, and Economic Progress illustrates the aggregate approach. Horowitz and Herrnstadt (1966) compared all jobs in five industries on detailed skill measures in the second and third editions of the U.S. Department of Labor's (1949; 1965) Dictionary of Occupational Titles (DOT). The time period ranges from just after World War II to the early 1960s. The industries included three from manufacturing (slaughter and meatpacking, rubber tires and tubes, and machine shop trades) and two from non-manufacturing (medical services and banking). The skill measures included general educational development (mathematical, language and reasoning development required), specific vocational preparation (total training time for an average performance at the job), eleven aptitudes (including verbal, numerical, spatial, motor coordination, and manual dexterity), and twelve work conditions (including variation, repetitiveness, discretion, direction, precision, and working under stress). For new jobs in the 1960s the study assessed average levels of complex work with data, people and things. The evidence showed that each of the different industries contained mixtures of upgrading and downgrading in the different skill measures. No dominant pattern of upgrading or downgrading appeared in any industry across indicators or in any skill indicator across industries. Spenner (1979) extended the earlier study to a sample of all jobs in the economy with the third and fourth editions of the DOT (1965-1977). Skill indicators for levels of involvement with data, people, and things showed little change; if anything, there was a slight upgrading over the twelve-year period. Other recent aggregate comparisons can be found in Berg, Freedman and Freeman (1978), Rumberger (1981), Karasek, et al. (1982), and Wright and Singlemann (1982).

Case studies offer a considerably more detailed picture of skill transformations for a particular industry, occupation or firm but at a cost of population coverage. Examples include Adler's (1983) study of the banking industry and computerization changes, and Wallace and Kalleberg's (1982) study of the impact of technological change on several printing industry occupations.

A recent example occurs in Vallas's (1988) study of the technological change from mechanical and electromechanical to electronic switching systems in the communications industry. Against a background of overall upgrading in the communications industry because of compositional shifts (i.e., more workers in higher skilled occupations) Vallas found mixtures of upgrading and downgrading that differed by occupation and dimension of skill for unionized workers in eight union locals in the state of New York. The study design relied on a synthetic cohort strategy to assess technological change and workers' reports of skills required by their jobs. It would have been difficult to obtain this detailed a picture of consequences of technological change with an aggregate study. In general, case studies show more change and volatility in skill levels as a function of technological changes, and offer a more detailed picture of change.

Composition and Content as Tracks of Change.
Transformations in skill occur along two tracks. Skill change in a
sector or the economy might occur through *compositional shifts*:
the creation or elimination of jobs of given skill level and the distribution of persons to jobs. Alternately, skill change might occur
through actual changes in work *content* (the technical nature of
work and the role relations surrounding work performance).

The social and economic forces that accomplish upgrading or
downgrading may operate on one front but not the other or may
operate in contradictory ways on the two fronts. There is no necessary isomorphism. In the short run, technological changes may be
more efficacious in generating skill shifts via changes in work content. In the long run, technological change may generate more
change via compositional shift because of increases in productivity,
lower costs, and economic growth. For example, there is some evidence that at upper levels of mechanization—automation narrowly
defined—work content is downgraded in some craft fields (Bright
1958; 1966), yet other changes offset the downgrading with upgrading
of content or upgrading via compositional shift (compare Wallace
and Kalleberg 1982 with Hull et al., 1982). Alternately, changes along
a single track may vary over the short- and long-term. In a study of
the effects of computerization on demands for clerical and managerial labor between 1972 and 1978, Osterman (1986) found lower
demand over the short-term followed by increased demand over the
long-term (that is, several years). Osterman interprets the offsetting
effects in terms of a bureaucratic reorganization hypothesis: over
the long-term firms reorganize as a function of technological changes
and assume new functions, products, and roles, generating new
demand for labor.

The collective body of evidence in economics and sociology—
aggregate and case studies, studies of composition, and content shifts
for a range of or a single technology—is far short of a comprehensive
sampling of time and space in the U.S. economy. Thus, sampling
limitations comprise a major source of uncertainty in our knowledge of technology and skill requirements. In general, case studies
afford greater coverage to the temporal dimension but with severe
restrictions on the coverage of the occupation-industry structure.
Aggregate studies are more limited in coverage of the temporal
dimension but are more expansive in coverage of the sample space. A
few studies offer quantitative projections of skill changes into the
future, but these are typically of composition shifts only and without
any direct measures of one or more dimensions of skill, or under

restrictive assumptions about the nature of content shifts (for example, see Rumberger 1984; Rumberger and Levin 1985).

Concepts and Measures of Skill Requirements. Several questions illustrate the issues. Is it workers who are skilled or jobs that require skill? Is skill a unidimensional feature of work with equivalent and equally meaningful application of the construct at different historical points and for different technologies? How can skill(s) best be measured? And do conclusions about the effects of technological change on skill requirements hinge on the specific concepts and measures of skill that are used? Unfortunately, the answers to these questions reinforce the conclusion about the uncertainty of the knowledge base.

The idea that skills reside in persons and are best studied at that level has precedent in human capital and related perspectives in economics (Becker 1964; also see Oakley 1954; Rumberger 1983). Workers acquire a stock of capabilities, knowledge and experiences that translate into productivity and that yield reward. As such, skills are portable from job to job within firms, and in some instances, across firms. This approach does not directly speak to the skill requirements of jobs because the possession of human capital cannot be equated with its use (Berg 1970). Indeed, the fit between the skill capacities of workers and the skill demands of jobs is notoriously "loose" and has been the subject of appreciable study under the rubrics of overeducation and underemployment (Rumberger 1981; Clogg 1979; Clogg and Shockey 1984; Smith 1986). Thus, the schooling, training, or wage levels of workers cannot be equated with the skill requirements of work, except under a very restrictive set of assumptions (Braverman 1974; Field 1980; Rubinson and Ralph 1984).

The idea that skill is a feature of jobs better lends itself to the study of the effects of technological change for several reasons. Classical and contemporary economic theories provide for positional differences among jobs, for example in John Stuart Mill's reasoning on positional components of wage inequalities or in Thurow's (1975) theory of job competition, where marginal products adhere in jobs and not people. Second, the supply of available education, training and skills in people enters the technological equation only indirectly and over the long-term, whereas the effects of technological change on the content and composition of jobs, hence skill requirements, are more immediate and direct. Third, a growing body of research suggests that the structure of work has a greater, more immediate effect on people (that is, their capacities, intellectual development, self-concept and so on) than vice-versa. The primary mechanism through which people shape their work and careers appears to be occupational selection over the longer term rather than "skilled" persons effecting immediate or substantial changes in the structure of their work (Kohn and Schooler 1983). Finally, theoretical perspectives on upgrading and downgrading address the skill in jobs rather than people. The suggestion that we study the skill requirements of jobs is not to suggest that people are unreliable reporters of the skill demands of their work or to gainsay the often tragic consequences of technological transformations for workers, or the importance of studies of related phenomena such as overeducation, skill transferability among jobs, or deindustrialization.

The major measurement strategies for job skills are nonmeasurement, indirect measurement, and direct measurement. The **nonmeasurement** strategy equates occupation groups such as white collar or blue collar with implicit skill levels (for examples, see the National Commission on Technology, Automation and Economic Progress 1966; Jaffe and Froomkin 1968; Bluestone and Harrison 1982; compare Jones 1980). This strategy contains substantial validity problems because the referent is not clear in the cross-section at one point in time, to say nothing of how an unknown referent may have changed between two or more points in time.

The **indirect measurement strategy** takes the schooling levels or wage rates of an occupational group as indirect indication of the skill level of one or more jobs (National Commission on Technology, Automation, and Economic Progress 1966; Wallace and Kalleberg 1982). Validity remains an issue with this measurement strategy because the isomorphism between the indirect indicator and the true skill level depends on a set of assumptions about other factors that generate variation in the indirect indicator. For example, such a use of wage rates requires a complex set of assumptions about constancies in the supply and demand for labor (see Field 1980: Appendix, for an exposition).

A more reliable and valid approach to studying technology and skill requirements involves the **direct measurement** of the dimensions of skill for jobs or workers. There are a variety of approaches to the direct measurement of skills. All of the approaches contain limitations. For example, job titles bear an unclear relationship to skill demands. The title can change but the skill demands may not or vice versa. Additionally, consensus does not exist on the relevant dimensions of skill. The available approaches range from the Position Analysis Questionnaire (McCormick, Mecham and

Jeanneret 1977), which measures nearly two hundred job features, to the Universal Skills System developed at Michigan State University, which purports to measure over 1,400 transferable job skills, to the Dictionary of Occupational Titles (U.S. Department of Labor 1965; 1977), to ad hoc systems that assess job skills from workers in jobs or from judgments of expert analysts.

Approaches based on the DOT are the most frequently used (for review and critique, consult Miller, Treiman, Cain and Roos 1980; also see Spenner 1980; and Cain and Treiman 1981). The DOT contains measures of over forty variables for over 13,000 third edition jobs and over 12,000 fourth edition jobs based on job analyses conducted by the Department of Labor (U.S. Department of Labor 1972). The measures include general educational development (mathematical, language, and reasoning development required), levels of involvement with data, people, and things; specific vocational preparation (total training time for an average performance at the job); eleven aptitudes (including verbal, numerical, spatial, motor coordination, and manual dexterity) and twelve work conditions (including variation, repetitiveness, discretion, direction, precision, and working under stress). The main advantages of the DOT include its comprehensiveness and national scope. The disadvantages include questions about sampling coverage, reliability, validity, and aggregation to job categories that ignore firm- and industry-level variations in skill requirements. For example, manufacturing jobs are overrepresented; service, managerial, and clerical jobs are underrepresented. Additionally, the construction procedures for the fourth edition may have built-in a stability bias (underestimating true change) compared with the third edition estimates (Cain and Treiman 1981; Spenner 1983). Thus, while the DOT is perhaps the best available system, its use requires extreme caution. These limitations add uncertainty to the knowledge base. Other, newer methodologies for the direct measurement of skill requirements exist but these are in experimental or developmental stages (for example, see Albin, Hormozi, Mourgos, and Weinberg 1984).

Dimensions of Skill. Empirical studies that partition job characteristics (for people or jobs) consistently find that substantive complexity defines the central core of variation in work content.[2] Skill as substantive complexity refers to the level, scope, and integration of mental, manipulative, and interpersonal tasks in a job. The subdimensions of mental, manipulative, and interpersonal capture well-known points of interface between people and jobs (U.S. Department of Labor 1972). These subdimensions are important because some recent arguments suggest past technologies primarily affected manipulative tasks whereas current and future technologies (i.e., microelectronics or computer-based) affect mental and interpersonal task complexity as well (for example, see Rumberger 1984). Substantive complexity of work includes subdimensions of cognitive, motor, physical, and related demands in a job. The level, scope, and integration subdimensions also capture important empirical variations among jobs. For example, a job that requires integrated mental, interpersonal, and manipulative activities across a wide scope of situations but at modest levels on each task dimension may be more complex in skill demands than a job that requires a high level of performance on one task dimension but in a narrow range of situations and without demands in other task domains (for example, a mid-level manager with a wide range of mental and data tasks may have a more complex job than an engineer whose task demands are more complex on a single dimension).

Theoretical and empirical studies also consistently show autonomy-control to be a second major dimension by which jobs are organized (Spenner 1983). Skill as autonomy-control refers to the discretion available in a job to initiate and conclude action, to control the content, manner, and speed with which a task is done. Whereas formal authority places a job within a formal network of jobs, autonomy-control designates within-role discretion, bounds, and leeway for action as provided by the job.

Across jobs in the economy, the two dimensions (substantive complexity, autonomy-control) are positively correlated, estimates placing the correlation in the range of $r = .5$ to $.7$ (Spenner 1980; Kalleberg and Leicht 1986; Vallas 1988). In general, case studies have afforded more attention to skill as autonomy-control while aggregate studies have given greater consideration to skill defined as substantive complexity. Further, some evidence suggests some technologies and the sum total of technological changes exert contradictory effects on the different dimensions of skill. If the dimensionality of skill requirements is greater than two organizing dimensions, then the possibilities for contradictory and offsetting effects are even more complicated. Some of the uncertainty in the knowledge base springs from no consideration or uneven treatment of the dimensionality of skill requirements.

Summary of Select Aggregate and Case Study Evidence

A compilation of major aggregate studies offers one way to summarize how technological changes alter the skill requirements of jobs, based on past research. Table 1 summarizes select aggregate studies that meet several criteria: (1) two or more points in time; (2) a sample that refers to a sizeable population of jobs, occupations, or industries; (3) some direct measurement of skill as substantive complexity or skill as autonomy-control. The criteria effectively exclude a large number of aggregate economic studies of the demand for labor but with no direct measurement of skill, or studies that indirectly infer the quality of jobs through wage rates, schooling levels, productivity indices, and so on. The table classifies each study by the sample or population, the time period, whether content or composition shifts are studied, the skill measures, and comments on possible threats to the quality of the inferences.

The most important conclusion centers on the uncertainty and serious limitations in the knowledge base. With a single exception, all studies refer to the post-World War II period. Many studies rely on the DOT as a source of skill measures, and are subject to the serious limitations of the DOT. Most studies investigate skill as substantive complexity and ignore variations in skill as autonomy-control. By definition, these studies average firm-specific and technology-specific variations in skill requirements. It is also important to note that popular judgments, conventional wisdom, and the knowledge base available to engineers and managers who design and implement technical innovations, and policy makers who legislate and administer about technical innovations—all share these limitations, uncertainties, and small reservoir of solid data.

In an earlier study, I offered several tentative conclusions and hypotheses that I repeat here (Spenner 1985).

1. The quantity of skill requirement change observed in particular studies depends on the indicator of skill. The GED indicator from the DOT offers the most optimistic upgrading estimates and is probably an anomaly.
2. In the post-war era there is no consistent evidence of dramatic change through content shifts in substantive complexity. All studies for time periods up to the mid-1970s suggest little net change or a small upgrading.
3. Studies of compositional shifts in skill as substantive complexity suggest the possibility of a small upgrading since World War II, but approximate stability since the turn of the century. The longer-term conclusion requires a strong set of assumptions about constancies in content shifts (Spenner 1982). There is some limited evidence of possible polarization effects: differential growth of the highest and lowest complexity jobs, where

Table 1. Summary of Aggregate Studies of the Effects of Technology on Skills Requirements that Employ Direct Measures of Skill

SKILLS AND THE DISTRIBUTION OF EARNINGS AND INCOME

Study	Sample/Population	Time Period	Content/ Composition Shift
Horowitz and Herrnstadt (1966)	All Department of Transportation (DOT) jobs in five industries (slaughter and meat packing, rubber tires and tubes, machine shop trades, medical services, banking)	1949-1965	
Spenner (1979)	5 percent sample of fourth edition (DOT) titles (N=622) matched to third edition titles	1965-1977	Content
Berg (1970)	1950-1960 decennial census distributions; 4000 DOT jobs rated in 1956 and 1965	1950-1960 (1956-1965)	Composition and content
Berg, Freedman, and Freeman (1978)	1950-1970 decennial census distributions; second edition DOT estimates for 1950; third edition estimates for 1960 and 1970	1950-1970	Composition
Rumberger (1981)	1960 and 1976 census and Current Population Survey (CPS), respectively; employed population fourteen and older; third and fourth edition DOT	1960-1976 (1965-1977)	Composition and content

Skill Measures	Outcomes	Notes— Design Threats
For jobs; 25 DOT indicators; most indicators reflect skill as substantive complexity; two or three indicators may approximate skill as autonomy-control	Mixture of upgrading and downgrading; little net change	Limited to five industries; depends on independence of DOT editions
For jobs; DOT indicators for data, people and things; skill as substantive complexity	Small upgrading; little net change	Depends on independence of DOT editions
For jobs; DOT general Educational Development (GED) indicator; skill as substantive complexity	Small compositional upgrading; for content, 54 percent of jobs had the same GED, 31 percent were higher and 15 percent were lower; apparent content upgrading	Depends on independence of editions; possible validity problems with GED; change in GED categories between editions may overestimate upgrading
For jobs; DOT GED indicator; skill as substantive complexity	Same as Berg (1970) for 1950-1960; small compositional upgrading for 1960-1970	Same as Berg (1970)
For jobs; DOT GED indicator; skill as substantive complexity	Modest compositional upgrading; small content upgrading but with some evidence of proletarianization as the number of very highest skill jobs decline	Depends on independence of DOT editions; possible validity problems with GED

(continued)

Table 1 *(continued)*

SKILLS AND THE DISTRIBUTION OF EARNINGS AND INCOME

Study	Sample/Population	Time Period	Content/ Composition Shift
Rumberger (1981): Table 4; also see, Eckaus (1964) and Rawlins and Ulman (1974)	See Rumberger above; 1940-1950 decennial census distributions	1940-1976	Composition
Reanalysis of Dubnoff (1978) data; see Spenner (1982)	Decennial census distributions for all gainful workers (1900-1930) or all employed workers (1940-1970)	1900-1970	Composition
Mueller et al. (1969)	National probability sample of 1967 labor force (N=2662)	1962-1967 (retrospective measure of job and machine change over five years)	Content (composition inasmuch as 1967 sample members changed jobs)
Karasek, Schwartz, and Pieper (1982)	National samples for 1969, 1972, and 1977; adult employed labor force working twenty or more hours per week (N=4531)	1969-1977	Content (composition partially adjusted for with demographic controls; otherwise assumed constant)

Skill Measures	Outcomes	Notes— Design Threats
For jobs; DOT GED indicator; skill as substantive complexity	Overall 18 percent compositional upgrading over thirty-six year; greatest increase between 1950 and 1960	Depends on independence of DOT editions; possible validity problems with GED
For jobs; DOT indicators for data, people, things, SVP, and combination of the first three indicators; skill as substantive complexity	Little net change; only one of eighteen skill-year or higher order effects significant in loglinear decomposition; for one interaction, evidence of skill polarization in recent years	Depends on the quality of the map of detailed occupations from one census year to another; comparison assumes constant work content to third edition DOT scores over entire time period

For people; detailed reports of level and type of machinery use over five years; self-reports of "skill required" and "own" influence in organizing the work"; mixture of skill as substantive complexity and skill as autonomy-control	For job changers over five years, modest upgrading in mechanization level and skill measures; for those who stayed in the same job but experienced machine change:
	
	        More Same Less
	"Skill" 53% 36% 7%
	"Influ-
	  ence 34% 54% 7%
	
	Across all respondents, small upgrading
		For job changers, conflation of compositional upgrading with seniority-career effects; short time interval; validity-reliability of self-report and retrospective report data; compositional shift via demographic replacement ignored

For people; aggregated to 240 occupation categories; four replicated questions combined into single scale (learn new things, "skill," creativity, and repetition); skill as substantive complexity	No change in skill discretion scale scores	Validity-reliability of self-reports; slightly different response categories in 1977 compared with 1969 and 1972

(continued)

Table 1 *(continued)*

SKILLS AND THE DISTRIBUTION OF EARNINGS AND INCOME

Study	Sample/Population	Time Period	Content/ Composition Shift
Wright and Singelmann (1982)	Decennial census distributions for thirty-seven industry sectors; the design decomposes 1960-1970 shifts into industry, class, and interaction component; skill levels implicit in class categories	1960-1970	Composition (industry and class shifts)
Sobel (1982)	National samples for 1970, 1973, 1976, and 1977; adult employed labor force working twenty or more hours per week	1970-1977	Composition and content

Skill Measures	Outcomes	Notes— Design Threats
For people; measured through class categories (self-employed, have employees, have subordinates, and level of freedom and decision-making in jobs); self-reports taken from 1969 National Survey of Working conditions; skill as autonomy-control	Overall small changes; mixed evidence for upgrading and downgrading in class and industry shifts; for upgrading more managers, for downgrading more workers; industry and class composition shifts tend to operate in opposite directions; some evidence for proletarianization in the class composition shift into the working-class	Depends on the validity of class measurement; validity-reliability of self-report; possible skill heterogeneity in class and industry categories; assumes constant work content over the time interval; skill is measured indirectly in class categories
For people; related questions in successive surveys taken to measure supervisory status; skill as autonomy-control	Decline in skill; percent classified as supervisors: 1970 36.1% 1973 34.1% 1976 31.4% 1977 31.1%	Different sampling designs at the time points; nonidentical questions to measure supervisory status at the time points; validity-reliability of self-reports; indirect measure of skill

subgroups of men and women differentially gain or lose in terms of new job growth and job elimination (Spenner 1982; Hartmann, Kraut and Tilly 1986).

4. Evidence on aggregate content shifts in skill as autonomy-control is mixed, with one study suggesting modest upgrading (Mueller et al. 1969) and the other suggesting slight downgrading (Sobel 1982). Since the studies use different indicators of autonomy-control, a firm conclusion is not possible.

5. Only one study addresses compositional shifts in skill as autonomy-control (Wright and Singelmann 1982). The evidence suggests a small net downgrading. The methodology of this study indirectly measures autonomy-control, but the larger conclusion is quite possible given the increased location of jobs in bureaucracies over the course of this century, and other evidence that shows jobs in bureaucratic settings are subject to greater constraints on autonomy-control—even though such jobs may involve higher substantive complexity—compared with jobs in more entrepreneurial settings (Kohn 1971; Spenner 1988).

Compared with the putative wisdom of upgrading and downgrading traditions, the collective evidence from aggregate studies shows no dominant trend in the twentieth century and suggests evolutionary not revolutionary rates of change. In summary, the dominant feature of aggregate study evidence is uncertainty; to the extent a conclusion is warranted it would suggest approximate net aggregate stability of skill requirements or a small upgrading.

The aggregate study by Mueller and colleagues (1969) warrants more detailed summary for several reasons. First, the study provides point estimates of the number of workers and jobs affected by mechanization changes (as a subset of technological changes) in a given time period. The sampled population included the U.S. labor force in 1967 (N = 2,662). Respondents provided detailed information on their current jobs in 1967, their jobs five years earlier in 1962, and select intervening work experiences. Detailed information on level and type of mechanization in the jobs and changes in such were coded into standardized categories by engineering students. The design can distinguish workers who experienced upgrading or downgrading at the same job versus workers who experienced upgrading or downgrading as a function of changing jobs. The period in question, 1962-67, involved an expanding economy and rapid economic growth, providing a resource-rich and demand-driven environment conducive to technological changes (although only mechanization changes are measured here). On balance, the workers experienced more upgrading than downgrading, a finding generally consistent with DOT-based results for this period.

Based on this sample, about 10 percent of the labor force experienced one or more mechanization changes in their jobs over the five-year period. Mechanization changes thus directly affected 2-3 percent of all jobs per year or about 1.5 to 2 million workers per year. Further, the Mueller study also found that mechanization changes directly generated little unemployment and existing employees were typically retrained. Consistent with more contemporary evidence on recent technological change (Office of Technology Assessment 1986), most displacent and adverse effects were for those already working at a low-skill level; most machine-change advantage went to those advantaged in other respects (higher education, higher status jobs). The final section returns to several of these issues.

A related compilation of select case studies can be found in Table 2. The number of case studies across several disciplines is substantial, and I have made no attempt to select a probability sample. Further the criteria are less stringent than those employed for aggregate studies (that is, direct measures).

The case studies show much more volatility in skill requirements as a function of changes in technology and the larger labor process. Few of the case studies give attention to issues of measurement validity or reliability, or to other sources of invalidity in design inferences. Comparisons across case studies are difficult because of different samples and methods, and different concepts of skill. Thus, designations of "unclear" or "apparent" in the table mean that I was unable to decipher the entry from the source material. The original study may have had a concrete position on the issue.

If rigorous methodological criteria are applied, then few generalizable and replicable conclusions are available. If the criteria are relaxed, then several general impressions (best viewed as hypotheses) characterize the case studies.

1. Case studies provide the strongest evidence for downgrading. Given the diversity of designs, sample, and method, the instances of downgrading are too varied to have all been artifacts. However, the volatility in skill requirements seen in case studies may occur in part because of sample selection effects, or overstudying changing occupations and work areas and understudying stable occupations and firms.

2. Case studies give more attention to content changes in work, reporting more instances of downgrading compared with aggre-

Table 2. Illustrative Case Studies of Skill Change

SKILLS AND THE DISTRIBUTION OF EARNINGS AND INCOME

Study	Sample/Population	Time Period	Content/ Composition Shift
Braverman (1974)	All work; concentration on operative, clerical, craft, and service occupations; some partici-pant-observation in England	1900-1974 (also late nineteenth century)	Primarily con-tent
Bright (1958, 1966)	Highly automated manu-facturing firms, principally auto engine assembly parts, machine shops, and metal working	1950s to mid-1960s	Primarily con-tent
Faunce (1958)	Random sample of workers from machinery depart-ments of Detroit automo-bile engine plant (N=125)	Mid-1950s	Content (Comparison of pre- and post-assembly line experi-ences)

CHANGE, SKILL REQUIREMENTS, AND EDUCATION

Skill Measures Dimensions	General Outcomes	Notes
Including: repetitiveness, responsibility, scope and variety of tasks, integration of mental, manipulative, and interpersonal task components; authority-supervision relations; skill as substantive complexity and autonomy-control; no direct skill measures	Overall deskilling; separation of conception and execution in work; polarization of jobs vis-a-vis skill requirements; growing mass of working class occupations	Sketchy coverage of composition shifts; unclear whether deskilling conclusions apply equally to all occupations or which fractions thereof
Twelve contributions of workers to tasks, including: physical and mental effort, manipulative and general skills, responsibility, and decision-making	Across seventeen defined levels of mechanization, have mixed effects, generally increasing skill requirements up to the middle levels of automation and decreasing thereafter	Sketchy coverage of composition shifts; applications to other areas and technology changes unclear; has been criticized for limited range of mechanization in studied plants and limited skill definition (Adler 1983)
Closeness of supervision, responsibility, control over work pace, attention, relationship with supervisor, interactions with coworkers	Deskilling in less control over work pace, more closely supervised, job requires more alertness and attention (could be interpreted as upgrading); upgrading in that the worker was responsible for a larger share of the production process; increased isolation from coworkers; altered relationship with supervisors	Validity-reliability of self-report; no consideration of composition shifts; short time span confounded with newness of technology change

(continued)

Table 2 *(continued)*

SKILLS AND THE DISTRIBUTION OF EARNINGS AND INCOME

Study	Sample/Population	Time Period	Content/ Composition Shift
Stone (1974)	Steel industry; skilled craft and heavy laborers	1890-1920 (secondarily through 1960s)	Primarily content
Kraft (1977)	Computer programmers (about 100 programmers interviewed, participant-observer study)	1940s-1970s	Primarily content
Glenn and Feldberg (1979)	Clerical work	1870-1880; principally twentieth century	Content and composition

Skill Measures Dimensions	General Outcomes	Notes
Unclear; apparently includes training, experience, dexterity, judgment, and general knowledge of production process; skill as substantive complexity and autonomy-control; no direct skill measures	Substantial deskilling of focal jobs; technology not primary cause but an instrument in larger control process (i.e., employer control over wages and labor unrest)	Quality of time one (nineteenth century) skill levels in the steel industry unknown; no consideration of composition shifts
No explicit definition or direct measures; apparently includes span and cognitive complexity of task, discretion and control over work; skill as substantive complexity and autonomy-control	Deskilling; management strategy to simplify, routinize, and standardize programming task; accomplished through canned programs, structured programming and chief programmer teams; some small fraction of systems analyst and engineer positions are upgraded	Sketchy coverage of composition shifts; applies largely to programmers in large business firms (versus smaller firms, academic positions, and so on)
No explicit definitions or direct measures; apparently includes task complexity and scope, control over work; skill as substantive complexity and autonomy-control	Progressive fragmentation, specialization, and routinization of clerical work roles; coupled with massive growth, substantial deskilling; upgrading for small number of systems analysts and supervisors	Quality of time one (nineteenth century) skill levels of clerical work unknown; study focuses most on secretary, typist, and stenographer, to the exclusion of other clerical roles

(continued)

Table 2 *(continued)*

SKILLS AND THE DISTRIBUTION OF EARNINGS AND INCOME

Study	Sample/Population	Time Period	Content/ Composition Shift
Burawoy (1979)	Engine division of Chicago-based multinational corporation, machine shop occupations; participant-observer study	1944 and 1974	Content
Wallace and Kalleberg (1982)	Printing industry occupations; principally compositors, machine operators, and linotypists	1931-1978	Content and composition as reflected in wage rates
Hull, Friedman, and Rogers (1982)	Printers for three largest New York newspapers in the sample at both time points (N=408 for 1950; N=245 for 1976)	1950 and 1976	Content

CHANGE, SKILL REQUIREMENTS, AND EDUCATION

Skill Measures Dimensions	General Outcomes	Notes
No explicit definitions or direct measures; apparently includes task scope and complexity, discretion, and autonomy in work role; skill as substantive complexity and autonomy-control but more as located in workers than job requirements	Larger changes in piece-rate and rate-fixing systems, bargaining relations, and redistribution of hierarchical conflict led to mixtures of upgrading and downgrading (i.e., more autonomy for a number of occupations); more important larger process involves the operations through which the factory social system contains struggles and manufactures consent	At times "skill" equated with experience and training; no consideration of compositional shifts; unclear how interactional dynamics in the labor process of this particular shop (given an important theoretical role) characterize other work settings
Indirect measure: wage rates	Steady, substantial decline in printing industry-skilled-occupation wages *relative* to several comparison occupation groups; regression and analyses indicate capital-intensity as the major proximate causal factor	Complex assumptions associated with indirect measure; change in wage rates may be due to factors other than skill change
Printers' self-reports of the *physical* and *intellectual* demands of new methods of printing; skills as substantive complexity	Percent of printers defining new methods of printing as *More Same Less* Physical demands 18% 24% 58% Intellectual demands 53% 21% 27% Overall, modest to strong upgrading in lowered physical and increased intellectual demands	Validity-reliability of self-reports; printers most subject to downgrading may not be in the sample in 1976

(continued)

Table 2 *(continued)*

SKILLS AND THE DISTRIBUTION OF EARNINGS AND INCOME

Study	Sample/Population	Time Period	Content/ Composition Shift
Adler (1983)	Clerical occupations in four largest French banks; observational study	1930s-early 1980s	Content
Kelley (1986)	Eleven studies that investigated introduction of numerical control technology; U.S., U.K., West German, and Japanese plants; twenty-two establishments, forty-one different blue-collar jobs	Primarily 1970s	Primarily content

Skill Measures Dimensions	General Outcomes	Notes
Same worker contributions as Bright (1958); some adjustment of dimensions for qualitative changes or new skills; skill as substantive complexity and autonomy-control; apparently no direct measures	As banks moved from lower to higher forms of automation, mixture of upgrading and downgrading effects; at highest level of automation, qualitative transformation of work so as to require new categories of skill: greater worker responsibility for production, more abstract tasks and greater interdependence of jobs; impact of technology substantially mediated by market factors, managerial strategies, and social definitions of skill requirements	No consideration of composition shifts; quality of time one skill levels in the banking industry unknown
Whether workers in affected blue-collar occupations (NC operations) perform any programming tasks; some mixture of skill as substantive complexity and autonomy-control	Mixture of upgrading, downgrading, and skill polarization that was largely establishment-specific; no evidence of singular managerial motives to deskill or upgrade; strong evidence of the role of managerial discretion and organizational variables (i.e., size); three managerial approaches: scientific management, technocratic, and worker-centered	Sketchy or no coverage of composition shifts; uneven skill measures; highly variable design quality in the eleven studies; involves cross-national comparison; unclear whether there were direct time one and time two skill measures

(continued)

Table 2 *(continued)*

SKILLS AND THE DISTRIBUTION OF EARNINGS AND INCOME

Study	Sample/Population	Time Period	Content/ Composition Shift
Webster (1986)	Eight British firms in Bradford, West Yorkshire that introduced dedicated word processing systems; clericals working in these service and manufacturing firms	1980s	Primarily content
Vallas (1988)	Eight New York and New Jersey locals (N=802; response rate=51%), representing operators, switching and maintenance craft workers, clerical workers, and customer service representatives in regional telecommunications industry; technology changes include industry shifts from mechanical to electromechanical to electronic switching systems	1984 for content shifts; 1950-1980 for compositional shifts	Composition and content

Skill Measures Dimensions	General Outcomes	Notes
Including: variety, discretion, task scope, repetitiveness, "complexity"; both skill as substantive complexity and autonomy-control	Mixture of upgrading and downgrading; the word processing technology expands the range of options for organizing clerical work; accordingly, some firms fragmented and specialized tasks (deskilling) while other firms expanded clerical jobs (upgrading); central role of management and organizational variables	No consideration of compositional shifts: apparently a short time span between, before, and after observations; unclear whether there were direct time one and time two skill measures
Direct measures of skill as substantive complexity and as autonomy-control taken from workers' self-reports; three levels of coded automation in the cross-section (synthetic cohort design to assess change)	Apparent upgrading between 1950 and 1980 via compositional shift (assumes constant work content); individual and aggregate (local) level effects of automation of work content showed deskilling of substantive complexity and autonomy-control across all sampled jobs; select jobs (outside craft workers) showed content upgrading on both skill dimensions	Strong assumptions of synthetic cohort design to measure change (workers at different technology levels, in 1984 assumed to reflect continuum of temporal change in work content in the industry); limitations of self-report measures; low response rate

gate studies. Recall that aggregate studies provided more evidence of upgrading through mixtures of content and compositional shifts.

3. Case studies strongly suggest regional, state and other geographic variations in skill transformations.

4. Case studies suggest the impacts of technology on skill requirements of jobs are not simple, are not necessarily direct, are not constant across settings and firms, and cannot be considered in isolation of larger classes of variables that I have summarized as managers, markets, and organizational cultures. Several recent case studies well illustrate the more complicated variations (Kelley 1986; Webster 1986; Vallas, 1988).

Two of the studies show that a specific technology—numerically control-led machinery in the studies reviewed by Kelley (1986) and dedicated work processing systems in the eight firms studied by Webster (1986)—can have opposite implications for the skill requirements of the same occupations, conditional on managerial discretion and organizational variables. Kelley reviewed eleven studies on the introduction of numerically controlled machines in U.S., western European and Japanese firms, concentrating on whether the machine operators did more advanced programming of the new machinery as an indicator of upgrading or downgrading. In some firms, operators' jobs were upgraded, particularly in the West German firm, involving new programming tasks as part of the technological change; in other firms, there was a clear downgrading, with less complex work, less autonomy-control in the role, and no programming activity. Smaller organizations seemed more likely to augment the computerization with programming tasks. Managerial approach played a major role, in some firms following classic scientific management principles, in other firms following more narrow technical criteria, and in yet other firms—the typical upgrading situation—there was advance effort to implement computerization changes around worker-centered participation and control. Webster's study of eight British firms but with a different computerized technology, confirms the important role of managers. This is not to suggest that upgrading or downgrading depends on spur-of-the-moment managerial **decisions**. More likely, a larger set of longer-term economic and sociological factors generate managerial implementation strategies that are more conducive to upgrading or downgrading.

The study by Vallas (1988), although subject to strong assumptions, suggests that the introduction of new microelectronic technology in the telecommunications industry (1) independently affects both dimensions of skill, substantive complexity and autonomy-control and (2) downgrades some occupations and upgrades others. The occupations that were downgraded lost on both skill dimensions; only outdoor craftworkers responsible for troubleshooting and repair experienced upgrading. So in this industry-technology situation, the technical features of work appear to play a larger role in determining where upgrading versus downgrading will occur.

When juxtaposed what do the aggregate and case studies suggest? The safest conclusion suggests offsetting trends, with a slow evolution in aggregate skill levels but substantial skill requirement change in particular sectors, occupations and industries. To the extent there is a trend in the aggregate and case studies, it might be summarized by a contradictory skill shift hypothesis (see Figure 1). The hypothesis raises the possibility that the substantive complexity of work environments has gradually increased across the economy in recent history while the skill levels as autonomy-control have gradually decreased. This hypothesis awaits a comprehensive test.

SKILLS AND THE DISTRIBUTION OF EARNINGS AND INCOME

Figure 1. Summary of Hypothesized Changes in the Skill Level of Work, by Skill Dimension and Nature of Change in Work

| | Skill Dimension | |
	Substantive Complexity	Autonomy-Control
Content shift	Approximate stability or small upward shift *Examples: Mueller et al. (1969); Rumberger (1981)*	Possible downward shifts, particularly since World War II *Examples: Kraft (1977); Sobel (1982); Stone (1974)*
Compositional shift	Approximate stability or small upward shift *Examples: Dubnoff (1978); Spenner (1982)*	Approximate stability or small downward shifts *Examples: Levin and Rumberger (1983); Wright and Singelmann (1982)*

(Change track)

Note: Each cell cites illustrative studies. For comprehensive citations and argument, consult Spenner (1983, 1985).

The case of engineering illustrates the contradictory skill shift hypothesis and associated forms of change. Several case studies suggest the engineers of one hundred years ago were independent professionals and business people compared with today's engineers, who typically are employees of large firms with a narrowed (but more complex) skill range and less autonomy-control (Braverman 1974, 242-246; Stark 1980). Consider the tremendous increase in the complexity of engineering over the years (largely driven by technology) on the one hand and the substantial fractionation and specialization of engineering on the other hand (aeronautical, astronautical, biological, biomedical, chemical, biochemical, civil, and so on). Further, the number of engineers in the United States grew dramatically from about 7,000 in 1880 to over 136,000 in 1920 to over 1.2 million today (or more depending on the classification). The work content shift in autonomy-control may well have been a skill downgrading for the original 7,000 compared with those that followed, even in the face of a substantive complexity upgrading in content because of technological change. The compositional shift in substantive complexity was massive in the upgrading direction because the substantive complexity of engineering far exceeds the average substantive complexity level for the U.S. labor force, whether assessed in the 1880s or 1980s. The compositional shift in autonomy-control for engineering is less clear; perhaps the dramatic increase of engineers in large firms and bureaucracies reflects a skill downgrading compared with the larger relative share of self-employed engineers before the turn of the century, but there is less direct evidence of this type of change.

Under the contradictory skill shift hypothesis, one reading of the collective evidence is that it approximately matches the trends suggested by engineering. If we consider the concept of an "average" occupation and work environment now compared with the turn of the century, then workers of today face skill demands that are slightly to modestly more substantively complex and, perhaps, jobs and skill levels that afford less autonomy-control compared with the past. These are characterizations of average aggregate shifts. Particular jobs, sectors and industries may have experienced more dramatic forms of upgrading and downgrading.

In summary, the dominant impression from the existing knowledge base on the relationship between technological change and skill requirements is one of uncertainty. The collective research has produced no simple satisfactory answer to the larger questions. The available data and methodologies are limited. The samplings of skill changes and technologies in time and space are extremely limited. The concepts and measures of skill are poor.

Further, the evidence suggests a complicated relationship between technological change and skill transformations. There are short- and long-term effects, direct and indirect effects, regional, occupational and other sector variations; and there are many apparent conditioning variables, including managerial discretion, markets, and organizational cultures. The next section considers some of the conditioning relationships and reviews arguments that the future effects of technology on skill requirements might differ from past relationships.

A Different Future?

There are several reasons to suggest the future relationship of technology to the skill requirements of work will differ from the past. The most general argument, the postindustrial thesis, suggests the economy and social system are in a qualitatively different mode compared with the past (for examples, consult Fuchs 1968; Bell 1973; Piore and Sabel 1984; Hirschhorn 1984). The variations in the argument are many: The white-collar service revolution is upon us; the exodus from agriculture has been exhausted; national economies face a new level of integration and dependence on the world economy; we are in the midst of a new industrial revolution, built around computers and microelectronics; industrial/finance/corporate capitalism face a new level of crisis; today's firms handle product, labor, and market uncertainties in fundamentally different ways; and so on. For each of these arguments and others, there are counterarguments (for example, compare Chirot 1986). The debates are ongoing and without a current resolution. If accurate, the arguments about qualitative shifts strongly limit the use of past studies of skill and technology to make judgments about the future.

One specific argument that suggests a different future and the inapplicability of past knowledge comes from the hypothesis that current "high" technology (that is, computers and microelectronics) differs from prior technological innovations. Among the proponents of the thesis, Rumberger and Levin have proffered the most detailed argument and predictions (Rumberger 1983; 1984; 1987; Levin and Rumberger 1983; 1987; Rumberger and Levin 1985).

Briefly, their argument suggests past technological innovations principally altered the manual, manipulative and physical features of work. Many of these changes were concentrated in agriculture, manufacturing and construction. Current (and future) technologies alter the mental demands of work in addition to physical demands. Rumberger and Levin suggest the effects of high technology on the composition of the labor force are several: (1) displacement of skilled mental labor; (2) job creation but in a polarized fashion, with a small relative and absolute number of "high skill" jobs (that is, measured with high wages and high education in their studies), and a large relative and absolute number of low skill jobs. Further, productivity increases may limit the ability of the economy to produce enough new jobs to offset the displacement. As evidence, they review the recent data and projections of occupation-specific and industry-specific growth and decline, in particular for "high-tech" occupations and industries (under a variety of definitions of high technology). High technology occupations and industries are growing at a rapid rate but begin with a small absolute base. Further, the occupations that will produce the largest number of new jobs are by a substantial margin medium and low skill by any definition (custodians, cashiers, waiters and waitresses, truck drivers, general office and sales clerks). Thus, a major part of the future of high technology is the creation of jobs that are of lower than average skill.

Although the argument sounds convincing, it has not been directly tested for several reasons. First, most of the evidence refers to recent and projected growth levels (relative and absolute) for occupations and industries across the economy. The specific effects of high technology have not been filtered out. The growth levels and projections reflect all sources, high technology, low technology, and otherwise (that is, as generated by demographic changes, productivity increases or declines, foreign competition, larger supply and demand variations in the economy, the movement of production to other countries, and so on). Their assertions may be correct, but overall growth levels of occupations and industries reflect all forces. Changes that are not high-technology could alter the projections. Thus, we are left with an interesting hypothesis but little direct data on high versus other technology forms and their compositional shift implications.

Second, the evidence considered by Rumberger and Levin makes no direct adjustments for content shifts in skill requirements caused by high technology, which could offset or augment the compositional shifts they hypothesize. In the absence of direct measures of multiple skill dimensions and some systematic sampling of time and space, their argument is more of an hypothesis awaiting test than a well-established relationship. Finally, let us suppose their thesis is correct: The net effect of high technology is compositional downgrading, even after adjusting for content shift. Uncertainty still enters the picture under the rubric of managerial discretion, markets, and organizational cultures, as these quantities might change or alter the relationship.

Managerial Discretion

Managerial discretion refers to the role that managers play in deciding whether to implement a technological change, what change to implement, when it is implemented, and how it is implemented. Managerial discretion includes the design of new technology, hence the important role of engineers, and firm or establishment policy and procedures with respect to displaced workers, job and task fractionation and redesign. The evidence from several disciplines is clear and unambiguous: Managerial discretion plays a central role in determining the consequences of technological change for the skill requirements of work. Indeed, one explanation for the substantial diversity of outcomes in the empirical literature suggests the highly variable but potent role of management generates a wide range of outcomes. Further, it is possible, but not proven, that managerial discretion plays a larger role than intrinsic features of a technological change in defining skill requirements. Technology defines a range of possibilities; other social and economic processes take over from there.

Two previously mentioned studies illustrate the central role of managerial discretion (see Table 2). Kelley's (1986) study reviewed several other studies and generated new data from several firms (eleven studies and firms in all) that involved the introduction of computerized numerical control technology in manufacturing firms. The various plants were located in the United States, the United Kingdom, West Germany, and Japan. One way in which management exercised choice in implementing the technical change involved which jobs and people would be responsible for the various levels of programming, monitoring, and trouble-shooting the new system. The options ranged from specialized roles where the earlier operators would only tend the machines and others would program and trouble-shoot versus a task arrangement in which the more complicated and discretion-based tasks were distributed across roles, including the earlier machine operator, even if this arrangement involved retraining. Kelley found a wide range of skill transformation outcomes, which included the original operative jobs being upgraded in some firms, downgraded in others, and experiencing little net skill change in others. The study considered the same narrow technology, in a fairly short span of history, in similar types of manufacturing concerns. Kelley attributes at least part of the different outcomes to the important role of management in designing and implementing technical change.

Webster (1986) reaches a similar conclusion for a different computerized technology—dedicated word processing—in a study of eight British firms. The occupations studied included clerical jobs, and the range of firms studied included a university setting, a mail order firm, a motor parts firm, and a building society. Similar to Kelley's major finding, in some cases secretarial/clerical roles were redivided and fractionated with the introduction of dedicated word processing: One job involved only entry, another involved set-up, another correction and final production, another supervision, and so on. In other firms, secretarial and clerical roles expanded with the introduction of word processing systems, with the work becoming more complex (that is, a single role involved judgments as to set-up, format, input, and correction) and more autonomy-control in deciding how the task would be done. Webster attributes some of the differences to varying managerial practice across the firms.

Thus, managerial discretion adds uncertainty to the relationship between technological changes and skill transformations. The uncertainty is not merely a matter of managers responding to an uncertain (market) environment according to a rational choice or decision-making model. It is additionally, the uncertain response of managers to uncertain environments. Although there are substantial traditions in economics and management science that model and generate theories of managerial behavior, firms and managers often behave in ways that are often at variance with textbook images. A number of studies document the idiosyncrasies when firms and managers implement technological changes (for review, consult Berg et al., 1981). For example, frequently management does not calculate or estimate the relative labor costs or skill mixtures associated with technology options. A growing number of studies are even less complimentary about the motives, strategies, and tactics of U.S. managers—for example, in short- versus long-term maximizing strategies, in takeovers, buyouts, plant shutdowns and international relocations (Bowles and Gintis 1976; Edwards 1979; Bluestone and Harrison 1982).

Markets

Another source of uncertainty occurs in market phenomena, broadly defined (Standing 1984). For example, larger variations in supply and demand, productivity change, and growth in the economy can substantially modify or overshadow skill changes that more directly derive from technological changes, assuming these various factors are analytically separable.

Osterman's (1986) recent study illustrates how market phenomena can obfuscate judgments about how technological change affects the skill requirements of work. In the period from 1972-78, Osterman found that the net effect of computers (as estimated by quantities of main memory available in industries in the Standard Industrial Classification) on the demand for clerical and managerial labor was negative (ignoring content shifts). But underlying the larger pattern was a reversal. Over the short-term (two to five years) computerization in the various industries depressed demand for labor. Over the longer-term (five to seven years) the effects were positive, with increased demand for clerical and managerial labor. The time period in question approximately spanned one short-term business cycle. Osterman interprets the empirical data with a bureaucratic reorganization hypothesis: In the short-term the technological change (computers) displaces labor because a substitution of technology for labor is more efficient in the production function of the firm, given the original purpose and scope of the innovation. Over the longer-term, computerization lowers unit cost, perhaps allowing expanding production, and induces structural reorganization in the firm, perhaps allowing the production of new products, movement into new market domains and so on.

With Osterman's study as backdrop, consider two dimensions underlying the socioeconomic environment in an industry: (1) resource-rich versus resource-lean environments and (2) the adoption-diffusion curve for a technological change within an industry, and the extent to which firms are staggered versus in synchrony in their rate of adoption of the technology. Further, let bureaucratic reorganization reflect a longer-term upgrading potential of a technological change that initially produces compositional downgrading. First, firms may be more or less likely to adopt an innovation, and second, to reorganize structurally depending on whether their local environments are resource rich or resource lean. Thus, in the cross-section, the location of an industry in the upgrading-downgrading cycle will depend on the resource richness or leaness of the environment, which is largely defined by larger market factors. Further, a study of an industry in resource-rich verus resource-lean environment might reach very different conclusions about the effects of technological change on skill requirements. Additionally, consider a situation in which the adoption-diffusion of an innovation is in synchrony for firms in an industry: Collectively, the firms would show initial downgrading then upgrading via structural reorganization. In this situation, the student of skill transformations would "see" a strong initial downgrading followed by skill upgrading. Contrast this situation with a highly staggered adoption-diffusion curve: Many firms in an industry are at different points in down-grading-reorganization-upgrading cycle described by Osterman. In **this** situation, the student of skill transformation would see a very different picture: approximate aggregate stability or slight down-grading.

In short, there are many ways in which market factors define and condition the relationship between technological change and skill transformations. Some of these we understand and some we do not. Further, there are even intricate ways in which market factors can obscure what our research studies show to be the relationship between technological change and skill requirements, in the absence of a complete specification and a long time series of data. The result is greater uncertainty, both in the intrinsic relationship between technological change and skill transformations, and in our knowledge of the relationship.

Organizational Cultures

A final source of uncertainty in our knowledge and in the technology-skill transformation relationship occurs in organizational cultures. By organizational culture I mean the social and cultural system of the work environment in which technological changes take place. Organizational culture so defined would include standard features of organizations such as size, age, differentiation, and hierarchy, but also the cumulative belief structures of employees, their images of technology, the norms and sources of power of managerial and worker groups, and more generally the demography and social psychology of organizations. Across the disciplines of anthropology, psychology, economics, management science, and sociology, there is nothing approaching a comprehensive theory of how organizational cultures operate, to say nothing of specific implications for skill transformations. Rather, there are many mid-level theories, concepts, and research programs (for examples, reviews and citations consult Ouchi and Wilkins 1985 or Pfeffer 1985). Here, I illustrate one or two ways in which organizational culture comes to bear on the relationship between technology and skill requirements.

No less than other social phenomena, "skill" is subject to social definition, change, and process (for example, see Jones 1980; Littler 1982; Adler 1983 or DiPrete 1986). For example, in the steel and automobile industries, what comes to be defined as "skilled" in relation to job titles, classifications and hierarchies is some complicated mixture of the technical features of tasks, the past and present of union-management negotiations over job classification systems, and even day-to-day politics of performance-norm definition, worker-supervisor interactions and other group dynamics. What workers define as skill and what researchers see and designate as skill in part depends on these relationships.

Another example of the conditioning role of organizational culture can be found in the studies of computerized typesetting in the printing industry. One of the major studies of the industry by Wallace and Kalleberg (1982) (see Table 2 above) documents the deskilling of hand compositor and typesetter occupations in the industry over the last forty years, as indicated by indirect wage comparisons. At first reflection, one would conclude that the consequences for workers in this industry were tragic. Nonetheless, a longitudinal study by Hull, Friedman and Rogers (1982) showed a group of printers from three large New York City newspapers experienced substantial upgrading in their subsequent work careers, even in the face of deskilling of their earlier jobs. Several years after the technological change, a majority of printers reported more expanded and challenging jobs, along with higher income and job satisfaction. What occurred? The severance package obtained by the printers and their union contained substantial benefits, including resources for retraining and a relatively long time period to accomplish the transition. This is not to suggest the printers' fate is the modal outcome for U.S. workers; tragically it is not. However, a study focusing on the original technological change and the affected occupations in this case would reach one conclusion; a study that followed the affected workers would reach another conclusion. Relationships defined by organizational cultures differentiate the two. Thus, organizational cultures provide an additional source of uncertainty, particularly if the focus shifts from affected jobs or occupations to affected workers.

Education and Training Policy
in the Face of Uncertainty

The central theme of this essay has been uncertainty: uncertainty because of inadequacies in the knowledge base, and in what we do know, an uncertain relationship between technology and the upgrading or downgrading of occupations. Many other things come into play that are difficult to predict. Just as there is no single, simple answer to the question of technology and skill requirements, there is no single, simple answer to the question of an optimal education and training policy in the face of uncertainty. And just as there are strong popular beliefs about technology and work, there are strong beliefs about the role of education and training in relation to skill change.

For some, education and training operate as leading institutions that anticipate and even modify the skill requirements of jobs (Levin and Rumberger 1987). For others education operates as a "trailing" institution that follows developments from other corners of society and has little to do with the skills needed for work. In between are those who suggest education and training systems slowly adjust to the requirements of the economy, affecting demand little in the short-term but more substantially over the long-term (see Rubinson and Ralph 1984 for review). In recent years, the policy counsel is frequent and varied on the topic of technology, and education and training. For example, some cite mathematics and science education in Japan as the chief factor fostering industrial robotics, and suggest mathematics and science education as a top policy priority (Lynn 1983). I know of no direct tests of the causal link. Ferman (1983) suggests a restructuring of all levels of community education to accomplish a closer link between new technologies in factories and training for work. Groff (1983) and others counsel bringing state-of-the-art technology directly into the curriculum and into methods of instruction. Werneke (1983) suggests more general skills that enhance adaptability to change; others counsel training in more specific skills linked to specific technologies. The calls for computer literacy at all levels of education abound (King 1985). And as if a diversity of counsel were not sufficient, a succession of national panels in the last five years has resoundingly indicted first, elementary education, second, high school or secondary education, and most recently post-secondary education, particularly colleges and universities. In each of these reports, there is both direct assertion and indirect suggestion that education and training—at the same time—are in a desperate failing situation, on the one hand, and on the other hand can or will play a crucial role in national productivity, technical innovation, adaptation to increasing rates of social change and so on. These are but a sampling of the views.

Many of the policy recommendations assume some knowledge of the relationship between technological change and occupational skill transformations. Based on this review such recommendations are on uncertain ground. A difficult and complicated enterprise to begin with—public and private policy on education and training—becomes even more tenuous in the face of uncertainty. Rather than a hopeless case though, education and training policy can attempt to take the uncertainty into account (versus ignoring it or assuming its nonexistence). It is here that the scientific literature can sharpen some of the policy issues and options.

Limitations and Possibilities

Education and training operate in different ways according to upgrading and downgrading perspectives. In the upgrading tradition, the relationship between education and jobs is a functional one: Schooling and training impart the general and specific skills required by the economy in general and by jobs in particular. Further, schooling and training are forms of human capital, subject to appreciation and reward in the workplace. Proponents would cite the broad range of relationships between work outcomes and schooling levels (Becker 1964; Cain 1976). In downgrading perspectives, schooling bears little instrumental relation to job performance or productivity. Proponents would cite weak relationships between schooling and employee performance within occupations, and the massive growth of education and training in the face of stable skill requirements, fluctuations in productivity, and related phenomena (overeducation, underemployment) (Berg 1970; for review, consult Rubinson and Ralph 1984). Rather, ours is a credential society where education and training provide the keys that open employment doors (Collins 1979). Further, education socializes workers into the values of the American workplace and more often reinforces existing inequalities rather than alleviating them (Bowles and Gintis 1976). Most downgrading theorists would assign a lesser role to on-the-job training, vocational training and other supply-side features, instead directing our attention to larger demand-side operations at the level of firms and the economy.

The evidence suggests schooling and training operate some-what in line with both perspectives. That is, workers with more education and training are advantaged in the labor force, types of jobs, earnings, stable work histories, job satisfaction, and so on. In part, the advantages flow from the general and specific skills that stu-dents acquire in schools and training programs; in part the advan-tages flow from credentialling effects, the values that students are assumed to acquire or hold with higher education and training, and locations in job access queues, where education gives people greater access to jobs but does not greatly affect job performances (Thurow 1975). Education and training are cited as cures for many contem-porary social ills: to arrest productivity declines, to provide the skills for high technology, to provide for job satisfaction, income, and per-sonal growth, to remedy the dislocations of structural unemploy-ment, and to assure equality of opportunity and the optimal use of human resources, to cite a few. Yet the research on education and training suggests important limits on its role as a solution to these and other problems.

First, if education and training modify the relationship between technology and skill requirements it is over the longer term. The ability of a well-educated population to innovate and solve its prob-lems with technology is constrained in the short-term and subject to a host of limiting economic relationships, time-lags in adoption and diffusion, an existing physical plant structure and capital base. *Changes* in education and training systems that affect a small frac-tion of the population might take an even longer time to exhibit even modest effects on technological innovation in the economy.

Second, education and various forms of training bear an imper-fect relationship to job acquisition and performance (Granovetter 1981; Thurow 1975). If anything, pre-labor force education and train-ing better predict access to jobs than job performance. There is little evidence to suggest education and training differentiate workers in the same occupation in terms of productivity (Berg 1970).

Third, the quality of the match between workers' capacities and skills, and job requirements is modest at best (Berg et al. 1981). The available pool of workers with sufficient skills is far less prob-lematic than the process that matches workers with given mixture and levels of skills to jobs with given skill requirements. Investments in better matching of workers to jobs might yield far greater return than across-the-board increases in schooling and training. For exam-ple, many workers are unwilling to migrate or are unaware of avail-able jobs, how to find jobs, or how to interview for a job; many jobs, perhaps one-half or more, are obtained in particularistic fashion (relatives, friends, inside recruiting and tips) (Granovetter 1974; U.S. Department of Labor 1976).

Finally, managers and organizations operate in a far less rational manner than suggested by textbook images. For example, the skill capacities of existing employees of a firm often guide decisions about technical innovations—versus skills estimated to be available from a larger local or regional labor pool or schools. The rational acquisition of schooling and training are of limited value if the labor market and organizations do not provide for its rational use.

Prelabor Force Education and Training

Education and training bear modest relationships to job acquisition and work outcomes. They will continue to be part of the skill acquisition and employment equations, if not in reality then in the minds of students and employers. There is nothing in this review thus far that would suggest a dramatically increased or decreased role for education and training. The modest levels of skill change, the mixtures of skill change, the forms of uncertainty including the role of modifying factors (managers, markets, and organizational cultures) provide the reasons for this conclusion. If a case for dramatic change in the general or vocational education enterprises were to be made, then the arguments and evidence must come from a domain broader than technology and skill requirements. There are perhaps two exceptions.

The first exception involves literacy. The national investment in bringing all of the population to a minimal level of literacy, with basic high school levels of language, reasoning, and mathematical skill, is worthwhile because those without these skills will be left out of the labor market entirely or restricted to the most menial jobs. If technology makes increasing or changing demands on workers, for example, in terms of added specific skills, then these workers will least be able to compete and survive in their jobs in the absence of basic literacy skills. At this most elementary level, workers of today need basic literacy skills, such as the ability to read, whereas a large fraction of the labor force of eighty to a hundred years ago (that is, those in agricultural settings) could easily survive without such skills.

The strongest case for more postsecondary and vocational education comes from those studies that show more educated workers are better able to adapt to technological change (in their current or next jobs) and are less likely to experience as many or as serious adverse consequences of technological change (Hull et al. 1982; Jaffe and Froomkin 1968; Mueller et al. 1969; Office of Technology Assessment 1986). In terms of policy, this means more schooling for the lowest one-third or one-half of the schooling distribution, versus the top half of the distribution, which might increase this form of inequality. The adaptability advantage seems to derive in part from having additional job-relevant skills that can be translated into a new job and from the more general skills such as cognitive ability, intellectual flexibility, and problem solving capacities as these are obtained in general schooling (versus vocational) and might apply to rapid adjustment to new technology or a greater capacity to quickly switch careers.

Some of the policy questions center on specific versus general skills. In the face of uncertainty, it makes no sense to stress one to the exclusion of the other. Further, reduced reliance on a single vocational skill makes sense for several reasons. American workers have more complicated careers now compared with fifty or a hundred years ago. Where a single vocational skill might suffice then, it may not now. For example, high school students of the mid- and late 1960s averaged over four different full-time jobs for men, and over three for women, before age 30 (Spenner, Otto and Call 1982). European societies provide one possible model, where vocational students often prepare in the skills of more than one field. In this sense, given the uncertainties, more specific skills seems reasonable, particularly for certain sectors of the economy.

Finally, the review of changing skill requirements should temper some of the enthusiasm for specific skills in computer literacy. The effects of computers on work, particularly clerical work, involve mixtures of upgrading and downgrading (Menzies 1981; Werneke 1983, Webster 1986; Hartmann, Kraut and Tilly 1986). Many jobs do not directly use or require computer literacy skills; many jobs that do require them frequently change systems such that the ability to learn a new system far outweighs knowledge of any single system, particularly at the lower levels likely to be taught in elementary and secondary education. A large fraction of jobs that use video display terminals and related systems involve less complicated skills that are rapidly acquired with on-the-job training. The impacts of the computer on our lives and our jobs are substantial but substantially indirect. Moreover, the **direct** impacts on our jobs and lives have been overemphasized, particularly in the short-term (Brooks 1983).

National versus Local Policies

In some ways, a coherent, clear national policy on education and training seems wise—for example, in standards for training or in uniform policies for notifying workers of displacement and providing retraining benefits. One way in which a national policy does not make sense involves local and regional variations in technological changes that depart from the national average. The research evidence shows such variations—for example, in the location of robotics innovations. Planning and policy should allow substantial room for local and regional variations, and should actively and periodically monitor such variations.

Structural Unemployment and Retraining

Recent studies document the tremendous diversity of layoff notification, severance packages, and retraining benefits for workers displaced by technological change, foreign competition, and so on (Office of Technology Assessment 1986). Some of the discussion has cast these issues in terms of education and training policy. The real issues are not whether to give workers advance notice of layoffs, or whether to provide retraining. If research can inform these questions, the answers are clear: The more advance warning the better in terms of minimizing adverse consequences and maximizing positive adjustment (psychologically and in terms of work) (for example, see Hull et al. 1982); and workers who have the time and resources for retraining fare better than those who do not (Office of Technology Assessment 1986). Rather, the issues and debate are more moral, ethical, and economic than education and training. Can firms economically afford to provide advance warning of layoffs, as is custom and law in a number of European countries (and one or two states)? Can firms morally afford not to provide such notice? And who will pay for the education and retraining? Can the society (business, government) afford such? Can it afford not to? No less important is the case for research on technology where social considerations play a central role, for the consequences of technology, policies need to be informed by both technical and social considerations.

Curriculum Planning in the Face of Uncertainty

Building a vocational curriculum around the skill requirements of a specific technology involves large uncertainties. The collective

research evidence suggests the effects of technology on skill requirements are governed as much or more by aggregate demand, macroe-
conomic policy, and managerial discretion compared with the intrinsic features of the technology. Curricula based solely on the
technical side are subject to greater uncertainties than curricula
based on the technical *and* broader social implications of a technology on skill requirements, however difficult that might be. Further,
few vocational programs can use approximate aggregate stability as a
basis for curriculum planning. The markets for vocational skills and
graduates are typically local and regional, not national. A specific
skill in low or declining demand nationally may be in high demand
in the recruitment area of a local vocational program (or vice versa).
For example, even under the worst-case predictions for manufacturing employment, this sector will still employ around one-fifth of
the nation's workers for the foreseeable future (Etzioni and
Jargowsky 1984). Wholesale and large-scale abandonment of training
areas in perceived decline does not make sense for the replacement
needs in some declining industries that will provide more jobs than
some of the high growth industries that start with a much lower
base.

Curriculum planning in the face of uncertainty should include
several features. Overreliance on single curriculum programs, unless
there is strong justification, seems unwise. Without spreading the
curricula too thin, there is strength in diversification of vocational
programs and curricula, if for no other reason than it cuts the loss in
the event of a major plant dislocation or change in the fortunes of a
particular industry.

Further, the uncertainty over skill requirements suggests periodic review by vocational and educational policy analysts and planners along several lines: (1) What are the occupational destinations
of local and regional program graduates? (2) What is the quality of
the match between graduates' skill training and the skill requirements of their jobs? (3) What are the likely local and regional
changes in the demand for labor in specific occupations, and possible major changes in the quality of the local/regional job structure?
Given uncertainty, some policies will be better and others worse;
but given knowledge of uncertainty, there is no excuse not to diver-
sify and periodically monitor and adjust to change. In short, the
best strategies in the face of uncertainty and lack of knowledge
about skill transformations include curriculum diversification and
periodic review aimed at eliminating programs no longer in demand
and creating ones where demand arises.

SUMMARY

The debate over the relationship between technology and work is long standing and comprises a substantial number of studies in several scientific disciplines. The major positions in the debate—the upgrading, downgrading and mixed-change or conditional arguments—have failed to receive a clear verdict from the collective body of evidence. There are a number of reasons for the uncertainty.

Empirical studies rely on aggregate and case study designs to assess the consequences of technological change for skill variations in work. Each type of design has strengths and weaknesses, and tends to reach different conclusions. Comprehensive judgments require assessments of skill change in terms of compositional shifts in jobs and content changes in the nature of work. Different theoretical approaches and different types of designs have afforded uneven coverage to changes in skill requirements along these two tracks. The empirical studies do suggest mixtures of upgrading and downgrading, offsetting and contradictory trends for some occupations, industries, technologies, and sectors of the economy compared with others. The available data base is far short of a complete temporal and spatial sampling for technologies or jobs in the American economy, even for the twentieth century.

The concepts and measures of skill in the research literature are uneven and poor. An optimistic reading of the empirical literature suggests two basic dimensions of skill: substantive complexity and autonomy-control. One interpretation of the evidence suggests the possibility of contradictory skill shifts over the course of this century: In the aggregate, a slow and gradual upgrading of the skill requirements of jobs in terms of their substantive complexity is counterbalanced by a small decline in the autonomy-control of jobs. This hypothesis awaits comprehensive test. A pessimistic reading of the empirical studies simply concludes that no conclusion is possible because of inadequate samples, concepts, and measures, threats to the validity of inferences based on the analysis and design, and other forms of noncomparability across studies.

Given the limitations, a review of select aggregate and case studies shows several provisional conclusions. The skill requirements of jobs in the U.S. economy are changing. The rate of change over the course of this century is slow for the labor force taken as a whole but particular occupations, industries, and sectors of the economy have experienced more substantial shifts in skill requirements. Compositional shifts appear to account for relatively more of the upgrading of skill requirements, particularly for substantive complexity; content shifts appear to account for more of the downgrading, particularly changes in the autonomy-control of jobs. Of far greater importance than these trends are the roles played by managers, market forces, and organizational cultures in conditioning the effects of technology on the number and quality of jobs. The empirical literature provides a number of illustrations of the same technology affecting similar jobs in opposite ways conditional on market forces, managerial prerogatives in how or when to implement a technology, and the organizational cultures in which technological changes occur. Several recent arguments suggest a changing relationship between technological change and the skill requirements of work, postulating new ways in which technology affects work, particularly current and future effects on the mental parts of work. An evaluation shows this thesis is plausible but has not yet been rigorously tested.

Perhaps more important than the intrinsic effects of a technology on skill requirements are the modifying role of managers (that is, in how and when to implement a technological change), markets (modifying or offsetting the effects of a technological change), and organizational cultures (also modifying or offsetting a technological change). Future research and policy deliberations should devote much more attention to the role of these modifying factors.

Finally, just as uncertainty characterizes the relationship between technological change and what we know about the relationship, education and training policy in relation to technological change faces considerable uncertainty. Education and training as policy vehicles are limited in many ways—for example, in the lag between schooling and greater productivity, the loose linkage between skills of workers and skill demands of jobs, and the uneven and uncertain responses of managers and firms to uncertainty. Arguments for increased education hinge primarily on bringing all of the population to minimal levels of literacy and additional schooling for the less well-educated because education and training appear to minimize the adverse consequences of technological change for workers, and workers with such training and education adapt to change better and quicker. The research evidence suggests the need for education and training policies that are sensitive to local and regional variation in labor demand and technological change and for periodic monitoring of the available supply and demand for education and training levels, along with monitoring the quality of match of local graduates to available jobs and changing job conditions.

Curriculum planning in the face of uncertainty should rely on curriculum diversification and periodic review aimed at adjusting available programs to demand. Thus, within modest limits, the research on technological change and skill requirements informs education and training policy, and within modest limits, education and training can be expected to inform and solve human problems associated with technological change.

NOTES

1. Portions and earlier versions of this section were originally presented in Spenner (1983; 1985).

2. For arguments and evidence, consult Baron and Bielby (1982), Braverman (1974), Bright (1958), Cain and Treiman (1981), Field (1980), Gottfredson (1984), Hunter and Manley (1982), Karasek, Schwartz, and Pieper (1982), Kohn and Schooler (1983), Littler (1982), Rumberger (1984), Spaeth (1979), and Spenner (1979; 1980; 1983; 1985).

REFERENCES

Adler, P. 1983. "Rethinking the Skill Requirements of New Technologies." Working Paper HBS 84-27. Cambridge, Mass.: Graduate School of Business Administration, Harvard University.

———. Forthcoming. "Does Automation Raise Skill Requirements? What Again?" In R. Gordon (Ed.), *Microelectronics in Transition: Industrial Transformation and Social Change.*

Albin, P. S., F. Z. Hormozi, S. L. Mourgos, and A. Weinberg. 1984. "An Information System Approach to the Analysis of Job Design." In S. Chang (Ed.), *Management and Office Information Systems.* New York: Plenum, 385-400.

Baron, J. N., and W. T. Bielby. 1982. "Workers and Machines: Dimensions and Determinants of Technical Relations in the Workplace." *American Sociological Review* 47:175-188.

Becker, G. 1964. *Human Capital.* New York: National Bureau of Economic Research.

Bell, D. 1973. *The Coming of Post-Industrial Society.* New York: Basic Books.

Berg, I. 1970. *Education and Jobs: The Great Training Robbery.* New York: Praeger.

Berg, I., R. Bibb, T. A. Finegan, and M. Swafford. 1981. "Toward Model Specification in the Structural Unemployment Thesis: Issues and Prospects." In I. Berg (Ed.) *Sociological perspectives on labor markets.* New York: Academic Press, 347-367.

Berg, I., M. Freedman, and M. Freeman. 1978. *Managers and Work Reform.* New York: Free Press.

Blauner, R. 1964. *Alienation and Freedom: The Factory Worker and His Industry.* Chicago: University of Chicago Press.

Bluestone, B., and B. Harrison. 1982. *The Deindustrialization of America.* New York: Basic Books.

Bowles, S., and H. Gintis. 1976. *Schooling in Capitalist America.* New York: Basic Books.

Braverman, H. 1974. *Labor and Monopoly Capital: The Degradation of Work in the Twentieth Century.* New York: Monthly Review Press.

Bright, J. R. 1958. "Does Automation Raise Skill Requirements?" *Harvard Business Review* 36:84-98.

———. 1966. "The Relationship of Increasing Automation and Skill Requirements." In National Commission on Technology, Automation, and Economic Progress, *The Employment Impact of Technological Change.* Appendix Vol. 2 of *Technology and the American Economy.* Washington, D.C.: U.S. Government Printing Office, 203-222.

Brooks, H. 1983. "Technology, Competition, and Employment." *Annals of the American Academy of Political and Social Science* 470:115-122.

Burawoy, M. 1979. *Manufacturing Consent.* Chicago: University of Chicago Press.

Cain, G. G. 1976. "The Challenge of Segmented Labor Market Theories to Orthodox Theory." *Journal of Economic Literature* 14:1215-1257.

Cain, P., and D. J. Treiman. 1981. "The Dictionary of Occupational Titles as a Source of Occupational Data." *American Sociological Review* 46:253-278.

Chirot, D. 1986. *Social Change in the Modern Era.* San Diego, Calif.: Harcourt, Brace, Javanovich.

Clogg, C. C. 1979. *Measuring Underemployment.* New York: Academic Press.

Clogg, C. C. and J. W. Shockey. 1984. "Mismatch Between Occupation and Schooling: A Prevalence Measure, Recent Trends and Demographic Analysis." *Demography* 2:235-257.

Collins, R. 1979. *The Credential Society: An Historical Sociology of Education and Stratification.* New York: Academic Press.

Crossman, E. R. F. 1960. *Automation and Skill.* London: HMSO.

Davis, L. E., and J. C. Taylor. 1976. "Technology, Organization, and Job Structure." In R. Dubin (Ed.), *Handbook of Work, Organization and Society.* Chicago: Rand-McNally, 379-419.

DiPrete, T. A. 1986. "The Upgrading and Downgrading of Occupations: Status Redefinition vs. Deskilling as Alternative Theories of Change." Unpublished manuscript, Department of Sociology, The University of Chicago.

Dubnoff, S. 1978. "Inter-occupational Shifts and Changes in the Quality of Work in the American Economy, 1900-1970." Paper presented at the annual meeting of the Society for the Study of Social Problems, San Francisco, August 17-20.

Eckaus, R. 1964. "The Economic Criteria for Education and Training." *Review of Economics and Statistics* 41:181-190.

Edwards, R. C. 1979. *Contested Terrain: The Transformation of the Workplace in the Twentieth Century.* New York: Basic Books.

Etzioni, A., and P. Jargowsky. 1984. "High Tech, Basic Industry and the Future of the American Economy." *Human Resource Management* 23:229-240.

Faunce, W. A. 1958. "Automation in the Automobile Industry." *American Sociological Review* 23:401-407.

Ferman, L. A. 1983. "The Unmanned Factory and the Community." *Annals of the American Academy of Political and Social Science* 470:136-145.

Field, A. J. 1980. "Industrialization and Skill Intensity: The Case of Massachusetts." *Journal of Human Resources* 15:149-175.

Fuchs, V. R. 1968. *The Service Economy.* New York: National Bureau of Economic Research, 1968.

Gallie, D. 1978. *In Search of the New Working Class: Automation and Social Integration Within the Capitalist Enterprise.* Cambridge: Cambridge University Press.

Ginzberg, E. 1982. "The Mechanization of Work." *Scientific American* 247:67-75.

Glenn, E. N., and R. L. Feldberg. 1979. "Proletarianizing Clerical Work: Technology and Organizational Control in the Office." In A. Zimbalist (Ed.), *Case Studies on the Labor Process.* New York: Monthly Review Press, 51-72.

Gottfredson, L. S. 1984. "The Role of Intelligence and Education in the Division of Labor." Report No. 355. Baltimore, Md: The Johns Hopkins University, Center for Social Organization of the Schools.

Granovetter, M. S. 1974. *Getting a Job: A Study of Contacts and Careers.* Cambridge, Mass.: Harvard University Press.

———. 1981. "Toward a Sociological Theory of Income Differences." In I. Berg (Ed.), *Sociological Perspectives on Labor Markets.* New York: Academic Press, 11-47.

Groff, W. H. 1983. "Impacts of the High Technologies on Vocational and Technical Education." *Annals of the American Academy of Political and Social Science* 470:81-94.

Hartmann, H. I., R. E. Kraut, and L. A. Tilly. 1986. *Computer Chips and Paper Clips: Technology and Women's Employment*, Vol. I. Washington, D.C.: National Academy Press.

Hirschhorn, L. 1984. *Beyond Mechanization: Work and Technology in a Postindustrial Age.* Cambridge, Mass.: MIT Press.

Horowitz, M., and I. Herrnstadt. 1966. "Changes in Skill Requirements of Occupations in Selected Industries." In National Commission on Technology, Automation, and Economic Progress, *The Employment Impact of Technological Change.* Appendix Vol. 2 of *Technology and the American Economy.* Washington, D.C.: U.S. Government Printing Office, 223-287.

Hull, F. M., N. S. Friedman, and T. F. Rogers. 1982. "The Effect of Technology on Alienation from Work." *Sociology of Work and Occupations* 9:31-57.

Hunter, A., and M. Manley. 1982. "The Task Requirements of Occupations." Paper presented at the annual meeting of the Canadian Sociology and Anthropology Association, Ottawa, Canada.

Jaffe, A. J., and J. Froomkin. 1968. *Technology and Jobs, Automation in Perspective.* New York: Praeger.

Jaikumar, R. 1986. "Postindustrial Manufacturing." *Harvard Business Review* November-December:69-76.

Jones, F. F. 1980. "Skill as a Dimension of Occupational Classification." *Canadian Review of Sociology and Anthropology* 17:176-183.

Kalleberg, A. L., and K. T. Leicht. 1986. "Jobs and Skills: A Multivariate Structural Approach." *Social Science Research* 15:269-296.

Karasek, R., J. Schwartz, and C. Pieper. 1982. "A Job Characteristics Scoring System for Occupational Analysis." Unpublished manuscript, Center for the Social Sciences, Columbia University, New York.

Kelley, M. R. 1986. "Programmable Automation and the Skill Question: A Reinterpretation of the Cross-National Evidence." *Human Systems Management* 6:223-241.

Kerr, C., J. T. Dunlop, C. Harbison, and C. A. Myers. 1964. *Industrialism and Industrial Man.* New York: Oxford University Press.

King, K. M. 1985. "Evolution of the Concept of Computer Literacy." *EduCom Bulletin* 20:18-21.

Kohn, M. A. 1971. "Bureaucratic Man: A Portrait and an Interpretation." *American Sociological Review* 36:461-474.

Kohn, M. L., and C. Schooler. 1983. *Work and Personality: An Inquiry into the Impact of Social Stratification.* Norwood, N.J.: Ablex Publishing.

Kraft, P. 1977. *Programmers and Managers: The Routinization of Computer Programming in the United States.* New York: Springer-Verlag.

Levin, H., and R. Rumberger. 1983. "The Low-Skill Future of High-Tech." *Technology Review,* 8618-21.

———. 1987. "Educational Requirments for New Techologies: Visions, Possibilities and Current Realities." *Educational Policy* 1:333-354.

Littler, C. R. 1982. *The Development of the Labour Process in Capitalist Societies, A Comparative Study of the Transformation of Work Organization in Britain, Japan and the U.S.A.* London: Heinemann.

Lynn, L., 1983. "Japanese Robotics: Challenge and—Limited—Exemplar." *Annals of the American Academy of Political and Social Science* 470:16-27.

McCormick, E. J., R. C. Mecham, and P. R. Jeanneret. 1977. *Technical Manual for the Position Analysis Questionnaire.* Lafayette, Ind.: Purdue University.

McLaughlin, D. B. 1983. "Electronics and the Future of Work: The Impact on Pink and White Collar Workers." *Annals of the American Academy of Political and Social Science* 470:152-162.

Menzies, H. 1981. *Women and the Chip: Case Studies on the Effects of Informatics on Employment in Canada*. Montreal: Institute for Research on Public Policy.

Miller, A., D. J. Treiman, P. S. Cain, and P. A. Roos. 1980. *Jobs, and Occupations: A Critical Review of the Dictionary of Occupational Titles*. Washington, D. C.: National Academy Press.

Miller, R. J., Ed. 1983. "Robotics: Future Factories, Future Workers" Special issue of *Annals of the American Academy of Political and Social Science* (November).

Mueller, E., J. Hybels, J. Schmiedeskamp, J. Sonquist, and C. Staelin. 1969. *Technological Advance in an Expanding Economy: Its Impact on a Cross- Section of the Labor Force*. Ann Arbor, Mich.: Survey Research Center.

National Commission on Technology, Automation, and Economic Progress. 1966. *Technology and the American Economy*. 2 Vols. Washington, D.C.: U.S. Government Printing Office.

National Resources Committee. 1937. *Technological Trends and National Policy*. Washington, D.C.: U.S. Government Printing Office.

Oakley, K. P. 1954. "Skill as a Human Possession." In C. Singer, E. J. Holmyard and A. R. Hall (Eds.), *A History of Technology*, Vol. 1. New York: Oxford University Press, 2-3.

Office of Technology Assessment. 1986. *Technology and Structural Unemployment: Reemploying Displaced Adults*. Washington, D.C.: U.S. Government Printing Office.

Osterman, P. 1986. "The Impact of Computers on the Employment of Clerks and Managers." *Industrial and Labor Relations Review* 39:175-186.

Ouchi, W. G., and A. L. Wilkins. 1985. "Organizational Culture." In R. Turner and J. Short (Eds.), *Annual Review of Sociology*, Vol. 11. Palo Alto: Annual Reviews, Inc., 457-483.

Pfeffer, J. 1985. "Organizations and Organization Theory." In G. Lindzey and E. Aronson (Eds.), *The Handbook of Social Psychology*, Vol. I, 3d edition. New York: Random House, 370-440.

Piore, M. J. and C. F. Sabel. 1984. *The Second Industrial Divide*. New York: Basic Books.

Rawlins, V., and L. Ulman. 1974. "The Utilization of College Trained Manpower in the United States." In M. Gordon (Ed.), *Higher Education and the Labor Market*. New York: McGraw-Hill, 195-235.

Rubinson, R., and J. Ralph. 1984. "Technical Change and the Expansion of Schooling in the United States, 1890-1970." *Sociology of Education* 57:134-152.

Rumberger, R. W. 1981. *Overeducation in the U.S. Labor Market.* New York: Praeger.

――. 1983. "A Conceptual Framework for Analyzing Work Skills." Project Report No. 83-A8. Stanford, Calif.: Institute for Research on Educational Finance and Governance.

――. 1984. "High Technology and Job Loss." *Technology in Society* 6:263-284.

――. 1987. "The Potential Impact of Technology on the Skill Requirements of Future Jobs." In G. Burke and R. Rumberger (Eds.) *The Future Impact of Technology on Work and Education.* Philadelphia: Falmer Press, 74-95.

Rumberger, R. W., and M. Levin. 1985. "Forecasting the Impact of New Technologies on the Future Job Market." *Technological Forecasting and Social Change* 27:399-417.

Scott, J. W. 1982. "The Mechanization of Women's Work." *Scientific American* 247:166-187.

Shaiken, H. 1984. *Work Transformed: Automation and Labor in the Computer Age.* Lexington, Mass.: Lexington Books.

Singelmann, J. and M. Tienda. 1985. "The Process of Occupational Change in a Service Society: The Case of the United States, 1960-1980." In B. Roberts, F. Finnegan and D. Gallie (Eds.), *New Approaches to Economic Life: Economic Restructuring, Unemployment and the Social Division of Labor.* Manchester, England: University of Manchester.

Smith, H. L. 1986. "Overeducation and Underemployment: An Agnostic Review." *Sociology of Education* 59:85-99.

Sobel, R. 1982. "White Collar Structure and Class: Educated Labor Re-Evaluated." Ph.D. dissertation, School of Education, University of Massachusetts, Amherst.

Spaeth, J. 1979. "Vertical Differentiation Among Occupations." *American Sociological Review* 44:746-762.

Spenner, K. I. 1979. "Temporal Changes in Work Content." *American Sociological Review* 44:968-975.

—————. 1980. "Occupational Characteristics and Classification Systems: New uses of the *Dictionary of Occupational Titles* in social research." *Sociological Methods and Research* 9:239-264.

—————. 1982. "Temporal Changes in the Skill Levels of Work: Issues of Concept, Method, and Comparison." Paper presented at the 10th World Congress of Sociology, Mexico City, Mexico, August 10-17.

—————. 1983. "Deciphering Prometheus: Temporal Change in the Skill Level of Work." *American Sociological Review* 48:824-837.

—————. 1985. "The Upgrading and Downgrading of Occupations: Issues, Evidence, and Implications for Education." *Review of Educational Research* 55:125-154.

—————. 1988. "Occupations, Work Settings and the Course of Adult Development: Tracing the Implications of Select Historical Changes." In P. Baltes, D. Featherman and R. Lerner (Eds.), *Life-Span Development and Behavior*, Vol. 9. Hillsdale, N.J.: Lawrence Earlbaum Associates, 243-285.

Spenner, K. I., L. B. Otto, and V. R. A. Call. 1982. *Career Lines and Careers*. Lexington, Mass: Lexington Books.

Standing, G. 1984. "The Notion of Technological Unemployment." *International Labour Review* 123:127-147.

Stark, D. 1980. "Class Struggle and the Transformation of the Labor Process: A Relational Approach." *Theory and Society* 9:89-130.

Stone, K. 1974. "The Origins of Job Structures in the Steel Industry." *Review of Radical Political Economics* 6:61-97.

Sullivan, A. 1978. *Marginal Workers, Marginal Jobs*. Austin: University of Texas Press.

Thurow, L. C. 1975. *Generating Inequality: Mechanisms of Distribution in the U.S. Economy*. New York: Basic Books.

United States Department of Labor. 1949. *Dictionary of Occupational Titles*. Washington, D.C.: U.S. Government Printing Office.

—————. 1965. *Dictionary of Occupational Titles*, 3rd edition. Washington, D.C.: U.S. Government Printing Office.

—————. 1972. *Handbook for Analyzing Jobs*. Washington, D.C.: U.S. Government Printing Office.

—————. 1976. *Recruitment, Job Search, and the United States Employment Service*. Research and Development Monograph 43. Washington, D.C.: U.S. Government Printing Office.

————. 1977. *Dictionary of Occupational Titles*, 4th edition. Washington, D.C.: U.S. Government Printing Office.

Vallas, S. 1988. "New Technology, Job Content, and Worker Alienation: A Test of Two Rival Perspectives." *Work and Occupations* 15:148-178.

Wallace, M., and A. L. Kalleberg. 1982. "Industrial Transformation and the Decline of Craft: The Decomposition of Skill in the Printing Industry, 1931-1978." *American Sociological Review* 47:07-324.

Webster, J. 1986. "The Impact of Dedicated World Processors on Office Labour in the UK." Paper presented to the 11th World Congress of Sociology, New Delhi, India, August 16-22.

Werneke, D. 1983. *Microelectronics and Office Jobs: The Impact of the Chip on Women's Employment*. Geneva, Switzerland: International Labour Office.

Wright, E. O., and J. Singelmann. 1982. "Proletarianization in the Changing American Class Structure." In M. Burawoy and T. Skocpol, (Eds.), *Marxist Inquiries*. Chicago: University of Chicago Press, 176-209.

4

Vocational Education—
Meeting Manpower Needs
and Providing Student Opportunities

Chet Rzonca
Douglas Gustafson
Sandra Boutelle

Vocational education, as described in this chapter, reflects the intent of federal vocational legislation, the resultant state and local programs, major new initiatives, evaluation efforts, and selected model activities. The latter section of the chapter is devoted to documenting the important role of community colleges which has evolved during the last thirty years. Our purpose is to acquaint the reader with the goals of public vocational education and the programming offered to achieve these goals. These goals are to enable students to (1) choose, (2) prepare, and (3) advance in an occupational field. The career awareness and exploration function provides students the opportunity of choosing among the vast array of careers, ranging from several weeks of preparation to programs offered in graduate and professional schools. The preparation function is typically limited to occupations which require less than the baccalaureate degree. However, this preparation phase is enhanced by the increasing number of articulation agreements that exist between secondary schools and community colleges and between community colleges and traditional four year institutions. Career advancement opportunities are typically provided by a local community college or adult vocational education center. While many of the activities are limited to the upgrading of skills for individuals who do not hold a baccalaureate degree, increasingly the adult and continuing education entity of a local school provides educational experiences in areas such as computer skills and management techniques and coordinates activities which are offered to professionals.

FEDERAL INVOLVEMENT

Historians vary as to when vocational education was initiated; agricultural skills passed from father to son, and homemaking skills passed from mother to daughter are commonly recognized as early forms of vocational education. Still others cite the craft guilds and formal apprenticeship programs as a point of origin. Our discussion of vocational education begins with the federal presence and funding provided by the Smith-Hughes Act of 1917. This federal act followed the efforts of Northeastern states in their preparation of individuals who worked in agriculture, the textile industry, and the evolving machine trades of the 1880s and 1890s. The Smith-Hughes Act was enacted to prepare young people to work in agriculture, business and commerce, trades and industry, and home economics. The Act formed a partnership between the federal government and states, providing matching funds and requiring a state plan identifying labor needs and procedures whereby a combination of federal and state monies could be spent to prepare young people for employment. The primary objective of this legislation was economic. Better prepared workers would realize higher incomes and business and industry would be better able to compete in national and international markets.

The traditional objectives of vocational education are (1) meeting the labor needs of the nation, (2) providing options for choosing and preparing for a career, and (3) identifying the relationship between occupational and general education (Evans & Herr 1978). As refined and expanded, these objectives now form the foundation of vocational-technical preparatory programs offered at the secondary and postsecondary levels. The earliest efforts in vocational education were almost entirely limited to meeting labor needs. Counselors and teachers carefully selected students. These selected students were prepared in shops and laboratories that approximated the occupation, and the quality of their work performance was monitored. Later federal legislation added to the occupations for which federal funding could be used and increased the amount of those funds. Essentially, the purpose of this legislation was to prepare workers to meet growing labor needs.

The first major change to federal vocational legislation, and the resulting influence upon state vocational education programming, came with the passage of the Vocational Education Act of 1963. Formulas in initial federal vocational legislation specified monies for selected occupational clusters such as agriculture, home economics, and trades and industries. The new legislation eliminated these categories. States now met local labor needs as specified in their state plans. The new legislation included funding for target groups such as disadvantaged and handicapped students. The philosophy shifted from the selection of qualified students for specific job preparation to the acceptance of students with a range of abilities, and providing educational programs enabling them to succeed in the workplace. This shift initiated policies allowing for more flexibility in educational programs both in range of occupations and, more importantly, in curriculum development. Remedial programs and the development of English as a second language programs, as part of the allowable federal reimbursement, enabled more students to participate in occupational preparation. This was also a period of rapid growth for community colleges, expanding their roles beyond offering courses in liberal arts to include vocational programs. Federal vocational legislation is now viewed as both economic and social legislation. Current legislation provides for the addition of a variety of occupations that could be offered in educational institutions, relying heavily on new programming efforts that increased basic skills and helped to relate occupational training to general education.

The Carl D. Perkins Vocational and Applied Technology Education Act of 1990 continues the philosophy and policies initiated with the 1963 Vocational Education Act and subsequent federal legislation. The new Act reemphasizes service to targeted special populations including the poor, handicapped, educationally disadvantaged, disabled, single parents, foster children, those not properly served because of sex bias, and those with limited English proficiency (American Vocational Association 1990). The basic state grant requires that 75 percent of the federal funds be used at the local level with the remainder of funds distributed among state administration, state leadership, correctional institutions, and equity issues including displaced homemakers and sex equity. Sex equity, services to handicapped and disadvantaged individuals, and services to displaced homemakers are traditional funding areas that have been reaffirmed in the current legislation. New emphases support further interaction of vocational and general education and the establishment of technical preparation programs.

The technical preparation program is four years in duration and allows for a consortia of local education agencies and postsecondary institutions. The intent is to provide for better prepared students who can initiate career preparation at the secondary school level and culminate their occupational preparation at a postsecondary institution. These planned four-year programs allow for articulation and in some cases the use of high school credits to partially complete a postsecondary program. Business and industry require that new employees have excellent basic skills as well as technical training. The tech-prep programs prepare individuals who are able to meet the increasing skill levels of business and industry. A current omission in these programs is the identification of one-year postsecondary programs which can be articulated with local high schools. In spite of educational programming, many students delay their career decisions until the senior year of high school. There are many entry level occupations requiring less than two years of postsecondary education. The effect of the tech-prep model can be enhanced if shorter periods of articulation are included to accommodate late bloomers and occupations that require less than associate degree preparation.

In addition to reemphasizing programming efforts and increasing funding authorization, the new Act also requires states to assess the effectiveness of their vocational education programs. Similar efforts are to be conducted on the national level. Funding is also provided for exemplary and demonstration projects of national significance.

INSTITUTIONS AND PROGRAMS

Federally reimbursed vocational education programs are offered as early as the middle schools and continue into community colleges and vocational-technical institutes. The objectives of these offerings vary from an awareness and exploration of occupations at the middle school level to specialized preparation at the postsecondary level. Vocational education is classified into two broad categories: general vocational education programs and occupationally specific education programs (Bottoms & Copa 1983). The five general vocational education programs provide a foundation for career decisions, prepare students in prerequisite skills and for the mastery of general skills useful in both work and everyday life. These five general programs are further classified into consumer and homemaking, pre-vocational, basic skills, related instruction, and employability skills programs. The second area, that of occupationally specific vocational programs, is subdivided into four major areas: occupational-cluster programs, occupationally specific programs, job-specific programs, and employer-specific programs. This progression from the general to the specific prepares a broadly trained individual to seek employment in a group of similar occupations while allowing for very specific training or retraining in the last category of employer-specific programs.

Bottoms and Copa also identify the types of institutions offering vocational programs. Vocational programs are offered in middle schools, general, comprehensive, and vocational high schools, area vocational centers at both the secondary and postsecondary levels, community colleges and technical institutions, specialized postsecondary vocational schools, some four year institutions, and in skill centers. An array of programs, complemented by the types of institutions, make vocational education available to almost everyone.

EVALUATION OF VOCATIONAL PROGRAMS

For the most part, the evaluation of vocational education programs is limited to the rate of job placement in the occupation for which the student has been prepared or in related occupations, hourly wages, or annual income. States generally conduct follow-up surveys in cooperation with local education agencies. Surveys show that vocational education graduates earn above average hourly and annual wage rates. The surveys also show that most students available for job placement find employment in their field or one closely related to it (Evans & Herr 1987). Favorable placement rates exclude those students typically considered unavailable for placement, such as those who pursue additional education or have entered the military. While these data tend to be positively related to the vocational education programs, the relationship is affected by the economy and assumptions about student goals. For example, a period of general economic decline tends to affect the employability of graduates from even the best vocational education programs. Students who have performed well in secondary vocational education programs and desire to continue their education, depending on the methodology used, are excluded from job placement data since they are not available for placement or placed in the category indicating they have not found employment related to their field of preparation.

Another complicating factor is the definition of who is a vocational education program student or graduate. As indicated by Bottoms and Copa (1983), there are an array of vocational programs available to students in public education agencies. It is often difficult to separate students who have taken one or two vocational education courses in a comprehensive high school from students who have actually completed a planned vocational education program. To the extent that data describe students who have completed vocational education programs, results tend to substantiate current policies that support work-related training at the secondary school level. An argument could be made that since aggregate data are evaluated (that is, some course work versus a complete program), students in vocational education programs perform better than state reports indicate. Conversely, there may be more able students with higher degrees of self-confidence that have enrolled in one or two vocational education courses which tend to unduly influence the placement rates of follow-up data. Comparisons among major high school classifications such as general education, college preparatory, and vocational programming are therefore difficult. While the schools can clearly delineate the courses required for various programs, students often mingle their selections among these areas. The college preparatory classification would appear to be the best defined, but a clear definition between general education and vocational education tends to be less common. Studies tend to compare students who have taken courses in each of the major traditional high school areas and then analyze data by student intent at the time of graduation.

Evaluation Through Research

In addition to the requirements placed upon states for reporting the success of their vocational programs to the federal government, researchers have attempted to evaluate vocational education from a contextual and philosophical basis. Among these efforts have been studies conducted by the former National Center for Research in Vocational Education located at the Ohio State University. As part of the Center's research and development series, Desy, Campbell, and Gardner (1984) compiled information from four studies based primarily on data taken from a subsample of the national longitudinal survey of labor market experience—youth cohorts (NLS Youth) combined with information from respondents' high school transcripts. This study determined the degree of participation in vocational education, the relationship between school and the tendency to leave, job satisfaction, and student employment. The availability of vocational education and the extent to which it is pursued in high school is an important contribution of this study. Only 22 percent of the students indicated that they had *not* taken any vocational education credits. Forty-nine percent took, on the average, slightly less than one credit to slightly more than two credits of vocational education; while 29 percent of the sample completed from three to at least six or more credit hours of vocational education course work. This classification helps to crystalize some of the problems associated with the evaluation of vocational education programs and the inflated figures representing the number of students enrolled in vocational education. Overall, 22 percent of the sample consisted of non-vocational students while 78% had some vocational education experience. Clearly the employment expectations are different for those students who take one or two credits from those who have completed a six credit vocational education program.

A consistent claim of vocational educators is that vocational education students are less likely to drop out of high school and are better prepared to enter the work force. While dropping out is a complex phenomenon related to many factors, Desy et al. reported that students who had taken more vocational education course work were more likely to persist and finish school the following year. The study differentiates by grade levels, ethnicity, and in the twelfth grade, by gender. While this positive association is important, the study also identifies that given the complexity of the issue vocational education must be used in concert with other interventions to assist dropout prone students.

Individuals who participate in vocational education are more likely to be employed after high school. The data suggest that vocational education students are more likely to be more satisfied with their jobs than other high school graduates. To some extent, this satisfaction may be related to student expectations. Vocational graduates, who have either prepared for or explored an occupation, have more realistic goals of what will take place in the work setting than students who enter the work place without orientation. While vocational educators point to a higher level of job satisfaction as a positive result of vocational programming, the authors suggest that vocational programs may be used to influence students into accepting employment below their potential.

Desy et al. also address the hourly earnings of students who held jobs in high school and their participation in the labor force after high school. They found that for both males and females, vocational education program students earn less per hour than either students with limited vocational credits or students with no vocational credits. The major factor influencing income for females is the supervision of the work experience by the school. Female students who participated in school-supervised employment earned considerably more, though there was essentially no difference in earnings for males. There were no differences in weekly earnings for men, but women with high concentrations in vocational education reported higher weekly earnings than those who did not participate in vocational education.

An earlier study by Gardner, Campbell, and Seitz (1982) found that, in general, students with any concentration in vocational education were more likely to be in the labor force for a full year than those students who had either no vocational courses or had less than one vocational course in high school. This study eliminated students who were participating in postsecondary education.

Desy et al. (1984) consider other aspects related to retention, employment, and the assessment of vocational education programs as well as providing recommendations for further research. Readers interested in the assessment of vocational education related to high school participation are referred to their "High School Vocational Education Experiences: In School and In the Labor Market."

PLANNING TO MEET LABOR NEEDS

Historically, states have been required to submit planning documents, fiscal information, and narratives describing the effectiveness of programs to receive federal vocational funding. This requirement has been in effect since the passage of the Smith-Hughes Act in 1917. To meet the requirements of early legislation, documentation was directed toward accounting for funds spent in specified occupational categories such as home economics, trade and industry, and agriculture. In addition, states specified student selection requirements used by local education agencies, laboratory space, and clock hours of instruction. These early efforts towards planning and documentation of results had become increasingly more complex as set asides and funding categories were added to the federal legislation. States now plan for vocational programs to meet state and local labor needs without regard to traditional vocational education specialty areas. Recently efforts have been geared to the documentation of fiscal accounting procedures, students served, and student success as measured by job placement and hourly earnings. Each state is required by federal law to have a state advisory council on vocational education. The council is made up of business, industry, and education leaders and serves as a third-party evaluator to determine the appropriateness and success of vocational education offerings. For the most part, state plans for vocational education encompass activities which are conducted at the secondary school level or through area vocational centers that serve adults in either initial or retraining activities.

The state plan for vocational education requires of each state as a condition for receipt of federal funds fiscal accountability and responsiveness to labor needs. Coupled with the need to eliminate unnecessary program duplication, state efforts are directed to fostering articulation between community school districts and post-secondary institutions. This is difficult since in many states separate boards govern the comprehensive community colleges and local education agencies. There are some notable exceptions. As an example, the state of Iowa has designated the State Board of Education as a common Vocational Education Board that oversees both secondary and community college vocational education. For organizational purposes this section will describe state planning activities which are primarily aimed at the secondary school level. A latter section of this chapter will describe activities conducted under the auspices of the comprehensive community college.

During the past fifteen years the employment needs of business and industry have required increases in technical skills and in the basic skills of reading, writing, and ability to compute. Fewer resources have made it difficult to provide for the increased level of technical knowledge and the necessary remedial education required by some students. The great American dream of higher and more education has allowed schools to cater and devote a majority of their resources to students who are bound for the traditional colleges.

Stable federal vocational funding, increased accountability requirements and increases in entry level skills requirements, have combined to provide a climate for states to experiment with innovative curricula and formalize state and regional planning procedures. The remainder of this section is devoted to innovative cur-

ricula efforts in the states of New York and Iowa. The section also
describes the statewide planning efforts conducted by New Jersey,
Texas, and Indiana. The section concludes with a description of a
study conducted by the National Center for Research in Vocational
Education which analyzes the relationships among job training entities.

New York

Faced with decreasing resources and increasing demands, states
have initiated comprehensive planning procedures to use limited
resources effectively. One of the earliest efforts in the vocational
education area was initiated by the Department of Education in the
state of New York. Leaders from business, industry, and education
representing the major vocational specialty areas were brought
together to plan for future occupations. The "Futuring Project"
attempted to look at emerging occupations, the existing vocational
education delivery system, and recommend changes necessary to
more effectively serve business, industry, and students (Tobias &
Zibrin 1982). The results of the project activities help to reconcep-
tualize how vocational education services are offered to help young
people prepare for occupations. New and emerging occupations presented problems in the state approval process. The approval of a new
program required the establishment of an advisory committee, the
identification of labor needs, curriculum planning, teacher inser-
vice, and an approval process which attempted to assess each of the
preceding steps. In order to shorten the time of the approval process, as well as to provide flexibility for student choice and preparation, planners developed a multi-tiered curriculum model.

The first level provides to all students interested in vocational
education an opportunity to strengthen basic skills, explore a variety
of occupations, develop meaningful attitudes toward work, job seeking, and interview skills. Following this initial level (using the health
field as an example) students are encouraged to further explore either
patient or non-patient care employment opportunities in the health
care field. The exploration phase encompasses career opportunities
from aide level training to those provided through graduate and professional schools. Included in this phase are the supporting sciences
which would be necessary by students regardless of the type of
health care occupation. The last level provides the necessary cognitive, psychomotor, and affective skills necessary for practice in an
entry level health career.

The model provides several important benefits compared to traditional vocational education programming. The initial level is taught without regard to traditional vocational specialty areas. Skills in this area are general and are taught by an instructor employed in health occupations or other vocational specialties. Classwork allows for student information exchange, thus exposing the individual to many more occupations than if a single vocational specialty area was initially selected. In the second level the emphasis is on exploration of careers in an occupational family. Students are not limited to those occupations in which a given school provides preparatory programs, nor are students limited to occupations requiring less than a baccalaureate degree. Basic skills and related course work in the sciences are provided, giving the student necessary prerequisites for a variety of health occupations. The last level of specialized training is easily modified to include emerging occupations. Students are given a wide array of choices. Only the last two years of a program provide specific job skills which can be modified to reflect the changing needs of business and industry. Variations of the planning strategies and the resultant model serve as a basis for curriculum revision in other states.

Iowa

Kirkwood Community College in Cedar Rapids, Iowa, uses a variation of the New York approach to provide entry level skills for secondary school students. The College coordinates the curriculum and allows advanced standing for students who have completed the secondary school program if they choose to prepare for a health career at the community college level.

Using consultant services from the New York Department of Education, the state of Iowa has passed legislation to provide for competency based vocational education at the secondary school level with provision for articulation to the state's community colleges. As is true of other states, committees representing occupational clusters and specific occupations were utilized to identify competencies necessary for entry level employment. The second phase of this activity requires that curricula be developed to follow the recommendations of the business and industry committees. The legislation requires that skills being taught are those needed by business and industry and that students who participate in secondary school vocational programs would not unnecessarily repeat educational activities if they chose to attend a community college. While the process and generated activities are not without critics, implementation of the model is currently underway.

A model cooperative program exists in Council Bluffs, Iowa (Cetron & Gail 1991). Eighteen vocational programs are offered to secondary students in the community school district by the local community college. Among the model's attributes are: (a) new and revised courses based on job surveys conducted in the metropolitan area, (b) continued emphasis on academic skills, (c) courses offered by the community college for both high school and college credit, and (d) low cost to the community school district in view of state subsidies.

New Jersey

The state of New Jersey has initiated a comprehensive planning activity to set directions for secondary vocational education (Ascher, 1987). The planning process takes into account the changing student demographics and the needs of business and industry. A panel representative of business, education, and parental groups provides recommendations for secondary vocational education. In addition to the concern that vocational education programs provide viable options for students to enter the labor force, the New Jersey plan recommends that both vocational and non-vocational students be held to the same level of basic skill attainment. Data from the statewide testing program evaluating basic skill attainment indicate that students from the business and vocational program areas do not achieve basic skills scores as high as students in the general or academic program areas. The statewide planning report identifies changes in employment opportunities and suggests the fostering of relationships with private schools, community colleges, and programs sponsored by other legislation designed to prepare individuals for employment.

Texas

In a similar effort, the state of Texas developed a master plan to provide direction for technical and vocational education. As with efforts of other states, consideration is given to emerging labor needs, cost effective relevant training, and the use of resources in cooperation with the private sector. This initiative applies to the state's postsecondary institutions including both community colleges and technical institutes. Specific recommendations include the development of a strategic plan and refinement of procedures to develop state, regional, and local employment projections. In addition to these major goals, recommendations include process objectives such as the provision of technical assistance, coordination, and help in developing strategic plans. The report (Back et al. 1987) identifies priority training activities for the state in the following areas: (a) agriculture, biotechnology, biomedicine; (b) energy, (c) material science, (d) marine science, (e) aerospace, (f) telecommunications, (g) manufacturing science, and (h) automated manufacturing and office automation. The training and development areas are targeted for various regions throughout the state.

Indiana

Another example of statewide planning for the future was a project conducted in the state of Indiana (Indiana Commission on Vocational and Technical Education 1989). The project was sponsored by the Indiana Commission on Vocational and Technical Education and employed CAPS Jobs for the Future, Inc. of West Somerville, Massachusetts. As in the case of previously mentioned state planning efforts, the Commission was interested in identifying jobs of the future and the resultant changes in existing or modified vocational education programs. This research surveyed 7000 business firms about their future employment needs, which included the type of occupations and essential basic skills desirable in future employees. Recommendations of the report stress the need for vocational education programming directed toward future employment needs including technical expertise, basic skills, and critical thinking. The report indicates that: (a) vocational programming ties with business and industry need to be strengthened through greater involvement from the private sector, (b) the economic development activities within the state need to be strengthened, and (c) exploring ways of communicating the occupational needs to potential students and citizens need to be considered.

*The National Center for
Research in Vocational Education*

A research study describing vocational education and job training efforts was directed by Charles S. Benson at the National Center for Research in Vocational Education, University of California, Berkeley, and described by W. Norton Grubb and Lorraine M.

McDonnell (1991). Their study was based on data collected from eight communities in four states and was designed to look at the relationships among various job training entities and their potential effectiveness. At the outset, the authors' attention focused on the dramatic growth of education and training for employment. In addition to previously described vocational education opportunities (Bottoms & Copa 1983), the authors call attention to the contributions of the Job Training Partnership Act (JTPA), the Job Opportunities and Basic Skills (JOBS), and Community-Based Organizations (CBOs). Looking at the many antecedents which either allowed or directly fostered a multiplicity of local job training efforts, the authors identify five models which provide employment training: (a) the "standard model," (b) the parallel systems model, (c) education versus training model, (d) the dominant-community college model, and (e) the autonomous institutions model.

While obvious differences are noted in each of the models, the authors conclude that there is little duplication or competition among the institutions involved in the various models. The programs offered by the institutions tend to be similar in the training provided and the clients served. "Even though they emphasize their local orientation and responsiveness to unique community needs, most community colleges, technical institutes, and Area Vocational Technical Schools (AVTSs) look roughly similar, as do most welfare-to-work in job training programs" (Grubb & McDonnell 1991, 35).

In addition to identifying the models and their attributes, the report suggests the initial indicators related to accessibility to individuals, accessibility to employers, adaptability to labor market changes, employment effects, program quality, and costs. These initial indicators draw attention to data needs and the lack of information available to make qualified judgments about a system's effectiveness or among the models identified in the study. The conclusion describes the need for multiple indicators of effectiveness and a system-wide objective. It is difficult to ascertain the effectiveness of individual programs or their role within the system when the demand for services greatly exceeds available resources. While the efforts of individual programs in schools are important, the authors argue that the relationships among providers are equally important to determine if local community needs are met.

> For this reason, we urge that future research on a work-related education and training take a system perspective and that efforts to

assess effectiveness use indicators that focus on the entire system as well as its individual components (Grubb & McDonnell 1991, 64).

THE COMMUNITY COLLEGE AND EMPLOYMENT TRAINING

Although there are many facets of postsecondary vocational-technical education, the American community college has emerged as an important provider in the education of the existing labor force and that of the future. Indeed, the community college has through its diversity come to provide, or co-sponsor, many of the functions of other institutions, and will therefore serve as a framework for examination of the postsecondary vocational-technical phenomenon. We note, however, that this very diversity has come under attack by critics questioning if such institutions are trying to do too much with too few human and financial resources.

The facets and functions of the contemporary American community, or peoples', colleges, are legion. From the provision of basic living and job skills, literacy education, high school completion programs, one year vocational certificates, the articulation of their two year associate of applied science degree to four year colleges and universities, the community colleges exhibit little resemblance to their forebear, Joliet Junior College, founded in 1901, by William Rainey Harper to prepare freshmen and sophomores for the University of Chicago.

CURRICULA INTEGRATION AND DIRECTION

Today's comprehensive community colleges still provide college parallel/transfer curricula for the arts and sciences. This facet is germane in view of the trend to integrate academic study and vocational-technical curricula for the purpose of improving work force quality.

This trend came about as a response to the American Association of Community and Junior Colleges' (AACJC) reception of complaints from industry that many postsecondary vocational-technical education graduates were often technically prepared but were lacking in areas such as written communication, interpersonal communication, value awareness, and ethical analysis. In a pioneering effort, community colleges such as Kirkwood Community

College and Clinton Community College (Iowa) have responded to AACJC's challenge by developing humanities courses designed for the vocational-technical student. Kirkwood Community College completed a three year grant from the National Endowment for the Humanities which was used to develop three new courses entitled, Working in America, Culture and Technology, and Living in the Information Age. It is too early to assess the impact on the vocational student, although the expected (and possibly warranted) objections from the vocational faculty as to the courses' content and even necessity have been documented (Collins 1991).

A survey of the education literature indicates a plethora of studies, commissions, committees, and reports on the crisis the United States faces with underprepared workers and their inability to drive the country's manufacturing and service industrial machine to full capacity to maintain the strong present position and future global economy. Critics of the push for more technical education for everybody (Silberman 1987) are not without a significant number of worthy complaints. Silberman cites the leveling off, according to some studies, of the need for highly skilled workers in certain segments of the future labor market. Although most researchers note the pressing need for basic interpersonal skills, and in a business sense, the related written communications and mathematical skills, not everyone believes that higher quantities of technical education will benefit all.

Career Choice

In their mission of providing career choice, preparation, and advancement, the community colleges' impact on the future labor market ranges from the obvious to the subtle and possibly questionable. Obvious to anyone perusing the program catalog of most community colleges is the breadth of associate of applied science degrees (AAS) within the divisions of vocational-technical education. The National Council on Vocational Education (NCVE) (1989) notes the need for a two year associate of applied science degree to gain entry into eighteen of the twenty fastest growing occupations, and professes that Bureau of Labor Statistics data indicate that vocational-technical education prepares students for 26 of the 37 occupations that will account for the largest number of new jobs by 1995. An AACJC report (1990) makes use of government census data to highlight significant work force earning differentials between those with the high school diploma as a terminal degree and holders of the AAS degree (29% more).

As always, caution in interpreting numbers such as the NCVE data is prudent; they are not absolute numbers needed for the future labor force. As an illustration, the percentage change in the number of custodians needed is small compared with that of bioengineering technicians, but in absolute numbers there will still be thousands of times as many positions for custodians, an occupation which does not require postsecondary vocational-technical education. However, in areas such as engineering technology, environmental mainte- nance, health occupations, and computer programming the compre- hensive community college is one of the leaders in preparation of workers for these fields through its provision of the AAS degree.

The career advancement function of the community college is becoming more widely known through tech-prep programs, men- tioned earlier in this chapter. Such programs are growing as signifi- cant partnerships in the community colleges' endeavor to provide convenience and streamlined programs to both high school students and seekers of the applied bachelor's degree, such as in Oregon's 2+2+2 (Portland Area Vocational Technical Education Consortium, 1990). PAVTEC provides an integrated career path for high school electronics students seeking a bachelor's degree in Electronics Engineering Technology, via Portland Area Community College, at Oregon State University. Engineering technologists will be in heavy demand by American industry according to projections, such as those for the state of Colorado calculated by Ward and Wolff (1984). The provision of such a streamlined program to high school stu- dents, giving them a sense of direction as well as an assurance of eliminating unnecessary duplication in skills taught, will also ben- efit industry interested in efficient use of the tax base for public educational purposes.

Economic Development

The topic of industry's involvement and its direct or indirect financing of education for its workers, often for career advancement, is perhaps the most important subissue under the overall labor crisis discussed earlier. Billions of dollars are spent every year by industry to train or update its labor force. In the mid-1980s, 31 percent of U.S. firms purchased education, often vocational-technical, for their employees (ASTD, 1987). Community colleges, along with private training firms, have been silent leaders in the forging of partnerships with industry to provide the flexible programs that other institu- tions of traditional learning, such as the research universities, have found difficult to provide because of their inherently large bureaucratic momentum and orientation to theoretical advances rather than direct action. Today it is hard for the watchdogs of public money and policy not to notice that most of the large community colleges have created departments of economic development as highly adaptive channellers of the colleges' resources. These educational programs are designed to meet the complex and rapidly changing needs of American firms trying to react to the dynamic forces of the global economy. The local policy control afforded the community colleges in Iowa, for example, seems to fit well into the decentralized business/educational systems envisioned by futurists J. Naisbitt (1982) and much earlier by E.F. Schumacher (1973) as necessary for efficient and environmentally responsible use of human and natural resources to meet humankind's future needs.

Accessibility

Community colleges are often the last hope for millions of disadvantaged Americans (NCVE, 1989), such as those with disabilities, minorities, single mothers, young adults from broken families, the elderly, and dislocated workers. Until the higher education system becomes truly free of physical, racial, sexual, and age biases it appears that the community colleges will continue to lead in providing programs and *choices* for millions needed in this country's future work force (Brock 1991). Tomorrow's labor pool will be older, more female, more ethnically and racially diverse, more physically disadvantaged, and more rehabilitated. Written testimony by former Secretary of Labor William Brock indicates that American industry cannot ignore shifting demographics if a sufficient number of appropriately skilled workers are desired for strong global competition. The vocational-technical programs found at the community colleges are and will continue to be major providers of skills, basic through degreed, for employment of disadvantaged Americans.

The strong representation of the disadvantaged in the community colleges has been the focus of attacks by critics such as Pincus (1980), who maintain that such colleges are actually acting as shunts or bypasses of the road to four year or even graduate degrees. This criticism is healthy and may be justified in some cases. Postsecondary vocational-technical institutions generally put much less stringent academic and financial demands on their students than do universities. Disadvantaged students who came up through a biased system and, therefore, put at an academic and financial disadvantage, may choose the community college path simply because they have no information about any other choice. The problem may be self-propagating if, for example, a black woman chooses a community college vocational-technical program over a university liberal arts program because, upon campus tours, she saw more black women on the campus of her final choice.

Another factor is that large portions of the huge federal Job Training Partnership Act (JTPA) are available to the disadvantaged, and as a result of action by local private industry councils, community colleges are often contracted to provide the vocational education funded by the JTPA program (NCRVE, 1990). A disadvantaged student seeking any postsecondary education for purposes of future employment will naturally be drawn to the institutions that offer him or her the best financial aid package, and employment relevant vocational-technical education paid for by the government is certainly tempting.

The reverse of this problem, that of a lack of one year tech-prep programs at the nation's community colleges, could be an indicator of overpreparation of some future laborers, who on a cost/benefit analysis may have fared just as well or better with one year of postsecondary vocational-technical work instead of the applied associate degree. The provision of literacy, basic work skills, a GED, and then a vocational certificate by a community college for some of those released from the correctional system, may pay off for some firm's labor needs. To expect all former inmates to initially obtain an AAS degree seems unsound. Perhaps the Deweyan philosophy of helping all citizens avoid the tragedy of not finding their "fit" in society, in this case the labor market, could serve as a guide in navigating the uncertain path of providing an adequately prepared work force for the future.

The American community college, in its endeavor to provide a range of programs from basic skills through articulation of the AAS credential into the baccalaureate degree, certainly has the ability to affect millions of the future labor force. But in the wake of waning budgets, only renewed financial commitment from government and industry will guarantee that scope of any substance is assured.

SUMMARY

As a nation we are faced with a shrinking qualified labor pool, the continual migration from rural areas to urban centers, and increased competencies required of entry level workers. Preparation which has been viewed as adequate in the past will not meet future labor needs. Emerging service occupations require a more highly skilled labor force, and the manufacturing technologies require computer ability and critical thinking skills. More effective ties with business and industry are needed to aid in the planning of programs and their role should not be to merely serve as consumers of the educational product.

Coupled with labor needs is the humanistic view of education in this country. Along with the concept that young people need to be better prepared is the idea that they must be able to select their field of work. The planning process, therefore, should go beyond the needs of business and industry and provide for curricula that enable young people to prepare, choose, and advance in an occupation. The delivery system must be both local and regional if it is to effectively provide for the many options that must be made available to high school students and adults in need of training or retraining. Comprehensive and strategic planning will enable vocational education programs to serve both the individual and the needs of business and industry.

REFERENCES

American Association of Community and Junior Colleges. 1990. A Summary of Selected National Data Pertaining to Community, Technical and Junior Colleges. *Report* (June):11.G.3.

American Society for Training and Development. 1987. *Annual Report.*

American Vocational Association. 1990. *The AVA Guide to the Carl D. Perkins Vocational and Applied Technology Act of 1990.* Alexandria, VA: American Vocational Association.

Ascher G. 1987. *Into the Twenty-first Century: Comprehensive Planning for Secondary Vocational Education in New Jersey.* ERIC Document Reproduction Service No. ED 286 064.

Back, K., G. Carter, C. Dede, P. Garrett, O. W. Markley, and T. Sullivan. 1987. *The Future of the Workplace in Texas: A Preliminary Identification of Planning Issues for Technical, Vocational and Adult Postsecondary Education.* ERIC Document Reproduction Service No. ED 293 001.

Bottoms, G. and P. Copa. 1983. "A Perspective on Vocational Education Today." *Phi Delta Kappan* (January):348-354.

Brock, W. 1991. Continuous training for the high-skilled workforce. *AACJC Journal* (February/March).

Cetron, M., & M. Gail. 1991. *Educational renaissance, Our Schools at the Turn of the Century.* New York: St. Martin's Press.

Collins, J. 1991. "A Description of an Attempt to Integrate the Humanities into Occupational Curricula at Kirkwood Community College." Unpublished master's degree project, College of Education, The University of Iowa.

Desy, J., P. B. Campbell, and J. A. Gardner. 1984. *High School Vocational Education Experiences: In School and in the Labor Market.* ERIC Document Reproduction Service No. ED 242 966.

Evans, R. N., and E. L. Herr. 1987. *Foundations of Vocational Education,* 2nd ed. Columbus, OH: Charles E. Merrill.

Gardner, J. A., P. Campbell, and P. Seitz. 1982. *Influences of High School Curriculum on Determinants of Labor Market Experience.* Columbus: The National Center for Research in Vocational Education, Ohio State University.

Grubb, W. N., and L. M. McDonnell. 1991. *Local Systems of Vocational Education and Job Training: Diversity, Interdependence, and Effectiveness.* Berkeley, CA: National Center for Research in Vocational Education.

Indiana Commission on Vocational and Technical Education. 1989. *Executive Report of the Jobs for Indiana's Future.* ERIC Document Reproduction Service No. ED 312 447.

Naisbitt, J. 1982. *Megatrends.* New York: Warner Books.

National Council for Research in Vocational Education. 1990. *Newsletter* (September).

National Council on Vocational Education. 1989. "America's Hidden Treasure." *Annual report of the NCVE.*

Pincus, F. 1980. "The False Promises of Community Colleges: Class Conflict and Vocational Education." *Harvard Educational Review* 50 (3):332-361.

Portland Area Vocational Technical Education Consortium (PAVTEC). 1990. "Preparing Workforce 2000 Through Vocational Technical 2+2 Programs." *Report of PAVTEC.* Portland, OR: PAVTEC.

Schumacher, E. F. 1973. *Small is Beautiful; Economics As If People Mattered.* New York: Harper and Row.

Silberman, H. F. 1987. "Raising Economic Competitiveness with Education." Paper presented at American Vocational Association Convention, Las Vegas, NV., December. *RIC Document Reproduction Service No. 291 876.

Tobias, S. and M. Zibrin. 1982. *Looking Towards the Future in the Health Occupations.* New York: City University of New York.

Ward, M. and W. Wolff. 1984. *An Assessment and Projection of Needed High Technology Training Programs in Colorado.* ERIC Document Reproduction Service No. 253.

II

Current Transformations
and the Future of Work

5

Temporary Work and
Labor Market Detachment:
New Mechanisms and New Opportunities

Donald Mayall

A quiet revolution in the workplace has been underway for nearly three decades. Five significant changes define this revolution: 1) in the way employers deal with uncertainties, both in product demand and labor supply; 2) in personnel policies and training methods; 3) in compensation and benefit policies; 4) in the way a significant portion of the labor market enters the job market and acquires skills and experience; and 5) perhaps most importantly, in the nature of the employment relationship itself. We can further characterize the revolution as the shifting of the temporary work market from an arena where informal processes predominate to more formalized systems and the growth of entire industries devoted to the marketing of temporary workers.

Temporary help supply (THS), an industry devoted entirely to serving the temporary work market, registered an incredible tenfold increase between 1963 and 1983. Voluntary part-time employment, a much broader indicator of the trend away from regular full-time work, doubled in the same twenty year period; this stands in sharp contrast to the civilian labor force as a whole which increased by just under fifty percent.

This revolution has clear implications for the fields of labor relations research, worker protection legislation, and career education and guidance, among others. Still, these changes in the economy received relatively little attention from researchers. Too often, temporary work has been regarded as a peripheral phenomenon making the study and evaluation of the permanent workforce more logical and significant. Traditional statistical databases ignore or lose the temporary worker; indeed there is no such category in the collection of labor force data by the Bureau of Labor Statistics or Census. Persons who work only a few hours a week or who do not appear on a monthly payroll may not be counted at all. For these reasons it is difficult to establish the overall dimensions of the temporary work market and how much this market is increasing relative to the total labor force.

Historically, temporary work emerged from a variety of causes and appeared in different forms and institutional arrangements. This paper presents profiles of five industries in which temporary employees have played a key role. It describes the economic reasons behind the use of temporary workers and the mechanisms and institutional arrangements that evolved under this system. Mayall and Nelson (1982) describe the background and methodology of the research upon which these profiles are based.

CONTRACT FOOD SERVICE

The contract food service industry consists of firms that prepare, deliver, and serve food for specific occasions such as conventions or banquets, or which operate restaurants or cafeterias in institutional settings such as schools, hospitals, businesses, or government agencies. This business differs from the restaurant industry in that there is a contract with a third party to provide food to an essentially captive clientele. Like other sectors of the food industry, it is highly competitive. Few workers in contract food service are covered by collective bargaining agreements.

Three characteristics commonly appear in the food industry. First, there is extensive reliance on workers on a temporary basis. Second, the pace and nature of the work—preparing and serving meals, and cleaning-up after—lends itself to split shifts or part-time workers. Finally, there is a great deal of turnover in the industry. Many of the jobs have no educational or skill requirements of any kind and are filled by anyone willing to take them. They offer little promotional opportunity, and pay scales remain at or below the federal minimum wage. In the food industry, the market for labor, especially for temporary workers, is probably about as informal as can be found.

There are basically three circumstances in which contract food services use temporary workers: emergencies, special events, and planned vacancies. An emergency need for a temporary worker occurs when the regular employee is not available for an assigned shift. The kitchen's only dishwasher or cook phones in sick or simply fails to show up. Such an occurrence is not unusual in any kind of food operation, including restaurants. The work has to be done and the manager is responsible for seeing that it gets done. Organizations that cater banquets, dinners, conventions and the like, either as an occasional activity or as their major business, generally use temporary workers to staff these special events. Finally, planned short-term vacancies, as when regular employees go on vacation or have elective medical treatments, are usually filled with temporary workers.

Because of the relatively low skill levels in food service work, there is the possibility of reassigning tasks among the available workers when temporary needs arise. Because of the tight cost constraints of the industry there is, however, not a lot of redundancy, and task reallocation is of limited effectiveness in meeting temporary needs. Sometimes employers will upgrade an existing regular worker temporarily. For example, a dishwasher may fill in for a missing waiter, and the somewhat easier to fill dishwasher spot is then filled with a temporary worker. In the case of a higher skilled job the manager may fill in.

A substantial portion of the food service work force is composed of persons working fewer than twenty hours per week. The number of part-time workers ranges from about ten percent to over thirty percent of permanent staff. One way of filling a temporary vacancy is to ask part-time workers to work additional hours, or an additional shift (but at regular, not overtime pay rates). Since these workers are already on the payroll, there is no hiring cost. Generally, overtime is not a desirable solution because there is very little in the nature of the work that can be backlogged and overtime pay requirements would raise costs significantly.

Large firms that have a number of work sites within commuting range of one another sometimes have a special group of workers that can be assigned to fill temporary vacancies. These workers are sometimes called "floaters".

The most common means for meeting the need for temporary workers in contract food services is through casual or spot hires of workers for assignments as short as a single shift. These workers often come from a list of persons who have applied for temporary work and who may be called in as needed. In some cases they may be referred by a union hiring hall, or a college placement office. Or they may be on an informal "hip pocket" list of persons available for temporary work maintained by the local service manager. Hip-pocket lists tend to be made up of former employees, friends, and friends of employees.

Schools, through their placement offices, are often the major intermediary in the temporary work labor market for contract food services. There appear to be two rather different reasons for this. Because it has low skill requirements and uses large numbers of part-time workers food service is a good source of income supplementation for students, and hence a likely placement target for school employment offices. Schools are also often involved in training for higher skilled food service jobs and eager to maintain contacts with potential employers.

Unions play a minor role in intermediating contract food service temporary workers. In some metropolitan areas restaurant workers are organized and the union may have a dispatch hall which can provide temporary help on short notice, but this would not be used unless the contract food service employees were working under contract with the union. Because they would have to pay union rates, non-organized employers would be unlikely to call the union. Union dispatch offices, where found, are often not a great deal more formal than the hip-pocket lists of food service managers.

The distinction between temporary and permanent work becomes blurred in low wage industries where turnover is high. If a worker quits with little or no notice, the employer may first attempt to fill the job on a temporary basis while looking for a permanent employee. If the temporary and the permanent worker are paid the same, have the same benefits and lack of opportunity to advance to better paying jobs, then the "permanent" workers may stay only a short time, resulting in another "temporary" hire.

The distinction between temporary and permanent workers is rather slim in contract food service. Both temporary and permanent workers usually get the same benefits and often these are only those required by law. Temporary jobs do provide a major means of entry into the industry, as temporaries move into permanent position.

MOTOR FREIGHT

The motor freight industry includes long-distance trucking, local trucking, and storage businesses. Long-distance companies are interstate common carriers, that is, they are available for hire to move commodities from any source, public or private. They are regulated by the Interstate Commerce Commission. Local trucking is similarly for hire but is not allowed to engage in transportation between states.

The motor freight industry, like other forms of transportation, is subject to continual fluctuations in demand, often on a day-to-day basis. These fluctuations arise from the nature of the demand for shipping. In consequence, the industry has developed mechanisms for adjusting employment levels to keep costs under control. It has long relied on a temporary workforce to perform certain kinds of sporadic tasks such as loading and unloading of vehicles. The need for drivers fluctuates with the volume of freight shipments and many of these jobs are temporary.

In earlier days this temporary work market was unstructured and chaotic. Loading and unloading jobs required no skills except physical strength, and such jobs were sought, particularly in times of slack employment. Often there was a morning "shape up" at which the day's crew was chosen. Favoritism, bribes, and political influence were common. Successful jobseekers were often those who took such initiatives as jumping onto a moving truck and asking the driver for work.

Collective bargaining provided a way of rationalizing this labor market and brought an end to most of the abuses. Union agreements insured that scarce work opportunities would be parceled out on the basis of seniority and competence rather than favoritism or influence.

The principle mechanism used for assigning temporary work under such collective bargaining agreements is the union-operated hiring hall. These halls dispatch drivers as well as loaders and unloaders. Once workers have worked a specified amount of time (e.g. 30 days out of 60) they can be placed on a secondary level seniority list known as the "B-list." When they have worked for a year in a specific occupation and geographic area they can be placed on the "A-list." Employers under contract to the union are required to list openings with the dispatch hall. The dispatcher offers the job to the unemployed A-list member with the highest seniority. When names on this list are exhausted, the dispatcher turns to the B-list. If workers fail to accept openings offered they may lose seniority.

Employers usually have the right to refuse applicants. They may also be able to specify that referrals come from a "preferred applicant list." This list consists of former employees in order of seniority and layoff date. If the preferred list is exhausted, the hall can refer other workers according to seniority. If the union cannot fill an opening within a specified time period, the employer can turn to other sources.

In general, collective bargaining brought a fair degree of equity to the temporary work market in motor freight. It also raised pay and benefits substantially, especially for full-time workers.

In recent years some large companies have contracted with third-party employers to supply drivers and other transport workers to operate company-owned trucks. These third-party employers are driver leasing companies. One motive for such arrangements is avoiding the high labor costs and work rules imposed by collective bargaining agreements. Although the leasing company may have a contract with the union, it will not be subject to the same agreements under which the truck owner operates, and it may have fewer benefits and lower pay. The truck owner, thus, gets the services of transport workers at considerably reduced costs.

The workers appear to be less well-off under such arrangements, but they have not had a great deal to say about it. Deregulation has brought new competition to long distance firms of the industry, reducing opportunities and hours of work in those sectors where pay was highest and jobs more secure. Unions have attempted to prevent the erosion of pay and benefits through employee leasing. Contractual agreements forbidding drive leasing appear to be hard to enforce, however. There also have been instances in which union officials have colluded with employers to allow such arrangements.

FINANCE

The finance industry consists of banks, savings and loan, thrift and related credit institutions. These institutions are labor intensive and have large numbers of low wage clerical positions. Although they have long been highly regulated and insulated from certain kinds of competition, this is changing. Competition is forcing these institutions to find ways to cut labor costs, particularly in the clerical areas. As a consequence they have been among the earliest to adopt labor saving computer and communications technologies. They also have developed a variety of organizational strategies to improve labor productivity. These strategies are found in the office portion of almost all industries, but the broadest range of techniques is found in finance. It represents the archetypal example of the rationalization of temporary office work.

The need for temporary work in financial institutions is primarily the result of recurrent phenomena, some of which are predictable, and some of which are not. In branch banks and savings and loans associations, for example, staffing demand tends to be greatest on Fridays, Mondays, and at the mid-points and ends of the month. Central units have work cycles based upon federal and state reporting and depositing requirements and various seasonal factors.

The need to replace temporarily absent workers is also of critical importance. A major component of the work consists of processing documents such as deposits and withdrawals in a standardized sequence. Any delay in processing these documents is very costly to the institution.

Because financial institutions are now competing for customers by offering new financial services, there has also been increased use of temporary workers to service the influx of new customers brought in by specific advertising campaigns such as for IRA accounts.

Finally, financial institutions have used temporary workers as a means of dealing with secretarial, word processing, and data processing shortages. In some cases, using temporary workers in these categories was simply a coping strategy to get the work done while hunting for a permanent employee. In other cases, such as the installation of a new computerized system, the temporary was regarded as a transitional specialist whose skills would be learned by regular workers.

There are two main categories of occupations in which temporary workers are used in finance, and the institutional arrangements for use are rather different for these two categories. The first category consists of standardized occupations which, although they may require considerable skill, do not vary in skill content from industry to industry. Examples of this category include file clerks, secretaries, compute programmers, systems analysts, bookkeepers, word processing operators, data entry clerks, messengers, and security guards.

The second group of occupations requires knowledge of the procedures and regulations specific to the financial industry. Included here are tellers, new account clerks, branch managers and operations managers. Persons in the second group also must be bonded if they handle negotiable items such as money or bonds.

Financial institutions have developed a variety of formal systems for meeting their temporary work needs. These involve using regular full-time employees, using less than full-time employees and using external employees. Most multi-branch banks have developed formal in-house systems for meeting temporary needs for clerical workers. These are called variously, the pool, the temporary pool, or service bureau.

The typical pool consists of regular full-time employees of the institution who receive all fringe benefits available to other employees. It may have separate sections, under separate supervision, for clerical and managerial occupations. The clerical group handles requests for secretaries, word processors, data entry clerks, proof clerks and the like. When a temporary vacancy occurs in a department an order is sent to the pool.

If they cannot fill the position they will arrange for a worker to be assigned from a Temporary Help Supply (THS) firm. Because of the need to insure continuous work for pool staff, the size of the pool is considerably below the peak need figure, and the number of THS workers called in may exceed the size of the pool staff several times over. The cost to the department requesting the temporary worker will be the same regardless of whether the worker is a pool or THS employee. Because THS employees cost more, pool management will try to limit their usage to openings of short duration and to true emergencies. They may restrict their services to positions of less than 45 days. If a vacancy lasts longer than that, the department must submit a new request.

Another section of the pool handles requests for tellers, loan clerks, and other specialized financial occupations including branch managers. Pool positions are filled primarily with persons already employed by the institution. These positions are considered to be an excellent way to learn about the firm and prepare for advancement.

Part-time workers who are on the company payroll but only called in to fill temporary needs are widely used in the finance industry. These employees usually receive fewer benefits than full-time employees. In some cases they may be paid at a slightly higher rate because of the lower level of benefits. Intermittent employees are used for general clerical positions such as secretaries and word processors and for specialized financial positions such as tellers and new account clerks.

Some companies use intermittent staff as a means of recruiting and training for full-time positions. New job applicants may be offered intermittent positions instead of full-time work. This is especially frequent if they are re-entrants to the job market or lack experience for current full-time openings. Such employees may receive training as tellers, data entry technicians, or other appropriate occupations. Often they move to full-time positions after six months to a year.

Financial institutions needing to meet their temporary work needs are one of the major users of THS's. Those with sizeable internal pools or rosters of intermittents use THS to supplement these systems. The kinds of occupations sought from THS firms are those requiring general, transferable skills rather than specific knowledge of the financial field. Among the occupations most commonly sought are secretaries, file clerks, word processors, account clerks, messengers, and security guards. A few THS firms have tellers and other specialized financial workers available.

HEALTH CARE

The health care industry includes hospitals, clinics, convalescent hospitals, doctors' and dentists' offices and laboratories. Employment levels have grown along with the populations the industry serves. Constraints on public financing for a portion of health care service, through medicare and medicaid have made the industry very cost conscious. Inflation in medical care costs, rising demand for medical services, and an increase in acutely ill persons as a proportion of total hospital patients have compounded the problems caused by tight constraints on public health care funding.

A major factor influencing lab or demand and costs in hospitals is the day-to-day fluctuation in the patient population, referred to as the "bedcount" or "census." If a bed is occupied there are costly staff services that must be provided, some on a 24 hour a day basis. If the bed is empty, there is usually no source of revenue to pay staff. This problem might not be so significant if hospitals operated at capacity. There is, however, an excess of bed capacity in many areas, and hospitals have had to find ways of adjusting staff in accordance with fluctuating demand. Occupations most affected are those closely associated with patient care and services, including nursing, laboratory, housekeeping, and food services.

Yet another complicating factor is that of labor supply. On many occasions during the past two decades, the number of nurses with the training and qualifications desired by hospitals that are willing to work at wages and working conditions being offered has been lower than the number of jobs available. In consequence, hospitals have partly restructured the nursing field, creating new lower-skilled, lower-paying jobs. They have also offered premium pay to those nurses willing to be part of the marginal labor supply, the temporary workers.

It has also long been the practice in the hospital industry that certain kinds of nursing services are separate and apart from those provided by the regular hospital staff. These services, referred to as private duty care nursing, include round-the-clock and specialized kinds of nursing. These services extend what the hospital is staffed to provide.

Hospitals use a variety of mechanisms ranging from maintaining lists of intermittents to using highly specialized labor supply services to meet temporary work needs. Not infrequently they will consider several alternatives for filling the spot.

Most hospitals maintain a roster of intermittent workers who are available for call-in. They tend to use these primarily for less skilled occupations such as clerks, housekeepers, receptionists, and food service workers. They also are used for patient care occupations, secretaries, and virtually any other short-term need. Typically, intermittents receive no fringes other than those which are mandatory, but they receive premiums up to one-third above base pay to compensate for the lack of benefits. This premium is more common in shortage occupations. Institutions usually try to keep the total amount of time worked below 1000 hours per year to avoid including intermittents in their retirement programs.

Nurses' registries are probably the oldest temporary work intermediary outside of union dispatch halls. Their initial function was to act as a clearinghouse for nurses who wanted part-time or supplemental work and persons needing private duty care nursing. The care might be provided at the patient's residence, in a convalescent hospital, rest home, or even in a regular hospital. Three levels of nursing care were available—registered nurses, practical nurses, and nurse's aides. The nurses were considered self-employed workers under contract to the patient or the patient's representative, which might be a health care institution. The registry collected a fee, usually ten percent of gross remuneration of the person sent on assignment. The registries thus operated in much the same fashion as a private employment agency, except that they had a registered nurse on staff to determine the level of medical need required in each assignment.

By the mid 1970s, some registries were supplying X-ray technicians, laboratory technicians and other medical workers on a temporary basis in addition to nursing specialties. They were also supplying nurses to fill vacancies of regular staff nurses at hospitals. The scope of these assignments did not fit the concept of private duty care, and did not meet the definition of self-employment under state Unemployment Insurance laws. Most workers sent out from the registry were considered "general employees" of the registry in the same way that persons on assignment from THS's are employees of those organizations. From this point onward, most nurses' registries have functioned as THS's with regard to all activities except private duty care nursing.

Paralleling the metamorphosis of Nurses' Registries into THS-like organizations has been the development of specialized medical THS's. Some deal in a single or small number of closely related medical occupations such as respiratory therapists, X-ray technicians, medical assistants, dental assistants, laboratory technicians, occupational therapists and medical social workers. These tend to be small operations, sometimes servicing only a few hospitals. Some are affiliated with proprietary schools that provide training in the medical specialty being offered by the THS. Some even maintain rosters of MD's who are available for temporary assignments. Most of the large national and regional THS's are active in serving the medical field, offering a full range of medical and other specialties. Some have separate medical divisions.

Employee leasing refers to the practice of placing all the employees of a company that are in a particular class or category in a separate business entity which is then leased to the parent firm. All the personnel in some doctor's and dentist's offices are leased. This arrangement is not so much a response to fluctuating labor demand as a means of reducing personnel costs and excluding lower paid ancillary staff from the pension plans of the highly paid professionals.

ELECTRONICS

The electronic components sector consists of firms engaged in the design and manufacture of such products as semiconductors, integrated circuits, magnetic tape, and computer peripheral devices. Firms in this sector are under considerable competitive pressure from one another and from foreign manufacturers. Employment levels have shown marked cyclical fluctuations in the past several decades.

The development of new products, or completion of special contract work are major generators of temporary work in the electronic components industry. These undertakings have a definite life cycle: planning, development, testing, revision, retesting, prototype, production. Each of these phases requires particular skills and work orientations. Such assignments may well be given to permanent staff, but due to their transitory nature it often makes sense to give them to non-permanent workers. Thus the preparation of the volumes of design drawings for a new product may be assigned to temporary drafters, and prototype model assembly may be done by a special shift of temporary assemblers, with another shift called in later to do the revision work.

The occurrence of deadlines, often a consequence of project work such as prototype model production, or the need to fill rush orders is another reason for the use of temporary workers in electronics. Since the overloads are expected to be of limited duration, there is a strong disincentive to hire permanent workers.

Because of the need to fill vacancies quickly, electronic components firms may use a temporary worker to fill a vacancy caused by the departure of a regular permanent employee, while recruiting to fill the position. In some cases employers regard temporary hires as one way of trying out new employees that may be offered permanent jobs.

Difficulty in finding workers with specific skills is another factor in the use of temporary workers in electronics. This appears to be one reason that firms will consider filling a permanent vacancy with a temporary worker. Shortages are a particular problem in technical occupations such as drafting, electronics engineering, programming, technical writing, and technical illustration.

Workers with particularly desirable skills frequently have been able to gain favorable combinations of pay and working conditions by taking temporary work assignments. It is not unusual for qualified specialists to be paid 20 to 25 percent more in temporary assignments than they could get in permanent positions. Although they forego security and certain fringe benefits, they believe that their particular skill mix is sufficient to assure continuing assignments. Such workers sometimes argue that the variety of work experience enhances their employability. The premium pay is at least equivalent to the benefits they have given up. Perhaps most important in this industry is the fact that some workers simply do not want to commit themselves to a firm, either in terms of full-time long term availability or in terms of giving the firm exclusive rights to their intellectual efforts. Some are engaged in second careers, entrepreneurial activities, and even avocational pursuits.

Electronics component manufacturers have used virtually every kind of mechanism for dealing with temporary needs. For short-term vacancies in office help they have tended to follow the patterns found in finance, a strategy which combines use of intermittents and internal pools with THS's. For technical and manufacturing staff and the longer term labor requirements implicit in project work the industry has developed more innovative approaches.

Almost every kind of business makes some use of limited duration hiring. This is usually a full-time job, but it is understood that the tenure is limited to a fixed period of time, usually less than a year and will usually not qualify one for inclusion in a company pension program. Sometimes called a project hire, electronics components manufacturers have used this approach to meet a variety of technical staffing needs.

Job shops are THS firms that specialize in supplying workers with technical skills. They are sometimes called technical temporary help services. The term originated in the auto industry with the subcontracting of design work to engineering services that employed crews of drafters. The design work was done "in-house" on the service's premises. Subsequently it proved desirable to have the drafters more directly supervised and they began working at the prime contractor's job site. The need for direct on-site supervision was particularly great at firms doing classified work under contract for the Department of Defense. As a result, job shops began operating like THS's. Some continued to do design work on their own (not the customer's) premises, which requires maintaining a technical staff to supervise the work. Most dropped this and became purely labor supplying organizations. As job shops evolved they began branching into non-technical occupations such as clerical and assembly work. Sensing a lucrative opportunity, some of the more traditional THS firms serving the electronics industry began expanding into the technical field as well.

Some job shops follow a brokering model. Prospective workers at the shop submit resumes which are carefully screened. When a request for temporary worker is received the resumes of workers best qualified for the position are forwarded to employers who make the final selection from among those offered.

Payroll servicing or "payrolling" refers to the practice of placing a THS payroll workers pre-designated by the customer. Employers advertise for, recruit, screen and interview potential employees, and when they have made a selection they notify the THS with whom they have made an arrangement for payroll servicing. The worker reports for duty at the customer's premises and is issued a paycheck by the THS, as in other THS situations. The employer often specifies the rate to be paid to the payrolled workers. In some cases the rate may be set equal to that paid for similar work at the customer's site, to avoid resentment among permanent staff. For highly skilled professional workers it may be higher to compensate for the lack of fringe benefits.

In payrolling the THS incurs virtually no costs for recruitment or selection of workers. Because of the competitive environment for THS's, the markups for payrolled THS workers have been negotiated down to a point where they are scarcely higher than the cost of mandatory fringes. Payrolling appears to be motivated entirely by employer desires to avoid benefit costs or long-term commitments to these workers.

Some individuals, primarily those with very specialized skills, such as programmers and engineers, work as independent self-employed contractors. These are the same general skill areas covered by the technical job shops. From the point of view of the skilled technical worker, independent contracting and jobs shops are alternative routes to the same end. Independent contracting can offer greater autonomy and higher income. Jobs shops, however, eliminate the costs of finding employers, and the necessity for keeping track of business expenses required of the self employed.

TEMPORARY WORK MECHANISMS

The various industries profiled above demonstrate that employers are using a variety of different approaches to deal with the same socio-economic factors. For want of a better term these different approaches can be called temporary work response mechanisms. Following is a taxonomy of the various types of mechanisms.

Redundancy

Redundancy is the policy of having a sufficient number of qualified persons on the regular payroll to meet foreseeable temporary work need contingencies. The consequences of such arrangements are generally that the employer will incur costs of a full-time staff, which will at times be underutilized. This policy is sometimes referred to as overstaffing.

Overtime

Overtime is the practice of assigning a volume of tasks to regular staff on the employer's payroll to be done in a time period exceeding the regular work day of the work week of the employee. Premium rates are often paid for overtime work.

Speedup

Speedup is an increase in workload without an increase in hours or pay.

Internal Pool

An internal pool is a unit within a firm whose function is to supply workers for temporary assignments to other units within the firm. Employees are regular permanent workers. They may work full-time or part-time or even adjust their hours of availability from week to week.

Floaters

Floaters are regular, permanent employees within a firm who are assigned wherever temporary needs occur. They are like pool workers except they are not part of a separately managed unit.

Regular Part-Time

Regular part-time employees work less than a forty hour week, but report to work at regularly scheduled times. This could range from nearly full-time to as little as one day per month. Fringe benefits are usually a pro rata share of those provided to regular full-time employees.

Formal Intermittents

Formal intermittents are persons who are on the payroll of a firm, but are only called in and paid to work on temporary assignments. The length of these assignments can range from one day to as long as nine months. They may receive the same fringe benefits as regular full-time employees of the firm, or they may receive fewer benefits.

Limited Duration Hires

Positions are sometimes filled with the express understanding that the job is not permanent and will terminate at some point. The duration may be fixed, or it may be indefinite. There may be a limit

specified by law, policy, or collective bargaining agreement, the purpose being to define and maintain boundaries around permanent
positions by limiting or controlling access to them. Limited duration
hires generally provide the same fringe benefits as for full-time permanent employees.

Informal Intermittents

Informal intermittents are persons known to employers that
they occasionally call in for temporary work. They may be former
employees, retirees, or even friends. They generally will not receive
any benefits beyond those legally required.

Casuals

Casuals are persons hired for jobs of very short duration who
are not known to the employer. Often employers find these workers
through the use of intermediaries such as union dispatch halls, the
public employment service, or school placement offices. They may
receive no more than mandatory fringe benefits, unless they are covered by a union contract.

Contract Labor Services

Contract labor services are formal arrangements between two
business enterprises in which labor services are provided to the contracting firm by a specialized enterprise, such as janitorial, steno-
graphic, or data processing work. These services could be performed by
employees of the contracting firm but are not for a variety of reasons.
These include restrictions imposed by laws, regulations or collective
bargaining agreements, and economies of scale or specialization.

Independent Contractors

Independent contractors provide personal services to businesses
in accordance with a contract, in the same way that specialized businesses provide services under contract to other businesses. The contract will almost always be of fixed duration, although there may be
the presumption that it can be renewed indefinitely. The chief difference from contract labor services is that the independent contractor is a single self-employed individual.

Self-employed workers are not on the payroll of the firm and
there are no deductions made for social security or withholding of
taxes. In order to comply with state and federal tax rules, indepen-

dent contractors are not supposed to be under the direction and control of the contracting enterprise. If the independent contractor is given a desk at the company, told to be present and report to a supervisor, tax authorities may make the presumption that the contractor is really an employee and require that taxes be withheld.

The employer saves on payroll bookkeeping costs as well as the payroll burden and benefit costs, but usually pay independent contractors a premium to make up for the loss of benefits. The independent contractor must ultimately account to the IRS and state and local taxing authorities for income received and pay appropriate taxes on it, including social security taxes at a higher rate than that paid by salaried workers.

Leased Employees

Leased employees are on the payroll of a service company, the leaser, but work under the supervision of the client company. Unlike independent contractors, leased employees work under essentially open-ended contracts, and the expectation is that the work attachment will be long-term. Their selection, tenure, and termination is entirely at the behest of the client company. In many cases the entire staff of the client company, except for the owner, may be leased.

Employee leasing, thus, saves the owner the costs of maintaining a personnel function. But the main advantage to the owner is in the area of pension plans. There may also be savings in the costs of health benefits and even better coverage for the leased employee than they could get by working directly for the owner. The cost of the leased employees to the owner is typically about 35 percent above salaries.

Under the Tax Equity and Fiscal Responsibility Act (TEFRA), an employer cannot set up a pension plan which favors highly-paid staff. Leased employees must be considered part of that staff unless the leasing company has a "safe harbor" pension plan. To qualify, the leasing company must provide immediate coverage and vesting and contribute 7.5 percent of wages for all its employees. In addition to pension plans, leased employees generally receive health, sick leave and vacation benefits. Where leasing companies have large numbers of employees, they can usually negotiate better terms with health plans than the small owner could.

Temporary Help Service Employees

THS employees are on the payroll of a service and work under the supervision of customers. In some ways they are very much like leased employees. The THS is responsible for the full range of employer responsibilities, withholding taxes, social security, unemployment (and disability insurance in those states that require it) and worker's compensation. They are also responsible for compliance with Occupational Health and Safety and Equal Opportunity requirements.

Unlike leased employees, THS employees receive relatively few benefits. Some get health coverage and vacation after working a certain amount of time. Pension plans are very rare. And there is no presumption of a long-term work relationship. There are two different types of work assignments.

THS payrolled employees are interviewed, screened, and selected by the customer without any intermediation by the THS. The customer very likely will set the pay scale the payrolled worker is to receive. The THS may insist on the right to interview and even reject the prospective worker, but in most cases the customer merely notifies the THS, who then adds the employee to their payroll. Such an arrangement requires an advance contractual agreement between the THS and the customer. The charges in excess of the worker's salary can be as low as 18 percent, since there are few if any benefits offered, and the THS has incurred almost no costs in bringing about the transaction.

THS assigned employees are screened and referred by the staff of the temporary help service to work assignments with customers. These assignments are usually of very short duration. The THS sets the pay of the worker and the amount charged the customer may be related to the worker's pay or it may be based on standard rates for specific occupations. Costs to the customers can be from 30 to 50 percent over wages, and higher. Assigned workers generally expect the THS to continue to find new assignments for them as long as they wish to be available.

FACTORS AFFECTING THE CHOICE OF MECHANISM

Fluctuations in the demand for labor, if not the sole reason for the temporary work market are at least a good starting point for analyzing it. As shown in Figure 2, the type of mechanism used is affected by a number of variables, labor needs, attachment costs, labor supply, and institutional constraints.

There are at least three quantitative dimensions in the demand for labor. These are volume, periodicity, and expected duration of the tem-

Figure 2. Temporary Work Response Model

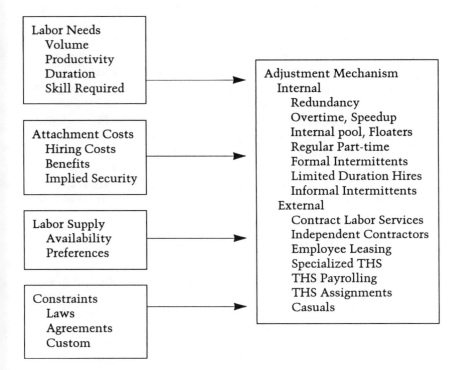

porary position. The type of skill required is a qualitative dimension.

A second factor in determining the type of response has been called attachment costs. These include the costs associated with hiring and placing workers on a company's payroll, screening, interviewing, training, and the like. Other costs are associated with the inducements to remain on the payroll, primarily in the form of benefits. Whenever a worker is placed into a non-temporary full-time position there is an implicit commitment of security, that the worker will remain in the job unless there is a major breach of expectations—misconduct or a major change in the fortunes of the business. This commitment reduces the employer's flexibility and adds to the cost of removing workers from the payroll.

Less well understood and less documented are worker preferences for a less than permanent full-time attachment to an employer. The limited data available indicate that a large majority of the workers in the temporary labor market are there because they want to be, not because they cannot find full-time employment. The most important consideration is the flexibility to set the hours that they work. A less common reason is the desire to gain experience in a variety of work settings. Some are using temporary work as a means to gain entry to permanent work.

There are also constraints on employers that affect the type of response mechanism that will be used. These include laws, institutional arrangements, and custom. Federal and state laws regulate the use of overtime hours, occupational health and safety, pension coverage, and require contributions for social insurance. Collective bargaining agreements may set up hiring halls for temporary workers or they may restrict the use of contracting or the use of employee leasing or THS's. Happenstance such as the existence of an especially effective school placement service or other long-term relationship with an intermediary can also affect the type of response.

THE PHENOMENON OF DETACHMENT

The various forms of temporary work are clearly part of a larger phenomenon. THS workers, independent contractors, and intermittents are used interchangeably by employers in virtually identical circumstances. Leased employees share many characteristics with regular full-time employees in the industries in which they work, yet in other respects they are indistinguishable from THS workers.

Employers want to avoid the costs of detachment associated with responding to temporary labor shortfalls. But they want to avoid attachment costs in other circumstances as well. They want to reduce benefit costs for all employees, and most important, they want to retain the greatest possible latitude to terminate employment relationships at will.

Several researchers have used dual labor market theory to explain the phenomenon of detachment. The dual market concept divides the economy into two sectors, large firms with substantial market power, called the monopoly or planning sector, and small firms with less power, called the competitive or peripheral sector. Monopoly sector firms have sufficient market power to develop internal labor markets and pass the costs on to consumers. In internal labor markets, much of the cost of worker training is borne by employers, who attempt to protect this investment by inducements to retain the workers.

Mangum, Mayall, and Nelson (1985) maintain that the dual market extends into large firms with internal labor markets. These enterprises have both core employees with job security and extensive benefits and a periphery of detached workers with fewer benefits and no job security. It is the existence of this peripheral work force that makes possible the promise of security for the core workers. A strong parallel is found in Japan. Ouchi (1981) points out that the guarantee of lifetime employment in large Japanese firms is made possible by the existence of a large force of temporary workers, mostly women.

Pfeffer and Baron (1988) argue that internal labor markets and continuous employment are relatively new phenomena which began in the late 1800s. The reversal of this trend is seen in the growth of the various modes of labor contracting: temporary help services, employee leasing, subcontracting for business services ranging from janitorial to data processing, and homework.

Applebaum (1986) also believes that the decline of internal labor markets is causing the growth of what she terms "alternative work schedules." Included in this concept are temporary work, part-time work, multiple jobholding and homework. Factors she cites in the decline of internal markets are increased emphasis on labor cost savings, the growth of higher education, and computer and communication technologies which permit job redesign.

Alternative work scheduling was the major workplace innovation of the 1970s, according to Nollen (1979). Defined as "any variation in the standard five day, 40 hour workweek," it clearly includes the detached work phenomenon.

Worker preference for non-standard worktime is an explicit factor in the growth of alternative work schedules. A third of all workers in the 1977 Quality of Employment Survey reported that they had problems with inconvenient or excessive hours of work. (See Quinn and Staines 1978.)

There is relatively little data on the preferences of detached workers, but nearly 80 percent of the part-time workforce is considered voluntary, that is persons who do not want full-time work (see Nardone 1986). Gannon (1984), in a study of THS workers, found that 86 percent wanted the flexibility to specify the days that they worked, and 57 percent preferred working at a certain time of day. Only eight percent viewed THS work as a stopgap measure until they found permanent work. Seventeen percent liked the greater variety that THS work offered.

The growth of detachment in the workplace is incontrovertible, but its precise magnitude is uncertain. One of the hallmarks of emerging social phenomena is that they are often hard to measure.

Like the labor movement, social insurance programs, and public policy in general, government statistical programs have focused primarily on the full-time worker.

There are two main sources of workforce data used by the US Bureau of Labor Statistics (BLS), individuals and business establishments. Individual data, gathered by sample surveys of households, provide information on work activities on a mid-month reference week. Establishment data are based upon payroll reports of employers.

The BLS individual data series provides an estimate of part-time employment, defined as those who work from 1 to 34 hours, during the reference week. They further distinguish between those who accept part-time work voluntarily and those who want full-time work, but are working part-time because of reduced employment opportunities and other economic reasons. This is probably the most inclusive indicator of detachment. Included are temporary workers, intermittents, casuals, and any independent contractors or leased employees who work less than a full week during mid-month reference period. It excludes workers in all these categories that happen to work full-time during the reference week, and any that did not work at all during the reference week. On the other hand, it includes permanent part-time workers who may not fit the definition of detachment.

There were nearly 19.8 million part-time employees in 1988, up 21 percent from 1980 (Belous 1989). Part-time employment has been increasing at a rate twice as fast as the total labor force since the 1950s.

BLS establishment data provide a measure of employment by a detailed industry. From this source it is possible to chart the growth in the number of persons working on temporary help services payrolls, employee leasing firms and certain other forms of sub-contracting.

Temporary help service payrolls numbered over 780,000 in mid-1986. Since this figure is also based on a mid-month reference week it excludes those not on a payroll at that time that work during other weeks. Because the average duration of a THS assignment is so short (11.8 days), the number of persons not counted is far larger than in any other industry. Mayall and Nelson (1982) estimated the total number of persons who work in a THS payroll at some point during a year to be five times the mid-month count. This suggests that as many as four million people may have worked for a THS during 1986.

The growth of the THS industry has been phenomenal. It grew from less than 400,000 employees in mid-1980 to 1.1 million workers in 1988. This 175 percent increase makes temporary work the fastest growing of all forms of contingency work (Belous 1989).

Most employee leasing firms are included in the "personnel supply services, not elsewhere classified" category. There were nearly 47,000 persons in this industry in mid-1986 according to the BLS estimates. Employment in this category grew about 50 percent from 1982 to 1986.

There is really no good basis for estimating the number of self-employed independent contractors or contract business service workers in the detached workforce. Audrey Freedman (1986), of The Conference Board, uses a somewhat broader concept of 'Contingent workers.' She includes all of the self-employed and half of all business service employment in this category, which totaled 29.5 million in 1985, a 25 percent increase over the preceding decade.

The rapid growth of the detached workforce has been seen as a cause for alarm by some and a source of new opportunities by others. John L. Zalusky, economist for the AFL-CIO (1986) believes that "new directions in staffing and scheduling, temporary or leased employees, working at home, flex-time, part-time work and job sharing are creating a sub-class in the economy that pits haves against have-nots" (quoted in the San Francisco Examiner, August 10, 1986). Observers inside and outside of the labor movement have pointed out that detachment has meant a loss of worker protection in terms of job security, pension and benefits. Others, however, have applauded the detachment phenomenon for bringing greater flexibility to the marketplace and providing new opportunities to the portion of the labor force that does not want permanent attachment or a forty hour workweek.

PROTECTING THE DETACHED WORKFORCE

Most American workers expect to be able to earn their living in healthy and hazard-free environments, not subject to exploitation, over-long hours of work, or a capricious management. They expect hiring and promotion based on qualifications, not prejudice or favoritism.

If laid off because of circumstance beyond their control, they expect unemployment benefits will be available to them. They expect compensation if injured in the course of working. If they are unable to continue working because of disability they expect to receive income support. When they reach retirement age they expect to receive medicare and old age income. These protections, embodied in federal and state laws, are guaranteed to virtually all American workers. Workers have also come to regard paid sick leave, vacations, health coverage, and retirement plans as rights, although they are not guaranteed by law. The promise of job security is a goal of many, if not most, workers.

Detached workers historically have received fewer protections than core workers, and they have been subjected to more abuses in the labor market. Casuals have no job security or non-mandatory benefits. If they work only a few hours for an employer, they may wind up without contributions being made on their behalf for unemployment insurance and social security coverage. Part-time and intermittent workers usually receive fewer employer benefits than those holding regular, permanent positions with the same employer. Limited duration workers may not qualify for inclusion in company retirement plans. Independent contractors receive neither the payroll-based federal and state social insurance nor any other employer-provided benefits. They must pay a higher rate for social security than salaried workers. THS and leased employees do receive all the payroll-based social insurance but THS employees receive few if any non-mandatory benefits. Only leased employees receive a full range of benefits comparable to those of regular, permanent workers, and they are effectively cut off from that elusive goal of long-term security.

The impetus for worker protection, above and beyond what they can obtain through individual action, has three roots: employer interest, the public interest, and collective bargaining. The employers' interest is in retaining good workers and protecting their investment in them and is expressed in personnel policies and practices. The public interest reflects the broad political consensus of the kind of protection all workers ought to have and is expressed in the form of laws and regulations. Labor union interests are expressed through collective bargaining agreements.

Employers have focused upon protecting certain workers at the expense of the others, because they represent their primary investment. They want to retain core workers because of their skills and knowledge. Employer actions thus can be seen as taking the form of incentives to core workers to maintain their attachment to the firm. These incentives include pay, benefits, and the promise of a continuing job. Because these incentives are costly, employers almost invariably try to limit attachment and exclude those workers on the periphery. Even though employers recruit permanent workers from the periphery they try to make it clear that detached workers have no vested rights in permanent jobs and there is no necessary expectation they may enter into the core.

Labor unions have won a great many rights for workers through collective bargaining (and through legislation). The areas of concern to the labor movement have, to a large degree, overlapped those of employers when it comes to the peripheral worker. In labor's view it is the responsibility of employers to provide permanent, stable job opportunities. Unions have sought, through collective bargaining, to prevent contracting out of work and the use of employee leasing, THS's, and self-employed independent contractors. The favored union solutions to temporary work needs are the more costly mechanisms of internal pools, overstaffing, or overtime hours at premium rates. Where large fluctuations in labor demand are in the nature of the industry, unions have sought to rationalize the temporary labor market through the use of the hiring hall.

Some unions have restrictions against intermittent or part-time employees running for union office, serving as convention delegates or otherwise participating in the union. On the other hand, other unions have attempted to require that THS workers pay dues after so many days on assignment with a THS customer where there is a union shop agreement. Where THS employees have entered into permanent employment with the company, unions have successfully argued that time spent in the THS assignment must count as part of the probationary period.

The number of statutory protections of workers is lengthy but includes wage and hour laws, old age, survivor's, disability and health insurance, occupational health and safety, the federal-state unemployment laws, and employee retirement income security. The intent behind this social legislation has been to provide broad coverage to the entire workforce. There have been many holes in the fabric, however. These have taken the form of exclusions of various categories, generally at the behest of employers or other special interests. Among the excluded groups have been farm workers, students, and employees of small businesses. To some degree the lowest paid, least advantaged, and most peripheral have had the least protection.

With the passage of time many but not all of these loopholes have been closed. Perhaps the most spotty coverage remains in the area of employer pensions. Such pensions are not required by law, but where such pension funds are tax-sheltered they must meet certain standards and cannot favor highly-paid workers. However, workers working less than full-time, defined as 1500 hours for the same employer in a year, can be excluded.

Presently the strongest pressure to close-up loopholes is coming from State and federal taxing authorities. Independent contractors can deduct as business expenses certain items that salaried employees cannot. There is also some under-reporting of income. The loss of revenue from this source is causing tax agents to review companies' use of independent contractors very carefully. In fact, the entire employee leasing industry exists principally because of a loophole in the laws affecting tax-sheltered pension plans. The use of such leasing is under review. The disappearance of the loophole could eliminate much of the rationale for the leasing industry.

New Routes to Skills and Work

A job in the core sector of a large internal market enterprise (or even a government agency) with all the attendant security, benefits, and good pay is a prize eagerly sought and not all that easily attained. Nor does it appear likely that this will change in the coming decades.

The increase in the number of core jobs has been less than in the labor force as a whole. Joblessness has moved up in the past decade to the highest levels in forty years, and this is likely to continue. As a result, there is great competition for the internal market opportunities that occur. Although large advertisements for such positions appear regularly in the metropolitan newspapers, they draw hundreds, even thousands, of responses. The large personnel departments that screen the volumes of applicants, are, along with the amounts spent on recruiters and search consultants, part of the price these firms pay to protect permanent employees.

Temporary work has always been an important route into permanent jobs. Part-time and intermittent jobs have been the employment of last resort for generations of young people with neither specialized training nor experience. Internal market firms with their firm or industry-specific training needs have used this peripheral work force as a recruiting ground. Skills are acquired through on-the-job learning and employers can identify those with greatest diligence and motivation without making any commitments.

Temporary jobs have also been a means by which workers with specialized training or experience have made themselves known to employers. Limited duration jobs on special projects have led to permanent hires. Providing a formal route into permanent work is not a major goal of THS's. If it were, they would be continually losing their productive resources. On the other hand, no one sees a series of THS assignments as a career.

THS's have not been reluctant to exploit the tendency of employers to recruit permanent workers from the temporary force. "Try before you hire" is a catch phrase that has been used to sell THS services to employers. More explicitly, employers are sometimes told that they can avoid screening costs and the risks of making commitments to unsuitable employees by filling vacancies with THS workers. The employer agrees in advance that if the THS worker is put on a permanent payroll liquidated damages will be paid to the THS. Or they may simply agree that the THS worker is to remain on the THS payroll for ninety days, or some other fixed period of time.

Only slightly less explicit representations are made to THS workers that there are chances for moving from temporary assignments into permanent jobs. A fair number of THS's are owned by, and operated in conjunction with private employment agencies. Clients looking for permanent jobs are sometimes offered, or advised to accept, THS assignments while waiting for a referral to a permanent position. Or they may be told that by working in a THS assignment they can obtain work experience that will be of value in a permanent job.

Job seekers new to an area can gain local experience that will improve their chances of employability. Re-entrants to the labor market, especially in the clerical field, can improve old skills and acquire new ones, such as word processor operation or computerized accounting systems and database managers. Those with backgrounds of quits and discharges can improve their work records with a string of successful THS assignments. They may, under the tutelage of a THS, return to work at places where they had former difficulties, and, in effect, clear the record.

The THS acts like a broker for the worker in the unstructured temporary job market, finding them assignments, selling their services to customers. Because they are the de jure employers of these workers, the THS has a strong incentive, quite unlike that of an employment agency, to take actions in the worker's best interest—to keep them happy, to enhance their earnings and productivity. Thus, they may at times act as the worker's advocate vis a vis the customer, seeking pay increases, adjudicating disputes. Of course, in the event of strong customer dissatisfaction they would remove the worker. They can and do, however, act in the role of counselor to the workers, helping them plot a career strategy, even acting as mentors to them. Such activities must be considered a substantial improvement in a temporary jobmarket that was once almost entirely chaotic, where chance, favoritism, and payoff were the factors in hiring and in moving into permanent work. The collective bargaining model has also brought order to chaotic temporary markets and, unquestionably, greater benefits and protection to permanent workers. The whole focus of the labor movement has been on securing rights to full-time jobs and benefit, often to the exclusion of the inexperienced entrant to the market. Collective bargaining rationalization of the temporary market has taken the form of hiring halls and the application of seniority to the labor force with seasonal or intermittent attachment to an industry.

The collective bargaining model has been on the decline for various reasons. Employers have sought to avoid the attachment implicit in these peripheral work forces. Federal laws requiring that hiring halls serve non-members have caused some unions to abandon them.

Private employment agencies never served the temporary market directly. Since fees are based upon annual salaries, the rate of return was simply too low. The public employment service once served parts of the temporary market quite effectively. Federal policy in the 1960s and 1970s directed them to concentrate on better paying jobs, however, and service to the temporary market declined.

Workers themselves have found innovative ways to utilize THS's, to enhance their income, change career fields, or pursue more individualistic lifestyles than may be possible in most permanent positions. THS assignments have provided ways for people to support themselves while completing the requirements for a degree, studying for a new career, awaiting approval on a consulting contract, or starting a new business. They provide ways for people to try out new fields in which they have training but not experience.

THS's relieve workers of the burden of making contacts and solicitation on their own behalf and of the record-keeping that goes with self-employment. Earning and perquisites are likely to be lower, however. Nurses and other health professionals who wanted to limit their hours of work have found it easier to do this as THS employees. In technical fields both independent contracting and THS's are avenues for greater individual control over hours and assignments. Programmers, engineers, and technical writers can follow the self-employed contractor route as do such high-level specialists as consultants in organizational design. Job shops, which at first provided drafters for design projects, soon branched into a variety of production and technical fields, from printed circuit board solderer to electronics technician. The list of occupations using job shops has grown to cover the entire professional spectrum below the managerial level. In addition to drafters, engineers and programmers are such specialties as statisticians and industrial psychologists.

Both contracting and job shops provide a means for professionals to reduce their attachment to specific employers while retaining high earning power. Reducing such attachment allows them greater latitude to reject assignments that they do not find interesting and consistent with their professional development. This also provides the freedom to gain experience in new areas and technologies as the opportunities arise. It is in contracting that the greatest autonomy and scope of work are to be found. Contractors and job shoppers also have the freedom to simply leave the labor force for leisure or avocational pursuits, and have an avenue of easy return. This option is, of course, open to persons in salaried positions but it is rare and considered risky.

Temporary work and other forms of labor market detachment are likely to account for an increasing share of work opportunities in the coming years. Despite the objections of critics, the phenomenon is clearly providing a satisfactory solution to a number of employer problems, while at the same time better meeting worker needs for employment flexibility.

REFERENCES

Applebaum, Eileen. 1986. "Restructuring Work: Temporary, Part-time, and At-home Employment" in Heidi Hartmann (Ed.), *Computer Chips and Paper Clips: Technology and Women's Employment*, Vol II. Washington: National Academy of Sciences, 268-310.

Belous, Richard S. 1989. *The Contingent Economy: The Growth of the Temporary, Part-Time and Subcontracted Workforce*. Washington D.C.: National Planning Association.

Carey, Max L. and Kim L. Hazelbaker. 1986. "Employment Growth in the Temporary Help Industry." *Monthly Labor Review* 109 (4):37-44.

Freedman, Audrey. 1986. Quoted in "Part-time Work, New Labor Trend." *New York Times*, 1 July, A1.

Gannon, Martin J. 1984. "Preferences of Temporary Workers: Time, Variety and Flexibility." *Monthly Labor Review* 107 (8):26-32.

Mangum, Garth L., Donald Mayall, and Kristin Nelson. 1985. "The Temporary Help Industry: A Response to the Dual Internal Labor Market." *Industrial Labor Relations Review* 38:599-611.

Mayall, Donald and Kristin Nelson. 1982. *The Temporary Help Supply Service and the Temporary Labor Market.* Salt Lake City: Olympus Research Centers.

Nardone, Thomas J. 1986. "Part-time Workers: Who Are They?" *Monthly Labor Review* 109 (2):13-19.

Nollen, Stanley. 1979. *New Patterns of Work.* Scarsdale: Work in America Institute.

Ouchi, William G. 1981. *Theory Z.* Reading, MA: Addison-Wesley.

Pfeffer, Jeffrey and James Baron. 1988. "Taking the Workers Back Out: Recent Trends in the Employment Relationship." In Barry Staw (Ed.), *Research on Organizational Behavior*, Vol 20, 257-303.

Quinn, Robert P. and Graham L. Staines. 1978. *The 1977 Quality of Employment Survey.* Ann Arbor: Institute for Social Research, University of Michigan.

6

Skills Shortage or Management Shortage?

Ruy A. Teixeira
Lawrence Mishel

I. INTRODUCTION

An oft-stated goal of the Clinton administration is the generation of high-skill, high-wage jobs for workers. A key question is the extent to which this goal can be attained through an improved education and training system. For instance, the administration echoes the increasingly common belief in the need for more "high-performance" workplaces, where high skill levels can be utilized to boost productivity and, therefore, wages. An issue then is whether an insufficiently educated workforce is currently a major constraint on the diffusion of such workplaces. If so, improved workforce skills might get us far along the "high-wage, high-skill path."

A related line of analysis has suggested that the U.S. faces a serious skills shortage, due to a rapid escalation in the skill requirements of jobs that is outstripping the poor educational preparation of U.S. workers. In this view, the skills mismatch between available jobs and available workers is preventing productivity and wage growth.

In both analyses, it is possible to discern a "field of dreams" approach to the high-wage jobs issue: "if we build the workers, they will come." That is, if we improve workforce skills through education and training then the rest will follow—first, high performance workplaces, then substantial increases in productivity, then high-wage economic growth, and so on.

We believe the "field of dreams" approach is mistaken. In reality, the main obstacles to attaining high-performance workplaces are factors such as: management myopia and fear of empowering workers; the lack of significant wage pressure; the ease of pursuing alternative low-wage options (producing offshore, depressing wages, benefits and working conditions); and a variety of institutional barriers to change (Appelbaum and Batt 1993). In the context of these factors, a poor supply of workers with necessary skills is at best a minor additional obstacle, especially in the high-wage durable goods sector. Indeed, as we show below, the available evidence does *not* indicate a skills shortage or skills mismatch, but rather a "management shortage," where U.S. employers have adapted to international competition by emphasizing low price rather than high skill production.

II. Supply: Trends in Skill Levels of the Workforce

One problem with the skills shortage diagnosis is that workforce skill levels have been rising rapidly, not stagnating and certainly not declining. For example, the educational attainment levels of the workforce have risen steadily over the past two decades (see Table 3). In 1973, 75 percent of the labor force were high school graduates. By 1991, that figure had risen to 87 percent, cutting the proportion of high school dropouts in the workforce by half. At the other end of the educational attainment scale, in 1973 only 16 per-

Table 3. Educational Attainment Levels of Workforce, 1973-1991

	High School Drop-out	High School Graduate	Some College	College Graduate
1973	24.8%	40.8%	18.0%	16.4%
1979	21.9	41.8	18.0	18.3
1987	14.2	41.3	21.9	22.6
1989	13.7	40.5	22.3	23.5
1991	12.6	40.0	23.1	24.3
Change:				
1973-1991	-12.2	-0.8	5.1	7.9

Source: Mishel and Bernstein (1993).

cent of the workforce had graduated from college. By 1991, that figure had risen to almost one-quarter (24 percent) of the workforce.

It might be possible, however, that educational *quality* (as proxied by test scores) could have fallen while educational *levels* were rising. To test whether or not this was in fact happening, we turned to the National Assessment of Educational Progress (NAEP), a survey of the cognitive achievement levels of students across the United States. The following is what we have found.

During the same time period that high school and college graduation rates were rapidly rising—the early 1970s to the present—NAEP scores remained stable (see Table 4). On a scale that theoretically ranges from 0 to 500 (over 90 percent of 17 year olds actually score between 225 and 375), scores for the total population fluctuated only a few points over the past two decades.

The only exception to this generally stable pattern of test scores is that blacks exhibited a significant improvement in mathematics and writing, 19 points and 28 points, respectively, over this time period. Thus, skill trends among minority workforce entrants, far from being a special source of concern, should properly be viewed as a special source of strength.

The fact that test scores have remained generally stable while education levels have rapidly increased, means that the education levels of the workforce have truly gone up substantially over the past two decades. Thus, if there is a skills shortage, it must be primarily attributable to a *very* rapid rise in the skill requirements of jobs, for which even the increased supply of more educated workers has not been adequate.

III. DEMAND: TRENDS IN SKILL REQUIREMENTS OF JOBS

There are two basic ways to look for evidence of changes in the skill requirements of jobs. The first is to look for direct evidence of such changes by examination of appropriate survey or case study data on the job structure. The second is to indirectly infer such changes from examination of patterns in wage data (i.e., from the existence of an increased "skill premium"). We consider both sources of evidence below.

A. Direct Evidence of Changes in Job Skill Requirements

Changes in the job structure can affect job skill levels in two basic ways, which, while they can and do take place simul-

Table 4. Educational Achievement Scores, Age 17, 1970-1990

Science

	Total Population	White	Black
1970	305 (1.0)	312 (0.8)	258 (1.5)
1973	296 (1.0)	304 (0.8)	250 (1.5)
1977	290 (1.0)	298 (0.7)	240 (1.5)
1982	283 (1.2)	293 (1.0)	235 (1.7)
1986	289 (1.4)	298 (1.7)	253 (2.9)
1990	290 (1.1)	301 (1.1)	253 (4.5)

Mathematics

	Total Population	White	Black
1973	304 (1.1)	310 (1.1)	270 (1.3)
1978	300 (1.0)	306 (0.9)	268 (1.3)
1982	299 (0.9)	304 (0.9)	272 (1.2)
1986	302 (0.9)	308 (1.0)	279 (2.1)
1990	305 (0.9)	310 (1.0)	289 (2.8)

Reading

	Total Population	White	Black
1971	285 (1.2)	291 (1.0)	239 (1.7)
1975	286 (0.8)	293 (0.6)	241 (2.0)
1980	286 (1.2)	293 (0.9)	243 (1.8)
1984	289 (0.6)	295 (0.7)	264 (1.0)
1988	290 (1.0)	295 (1.2)	274 (2.4)
1990	290 (1.1)	297 (1.2)	267 (2.3)

Writing

	Total Population	White	Black
1984	212 (1.7)	218 (2.2)	195 (4.4)
1988	214 (1.4)	219 (1.6)	200 (2.8)
1990	212 (1.3)	217 (1.5)	194 (2.3)

Note: Standard errors are in parentheses. Total population includes white, black and other.

Source: Mullis, Dossey, Foertsch, Jones and Gentile (1991).

taneously, are important to keep separate conceptually. The two basic ways are through *compositional shifts* in the job structure (changes in job mix), where the distribution of individuals into jobs with different skill levels changes, and through *content shifts*, where the actual content of the work individuals do within jobs changes. For example, both the proportion of bank tellers within the economy may change as well as the kind of work bank tellers do.

The Effect of Industry and Occupation Shifts on Job Skill Requirements. We turn first to the effect of changes in job mix, summarized in Table 5. These results suggest that job skill requirements are rising, but at a progressively *slower* rather than *faster* pace. That is, there is an ongoing *slowdown*, not *speedup*, in the upskilling of jobs. The slowdown is sharpest from the 1970s to the 1980s, and then is projected to continue at a more moderate rate (based on the 1990-2005 Bureau of Labor Statistics' occupational employment projections) into the next century.

For example, job skill levels, as measured by the verbal aptitude index, went up at a ten year rate of 2.3 percent between 1970 and 1979, but only 0.9 percent between 1980 and 1990. Similarly, skill requirements in terms of data-handling went up at a 4.1 percent rate

Table 5. The Effect of Industry and Occupation Employment Shifts on Skill and Education Requirements of Jobs, 1970-2005

| Job | | | BLS Projections |
Characteristic	1970-79	1980-90	1990-2005
	(Ten Year Rate of Change*)		
Skill Indices			
General Education Development—			
language	4.3%	1.8%	1.5%
General Education Development—			
mathematics	4.3	2.0	1.3
Numerical Aptitude	1.5	.7	.4
Verbal Aptitude	2.3	.9	.9
Handling Data	4.1	1.8	1.3
Handling People	2.2	1.1	.8
Education			
Average Years of Schooling	1.5	.4	.5
	(Percent Point Change)		
Shares of Employment Requiring:			
Less Than High School	-1.6%	.1%	-.4%
High School Graduate	-1.3	-1.3	-.7
Some College	.7	.4	.2
College Graduate or More	2.2	.9	.9

* To facilitate comparisons of these time periods which are of different length the data have been converted to ten year rates of change: the change if the annual rate of change in these time periods had continued for ten years.

Source: Authors' calculations, based on 1970 Census, 1979 March CPS, 1980 Census, 1990 CPS Earnings File and 1990-2005 BLS Projections.

between 1970 and 1980, but just 1.9 percent from 1980 to 1990. The other skill and education measures generally show a similar pattern: modest rates of change in the 1970s, followed by a sharp deceleration in the 1980s.

The projected rates of skill requirement growth in the 1990-2005 period are also far less than what occurred in the 1970s, and even slightly less than the 1980s experience. The bottom line is clear: future rates of job skill growth are projected to be startlingly anemic—the very antithesis of the explosion of high skill jobs postulated by the skills shortage viewpoint.

The Effect of Content Shifts Within Jobs on Job Skill Requirements. The analysis above strongly suggests that compositional change—that is, distributional shifts in the industrial and occupational composition of employment—has not, and most likely will not, produce substantial skill upgrading of jobs. This means that if substantial skill upgrading is taking place, it must be from changes *within* jobs in the content of task performance.

There are three sources of evidence on these possible content shifts. The first is *case studies* of jobs within particular industries. The second is *employer surveys*, where employers are asked to assess the skill requirements of jobs within their firms. The third and most direct source is *worker observation*, where job analysts actually watch work being performed and rate its skill requirements.

Turning first to the case study literature, the message is ambiguous concerning the direction and magnitude of within-occupation change. For instance, where technological changes within occupations have been large, has there been substantial growth in skill levels? The message of the literature on this question is: *It depends* (Spenner 1988; Bailey 1989). That is, there is no necessary relationship between technological progress and skill upgrading. The change in employment patterns due to a given technology can vary from large increases in skill levels to small increases to none at all, or even *downgrading*. For example, Jaikumar's (1986) cross-national study of flexible manufacturing systems shows essentially similar technologies being deployed in quite different ways in different countries.

Thus, the case study literature provides no clear evidence of the massive skill upgrading called for by the skills shortage thesis. Nor does the picture clear up much when we turn to evidence from employer surveys. Indeed, if anything, the picture becomes murkier.

To begin with, employer surveys consistently show the strongest employer interest, not in cognitive skills, but in worker attitudes (Natriello 1989). That is, when employers are asked what they are most likely to look for in prospective hires, they typically stress "finding workers with a good work ethic," "a good attitude," "reliable," etc., rather than, say, knowledge of statistics or even basic math. The Commission on the Skills of the American Workforce (1990) put the share of employers with this emphasis at about 80 percent, compared with only 5 percent who emphasized growing educational skill needs.

The latter figure is obviously of some interest. It suggests that the proportion of employers who have instituted "high-performance work organizations"—which would presumably call for higher worker skill levels—may be small. Consistent with this, the recent report (1991) of the Secretary of Labor's Commission on the Achievement of Necessary Skills (SCANS) put the proportion of employers who have reorganized work in this way at only about 10 percent.

Other estimates are more optimistic. A very recent study by Osterman (1993), based on a commendably careful and representative survey of 875 firms, put the proportion of employers (fifty workers or more) utilizing high-performance work organization at a comparatively robust 37 percent. However, Osterman's operationalization of high-performance work organization is based on employers' identification with only two of four (somewhat vague) work organization concepts. Simply ratcheting up the definition of high-performance work organization to three of four, rather than two of four, organizational attributes yields a far lower 13 percent estimate, based on Osterman's own data.

Employer surveys, therefore, also do not paint a picture of job transformation consistent with the skills shortage hypothesis. That is, the data are consistent with modest skill upgrading rather than dramatic changes in job content.

This leaves us with the last, and most direct, measure of job content changes: observation by job analysts of actual job skill requirements. The only two reasonably recent attempts to look at such data are by Cappelli (1992) and the present authors.

Cappelli's study uses data from the Hay compensation consulting firm, which rates jobs of a (nonrandom) sample of U.S. firms for various clients. This somewhat idiosyncratic dataset does suggest some skill upgrading within jobs between 1978 and 1988, but only within production jobs in manufacturing. Data on clerical jobs across industries (the other set of jobs Cappelli was able to examine) suggest no net upgrading of these jobs.

However, the best source of data on the skill content of jobs is the Dictionary of Occupational Titles (DOT), a rating of over 12,000 jobs in the U.S. economy by the Department of Labor. While no new edition of this dataset has been released since 1977, when the 4th edition was released, a substantial revision of the dataset was released in 1991. By painstakingly matching the revised and original 4th editions, we were able to isolate over 1,600 jobs that were re-rated by job analysts over the intervening years.

The results, displayed in Table 6, are perhaps the "hardest" evidence on changes in job content currently available. And these data clearly do not suggest massive upgrading within jobs. Indeed, they suggest much the same sort of modest job upgrading captured by the industry/occupation employment shift analysis in Table 5.[1]

The conclusion seems inescapable. Direct evidence on changes in job skill requirements indicates that the skills shortage thesis considerably exaggerates the limited upgrading actually happening in contemporary workplaces. Instead, the evidence suggests that the job structure is changing rather slowly and irregularly. This means, counterintuitively, there may not be *too much* upskilling of the job structure, but rather *too little*. Put another way, there may be more of a *potential* for upskilling than *actual* upskilling.

Table 6. The Effect of Content Shifts
within Jobs on Skill Requirements, 1977-1991

	10 Year Rate of Change
General educational development-language (GED-L)	2.8%
General educational development-mathematics (GED-M)	1.7
Specific vocational preparation (SVP)	0.2
Handling data	-0.8
Handling people	-0.4

Source: Authors' calculations, based on 1977 and 1991 versions of 4th edition of Dictionary of Occupational Title (DOT).

B. Indirect Evidence on Changes in
Job Skill Requirements (Wage Data)

But what of wage trends that show skill being rewarded so handsomely during the 1980s? This is the crux of many economists' arguments about a skills shortage. No need to look at the direct evidence, they cry, our *indirect* evidence shows conclusively that skill requirements are rising. No other possibility, they argue, would be consistent with the rising skill premia revealed by analysis of wage data.

The data on increasing relative returns to education—which simply means that the wages of more-educated workers (e.g., college graduates) have increased relative to that of less-educated workers (e.g., high school graduates)—are not in dispute. All observers agree there was a substantial increase in the wage gap between college and high school graduates in the 1980s (however, note that this increase flattened out in the late 1980s).

But the assumed link between these data and increases in *average* skill requirements is very much open to question. Note, to begin with, that the return to education is a *relative* indicator and therefore bears no necessary relationship to overall changes in *average* or overall skill requirements. For example, a substantial downskilling of the bottom half of the job structure would presumably *increase* the returns to education (since the wages of workers with little education would decrease relative to well-educated workers), while producing, at the same time, an overall *decrease* in job-skill requirements.

It is also important to note that, in Table 7, the relative returns to education for men increased in the 1980s almost entirely because of declining wages for the noncollege-educated workforce (e.g., down 12.7 percent for high school graduates from 1979-89), not because of increasing wages for the more educated (up only 0.2 percent for college graduates in the same time period). Thus, it has not been the wages of more-skilled workers that have been bid up—as one might expect in a "skills shortage"—but rather the wages of the less-skilled that have been pushed dramatically downward. Moreover, the wages of white-collar and college-educated workers have actually been *declining* since 1987, a further complication for the "bidding up of the wages of skilled and more-educated workers" story.

Further, econometric analyses suggest that the forces that have depressed wages of the noncollege workforce include a host of factors with no clear relationship to rising skill requirements in the work-

Table 7. Change in Real Hourly Wage for Men by Education, 1973-1991

Year	High-School Dropout	High-School Graduate	Some College	College	College 2+ years
Real Hourly Wage					
1973	$11.48	$13.50	$14.08	$18.99	$21.09
1979	11.01	12.77	13.80	17.08	19.16
1987	9.35	11.55	13.01	17.55	20.85
1989	9.01	11.15	12.65	17.11	21.02
1991	8.45	10.72	12.49	16.69	21.11
Percent Change					
1973-79	-4.2%	-5.4%	-2.0%	-10.0%	-9.2%
1979-89	-18.2	-12.7	-8.3	0.2	9.7
1989-91	-6.2	-3.8	-1.3	-2.5	0.3
1973-91	-26.4	-20.6	-11.3	-12.1	0.4

Source: Mishel and Bernstein (1993).

place: deceleration in the growth of the relative supply of college-educated workers; industry shifts in the pattern of employment; increased import competition; a lower minimum wage; declining unionization; and so on. It thus appears that skill upgrading may have been only one of a multiplicity of causes for the rising returns to education in the 1980s.

Now, this is not to say that some part of the rise in the returns to education for male workers (or other groups of workers) cannot be reasonably ascribed to rising skill requirements. But this is hardly enough to justify talk of a dramatic rise in these skill requirements. In fact, results on this level seem quite consistent with the analysis offered earlier in this article, which suggests relatively modest recent growth in skill requirements. And certainly it is not enough to justify overruling the weight of the *direct* evidence we currently have on changing job skill requirements.

IV. Conclusions and Policy Implications

The evidence reviewed above casts considerable doubt on the skills shortage diagnosis of U.S. labor market problems. This suggests that, instead of just increasing the supply of worker skills (which remains desirable and necessary), ways must be found of improving the demand side—chiefly the workplace organization strategies of U.S. employers—if a high-wage, high-skill growth trajectory is to be reached. In other words, the real shortage we must confront is a *management shortage*, not a skills shortage.

How might this management shortage be addressed? There are a variety of possibilities, all based on the idea that labor market policy must make relationships in the workplace and how the factors of production are combined a central concern. For example, labor market and technology diffusion policies should, wherever possible, be used as levers to transform work systems. This might include making training grants and other assistance contingent on the adoption of human resource plans leading to work reorganization and increased worker participation.

This is the "carrot" aspect of the approach: providing benefits if firms follow the "high road" to increased competitiveness. But, it may also be necessary to block access to the "low road" (wage and benefit reductions, increased use of part-time and temporary workers, union-busting, moving work overseas) if widespread adoption of high-performance work organizations is desired. This means we should consider policies on labor standards, labor relations, and trade that could inhibit employers' ability to use low road strategies. Examples here might include labor law reform and the supplemental North American Free Trade Agreements (NAFTA).

Of course, these kinds of policies present difficult tradeoffs and need much serious thought to be appropriately formulated and implemented. But, we believe it is time to start sifting through these policies in earnest before we adopt labor market policies designed to solve a problem—the skills shortage—that does not really exist.

NOTE

1. Whether these changes are "modest" or "large" depends on their size relative to prior historical trends. Unfortunately, there are no estimates of prior content shifts for several of the most important skill dimensions. However, where the available data do match up, they suggest that the rates in Table 6 are quite modest.

REFERENCES

Applebaum, E. and R. Batt. 1993. *Transforming the Production System in U.S. Firms*. Washington DC: Economic Policy Institute.

Bailey, T. 1989. "Changes in the Nature and Structure of Work: Implications for Skill Requirements and Skill Information." Technical Paper No. 9, Columbia University: Conversation of Human Resources.

Blackburn, M.L., D.E. Bloom and R.B. Freeman. 1990. "The Declining Economic Position of Less-Skilled American Men. In G. Burtless (Ed.), *A Future of Lousy Jobs?: The Changing Structure of U.S. Wages*, Washington, DC: The Brookings Institution.

Cappelli, P. 1992. "Are Skill Requirements Rising?: Evidence from Production and Clerical Jobs." Working Paper No. 3, University of Pennsylvania: National Center on the Educational Quality of the Workforce.

Commission on the Skills of the American Workforce. 1990. *America's Choice: High Skills or Low Wages!* Rochester, NY: National Center on Education and the Economy.

Jaikumar, R. 1986. "Postindustrial Manufacturing." *Harvard Business Review*, November-December, 69-76.

Johnston, W.B. and A.E. Packer. 1987. *Workforce 2000: Work and Workers for the 21st Century*. Indianapolis, IN: Hudson Institute.

Juhn, C., K. M. Murphy and B. Pierce. 1989. "Wage Inequality and the Returns to Skill." Unpublished manuscript 1989.

Katz, L. 1989. "Comment." Table 1, citing Katz and Murphy. In Brainard and Perry (Eds.), *Brookings Papers on Economic Activity*, Vol. 2. Washington, DC: The Brookings Institution, 269.

Levy, F. and R. Murnane. 1992. "U.S. Earnings Levels and Earnings and Inequality: A Review of Recent Trends and Proposed Explanations." *Journal of Economic Literature* 30:1333-1381.

Mishel, L. and J. Bernstein. 1993. *The State of Working America, 1992-93 Edition*. New York: M.E. Sharpe Inc.

Mishel, L. and R. A. Teixeira. 1991. "The Myth of the Coming Labor Shortage: Jobs, Skills and Incomes of America's Workforce 2000." Washington, DC: Economic Policy Institute.

Mullis, I. V. S., J. A. Dossey, M. A. Foerstch, L. R. Jones and C. A. Gentile. 1991. *Trends in Academic Progress: Achievement of U.S. Students*. Washington, DC: U.S. Department of Education, National Center for Education Statistics.

Natriello, G. 1989. "What Do Employers Want in Entry-Level Workers?: An Assessment of the Evidence." Occasional Paper No. 7. Columbia University: Teachers College.

Osterman, P. 1993. "How Common Is Workplace Transformation and How Can We Explain Who Adopts It?: Results from a National Survey." Unpublished manuscript, MIT: Sloan School of Management.

Spenner, K. I. 1988. "Technological Change, Skill Requirements, and Education: The Case for Uncertainty." In R. M. Cyert and D.C. Mowery (Eds.), *The Impact of Technological Change on Employment and Economic Growth*. Cambridge, MA: Ballinger Books.

U.S. Department of Labor. 1991. Secretary's Commission on Achieving Necessary Skills. "What Work Requires of Schools." Washington, DC: U.S. Department of Labor.

U.S. Department of Labor. 1972. *Handbook for Analyzing Jobs*. Washington, DC: U.S. Government Printing Office.

7

A Sociological Commentary
on Workforce 2000[1]

Nancy DiTomaso
Judith J. Friedman

Economic and labor force projections presented in *Workforce 2000* (Johnston and Packer 1987) caught the attention of corporate policy makers, public policy makers, and the national media. This Hudson Institute report is concise, yet complex. In just over one hundred pages, the authors describe projected changes between 1985 and 2000 in the composition of U.S. jobs, in productivity, in the skill levels of workers, and in the composition of the labor force; they link these trends together; and they present recommendations about the best way to deal with six "policy challenges."

The projection of labor force composition in *Workforce 2000* has attracted particular attention, although this projection is only a small part of the entire document. Many policy makers and media writers apparently think this labor force projection predicts a large drop in the percent of the total U.S. labor force that consists of native white males. Such a drop would mean a much more "diverse" workforce. Thus *Workforce 2000* has stimulated discussions about the implications of labor force diversity.

The labor force projection developed for *Workforce 2000* certainly predicts a more diverse workforce in 2000 than in 1985, but it also predicts that native white males will remain numerically the largest among the six categories of workers identified.

Workforce 2000 presents the projection for 2000 by showing the distribution of "net new workers." This form of presentation emphasizes the relative growth of the *other* five categories of workers (i.e., those not native white males), and hence change in composition. Thus understanding what the projection actually says about change in labor force diversity requires an understanding of "net new workers." Media discussions of the projection suggest, however, that many readers are unfamiliar with the distinction between *net* new workers and *all* new workers. As we discuss the projection of labor force composition presented in *Workforce 2000*, we will clarify the meaning of *net* new workers. We also will emphasize the importance of assumptions to any projection, including assumptions about public and corporate policy.

In addition, as Johnston and Packer (whose primary training is in economics and business) discuss projected changes in the labor force and other projected changes in the U.S. economy, they make assumptions about the operation of the U.S. economy and society that a sociologist is likely to question. Lawrence Mishel and Ruy Teixeira (1991) have an excellent critique of the report's projection that there will be an increasing mismatch between the skills of those entering the U.S. labor force and the skills required by future jobs. We will comment on the discussions of several projected economic trends in *Workforce 2000*, and on related policy recommendations.

Workforce 2000 has attracted substantial attention, and more sociologists need to enter this public discussion of the U.S. economy.

LABOR FORCE PROJECTIONS

Johnston and Packer divide the U.S. labor force into six categories based on gender, race (white/other) and nativity (native born/immigrant), and they project the number in each category to 2000. The presentation of this labor force projection is concise; for this projection is, after all, a small part of their total analysis. *Workforce 2000* includes just two sets of figures taken from the total labor force projection. Figure 3-7 (p. 95) and the executive summary (p. xxi) each present (1) the distribution of the 1985 (base year) labor force among these six categories, and (2) the distribution of projected *net* additions to the labor force (or net new workers) for 1985-2000 among these six categories. We reproduce these two sets of percents in Table 8.

Table 8. Hudson Institute Data on the Percent Distribution of the 1985 U.S. Workforce and of Net New Workers, 1985-2000

	Workforce 1985	Net New Workers 1985-2000
Native White Men	47%	15%
Native White Women	36%	42%
Native Non-white Men	5%	7%
Native Non-white Women	5%	13%
Immigrant Men	4%	13%
Immigrant Women	3%	9%
Total Percent	100%	99%
Total Number (in 1,000)	115,461	25,000

Source: Hudson Institute, *Workforce 2000*, 1987: xxi.

Workforce 2000 does *not* show crucial parts of the labor force projection, including the *overall* labor force projected for 2000 divided among these six categories. These percents are easy to calculate from the numbers provided (Table 8), and, as we will show later, these missing percents provide a different picture of change in composition between 1985 and 2000.

In addition, the brief discussion of the labor force projection within *Workforce 2000* mentions only a few of the assumptions used to develop the projection. Unfortunately, this means readers can miss the fact that this projection, like any projection, relies upon selected assumptions, including assumptions about public policy and about corporate practices.

Net New Workers

The projection of "net additions" to the U.S. labor force between 1985 and 2000 may be the most cited aspect of *Workforce 2000*. *Net* new workers (net additions) for a time period are people who enter the labor force during that time period minus those who leave during that time period. If 300 of those who are in a labor force at the beginning of a year leave that labor force by December 31, and 500 enter that labor force during the year and remain until December 31, that labor force gains 200 "net new workers." Thus the concept *net* new workers differs from the more common concept, *all* new workers (or "entrants"). In this example, there are 500 new workers in all, but only 200 *net* new workers.

This concept of *net* new workers is not part of everyday discussions of the labor force, and many labor force projections do not provide net figures. Further, it is easy to confuse *net* new workers with *all* new workers. We have found numerous examples in the media. Such misinterpretations exaggerate the projected decline in the percent of the total U.S. labor force that consists of native white men.

This will be clearer if we look at the projection as presented in *Workforce 2000*, and then look at some media discussions of the projection. Their Figure 3-7 (which is frequently reproduced in the media) consists of (1) a bar graph that shows the 1985 labor force classified by sex, race (white/nonwhite) and nativity (native/immigrant) and (2) a bar graph that shows the projected percent distribution of "net new workers" for 1985-2000 (or "increase 1985-2000") among these six categories. The first bar in Figure 3-7 (column 1 in our Table 8) tells us that in 1985, 47 percent of those in the U.S. labor force were native white males. The second bar (column 2 in our Table 8) tells us that this projection predicts that 15 percent of the *net new workers* as of 2000 will be native white males. Again, *neither* set of percents provides the percent of *all* new workers expected to be native white males, and *neither* shows the percent of the 2000 labor force expected to be native white males.

Readers seem to find the contrast between 47 percent and 15 percent striking. Discussions of *Workforce 2000* in the general news media, in the business news media, and in some internal corporation publications provide numerous references to this contrast. In some cases the reader apparently thinks that the 15 percent refers to *all* new workers rather than to *net* new workers.

A few of the many examples will illustrate this. A special issue of *Business Week* reproduced the two sets of percents found in *Workforce 2000* (Nussbaum 1988, 102-103). The discussion of the workforce, later in the issue, includes this typical quote: "Over the next 10 years, predicts the Hudson Institute, an economic think tank, only 15% of the workforce entrants will be native-born white males" (Ehrlich and Garland 1988, 110). Further, some writers connect this 15 percent native white male with the total pool available for management jobs. An article in *Time* (Castro 1990, 50), using a similar projection with 1988 as the base year; stated: "Most startling, only 9.3% of the new workers will represent the population from which nearly all top corporate managers have sprung: white, non-Hispanic-U.S. born men."

There are exceptions. A *Wall Street Journal* article (September 22, 1989) headed "Labor Force Change Is Greatly Exaggerated," for example, points out the distinction between "new" and "net" additions. However the vast majority of the discussions we have seen appear to misinterpret these figures for net new workers.

There are other problems in interpretation as well. A *Wall Street Journal* article (Fuchsberg 1990), again citing *Workforce 2000*, states that "white males would constitute only 15% of net additions to the workforce by the year 2000, down sharply from 45% [*sic*] in 1985." Here the meaning of the initial figure is unclear.

These examples (again, taken from many we have seen) suggest that even journalists who specialize in business are not conversant with the concept "net new workers" (or "net additions"). *Workforce 2000* does not include a definition of this key concept, and the text frequently substitutes "new entrants" or "new workers" for "net new workers." Discussions of Figure 3-7 do refer to "net additions," but they also encourage a direct comparison of the two bars. Thus the Executive Summary states that "only 15 percent of the net new entrants to the labor force over the next 13 years will be native white males, compared with 47% in that category today" (p. xiii). Similarly: "Non-whites, women, and immigrants will make up more than five-sixths of the net additions to the workforce between now and the year 2000, though they make up only about half of it today" (p. xx). Interpretation requires that the reader understand this term.[2]

The Projected Changes

What *does* the projection within *Workforce 2000* suggest about the composition of the U.S. labor force in 2000 and about *change* in U.S. labor force composition between 1985 and 2000?

The Executive Summary (pp. xix-x) presents the key predictions about the *direction* of change in the U.S. labor force in the form of five demographic "facts" (their term). Specifically:

1. "The population and the workforce will grow more slowly than at any time since the 1930s."
2. "The average age of the population and the workforce will rise, and the pool of young workers entering the labor market will shrink."
3. "More women will enter the workforce."
4. "Minorities will be a larger share of new entrants into the labor force."
5. "Immigrants will represent the largest share of the increase in the population and the workforce since the first World War."

In the body of the report, the authors emphasize the relative change expected in two sectors of the labor force, (A) native white males and (B) everyone else, i.e., all females, plus nonwhite males and male immigrants. Thus the report focuses upon the combined impact of "facts" 3-5. The contrast, here, is between the segment of the labor force from which corporations traditionally hire managers, and the rest of the labor force. The authors see any shift toward category B as evidence of increasing "diversity." They note: "For companies that have previously hired mostly young white men, the years ahead will require major changes. Organizations . . . will be forced to look beyond their traditional sources of personnel" (p. 95).

We agree that each of these changes is highly probable, although we comment on some of the assumptions behind them later in this chapter. Their impact depends, however, upon (1) their scale and (2) the extent to which they represent a *change* in direction or in scale. Were native white males *also* a small percent of the net new workers during the *preceding* fifteen years? Is any increasing diversity something new, or is it a continuation of past trends?

Net New Workers

Before discussing these points, we will further clarify the meaning of "net new workers."

Again, net new workers are *not* all new workers. Here, they are *not* all those expected to enter the U.S. labor force after 1985 and to remain until 2000. Instead, net new workers are a subset of all new workers: specifically, those new workers who do not "replace" someone present in 1985 who subsequently leaves the labor force.

A simplified example will clarify this. Suppose a university department had twenty professors in 1990, and fifteen of these professors were male. Between 1990 and 2000, six professors retire; no one leaves for another reason. Past hiring practices mean all six who reach retirement age are male. The department replaces the six who retire, and gains three new lines. Among all nine new professors (the six replacing retired professors and the three on new lines), six are male and three are female. How does the composition of this department change between 1990 and 2000? In 1990, fifteen of the twenty (75 percent) are male. Of the nine new professors, 66 percent are male. Each of the six men hired can be said to replace a male who retires. Thus there are three "net new workers" in the department, all female. All (100 percent) of the net new workers are female, but only a third of *all* new workers are female. Males, who were 75 percent of the department in 1990 (15/20), are now 65 percent (15/23). This is a decline of 10 percent in the percent male, but males are still in the majority and the department has hired twice the number of males as females.[3]

No statistics lie here, but presentation matters.

The second example involves the entire labor force. To calculate the number of "net new workers" in a given category, say native white males, one first "matches" each native white male present in 1985 who leaves the labor force by 2000 with a native white male who enters the labor force after 1985 and is present in 2000. None of these "matched" individuals is a "net new worker." The native white male *"net* new workers" are any *others* who are in the 2000 labor force. If more leave a category than enter, "net new workers" for that category is a negative number. If the total number of people in the 2000 labor force equals the number in the 1985 labor force, the sum of the *"net* new workers" across categories will be zero. The zero would *not* mean that the economy absorbed no new workers over the fifteen year period, but only that the number who entered the labor force equaled the number who left the labor force.

If patterns of leaving and entering are similar across the six categories—and if the six categories are close in initial size—the composition of net new workers will resemble the composition of all new workers (all new workers are net new workers plus the new workers who replace people leaving the labor force). Neither condition holds, however, for comparisons between native white males in the U.S. labor force and the other categories formed by sex, race, and nativity. The category "native white male" has been relatively large (e.g., 47 percent of the 1985 labor force), and the labor force participation rates of native white males have been especially high. These two characteristics suggest this category will have a relatively high number of leavers compared with entrants. Already high participation rates reduce the number available to enter the labor force, however strong the economy. Thus when the total labor force grows faster than the adult native white male population, a relatively high proportion of the "net new workers" are likely to come from categories with lower initial participation rates or from immigrants.

An additional process can work, to some extent, as a counterbalance. When native white males respond to opportunities produced by periods of overall labor force growth, their response is likely to take forms such as a rise in the average age of retirement. The corresponding reduction in the number of leavers puts more of the native white male entrants into the category "net new workers."

The actual calculation of net new workers (or of net change, the term used by the U.S. Department of Labor), involves projecting each component of the labor force forward to the year 2000. The difference between the number in a category in 1985 and the number in that category in 2000 is the number of net new workers. A recent projection in *Monthly Labor Review* (Fullerton 1989, 10-11) includes a table showing net change figures, but Fullerton notes that net change figures "must be interpreted with caution."

THE SCALE OF THE PROJECTED CHANGES
IN LABOR FORCE COMPOSITION

What *does* the projection developed for *Workforce 2000* actually suggest about the composition of the U.S. labor force in 2000, about the composition of those expected to enter the U.S. labor force between 1985 and 2000, and about the *scale* of the change in composition?

To see this, we calculated the composition of the labor force of 2000 using numbers from *Workforce 2000* (p. xxi) for the base year (1985) and for net new workers. Table 9 presents our figures in columns 1, 3, 5, 6, and 7. Columns 2 and 4 are from *Workforce 2000* (p. xxi and p. 95). The only thing new here is the form of the presentation; we have not changed the assumptions used in *Workforce 2000*. The total number projected for each category of the labor force in 2000 (column 5) is the sum of the number within that category in 1985 (column 1) and the projected number of net new workers (column 3). The percents for 2000 (column 6), calculated from the numbers in column 5, can be compared directly with the percents for 1985 in column 2. (These are the percents in the first bar of Figure 3-7 in *Workforce 2000*).

The projection predicts change in composition, and it predicts a decline in the percent native white male. Thus it predicts increasing labor force diversity. The projected figures for *net* new workers show this in the most striking way: 85 percent of the net new workers will be people other than native-born white males, i.e., they will be native white females or immigrants or blacks, Asians, and other native non-whites. (Native white Hispanics are part of the native white categories.)[4]

At the same time, the projection predicts that native-born white males will continue to enter the U.S. labor force each year in substantial numbers, while other native-born white males leave the

Table 9. Number and Percent Distribution of the U.S. Workforce in 1985 and in 2000 (projected), Projected Net New Workers for 2000, and Projected Percent Change between 1985-2000, by Nativity, Race, and Gender

	Workforce, 1985		Projected Net New Workers 1985-2000		Projected Workforce, 2000		Change in Percent 2000-1985
	Number	Percent	Number	Percent	Number	Percent	Percent
	(1)	(2)	(3)	(4)	(5)	(6)	(7)
Native White Men	54,267[1]	47%	3,750[1]	15%	58,017[1]	41%	-6%
Native White Women	41,566	36	10,500	42	52,066	37	+1
Native Non-white Men	5,773	5	1,750	7	7,523	5	+0
Native Non-white Women	5,773	5	3,250	13	9,023	6	+1
Immigrant Men	4,618	4	3,250	13	7,868	6	+2
Immigrant Women	3,464	3	2,250	9	5,714	4	+1
Total	115,461	100%	25,000[2]	99%	140,461	99%	0%

[1] In 1,000.

[2] Column 3 actually sums to 24,750 because of rounding errors in the percents on which it is based (column 4). Similarly, column 5 sums to 140,211, and column 7 does not sum to 0. The percents in column 6 are the same, whether based on 140,461 or 140,211.

Sources: *Workforce 2000* (1987: xxi) provided the percents in columns 2 and 4 and the total number in the 1985 and the 2000 labor forces. Using these numbers, we calculated the numbers in the other columns.

labor force as they retire, die, lose their job and drop out of the labor force, and so forth. There will be substantial turnover—plus some net growth—for this category. In 2000, native white men will remain numerically the largest category within the U.S. labor force (58 million, col. 5). This is an increase of 3.75 million since 1985 (col. 5 minus col. 1).

Turning to the percent distribution for the projected labor force (col. 6), again we see that "native white men" remains the largest among these six categories, 41 percent in 2000 (col. 6). This percent has declined since 1985 (col. 1), for other categories are projected to grow *more* rapidly. The drop is six percent (47 percent minus 41 percent). Conversely, the other five categories together increase from 53 percent to 59 percent of the labor force. Thus an increasing percent of the labor force consists of women, native non-white men, and immigrant men. The *scale* of the change in percents, however, is 47 percent minus 41 percent—far less than the change implied by comparing 47 percent with 15 percent.

Change since 1970

Now that we have a measure of the extent of the change in composition for each category between 1985 and 2000, we can compare the direction and the scale of change between 1985 and 2000 with the direction and scale of change in the preceding fifteen years. Certainly the implications of a projected change depend, in part, on the extent to which the projected change is out-of-line with the recent trend.

To do this, we compare the projected change for "all white males" between 1985 and 2000 with the actual change for "all white males" between 1970 and 1985. We look at *all* white males rather than just *native* white males because neither the Bureau of the Census nor the Department of Labor provides labor force information separately for the native-born and immigrants. In 1970, white males comprised 56 percent of the U.S. civilian labor force; by 1985, they comprised 49 percent (U.S. Bureau of the Census 1987). This is a drop of seven percent over fifteen years, years in which women's labor force participation rate increased sharply.

To calculate the corresponding percent for 2000 using the *Workforce 2000* projection, we must make an assumption about the percent of the immigrant males who are white. If all immigrant males in the 2000 labor force are white, white males would be 47 percent of the labor force (see col. 6, 41 percent plus 6 percent). If two-thirds of the male immigrants are white, the estimated percent white male in 2000 would be 41 percent plus 4 percent, or 45 percent.[5] This second percent corresponds to the percent predicted by a Department of Labor "moderate" projection of the labor force in 2000: 44.9 percent (Fullerton 1987, 25). Using 45 percent, the change between 1985 and 2000 is 49 percent minus 45 percent, a decrease of 4 percent. The best description of this thirty year trend for the percent "all white males" in the U.S. labor force (minus 7 percent, minus 4 percent) is, we feel, a continuing, but somewhat slowing, decline.

Implications of Increasing Labor Force Diversity

The exact meaning of "net new workers" is not trivial. The projection of the percent of the net new workers in the U.S. labor force who will be native white males seems to be one reason for increased interest in workforce diversity. Managers can perceive successful "multicultural management" as a way to get a crucial competitive advantage as the U.S. workforce becomes more diverse and businesses increasingly operate on a global scale.[6]

Labor force diversity *is* important, but *not* because the U.S. labor force will lack native white males. Indeed, the very importance of creating workplaces that provide opportunities for *all* employees makes any perceived link between increased labor force diversity and changes in corporate practice dangerous. If corporate managers consider changing company practices primarily because they expect the pool of potential managers to change, what will happen to their efforts when they find the pool actually is not changing as much as expected? If a slowing economy or corporate restructuring means they are hiring few new managers overall?

And why assume that managers' concern with labor force diversity will mean an *actual* change in hiring and promotion practices? Other possibilities exist, including reduction in middle-management. Indeed, the authors of *Workforce 2000* do *not* predict a major improvement in overall job prospects for minorities.

THE NATURE OF PROJECTIONS

Media discussions of this labor force projection from *Workforce 2000* convey a sense of inevitability: this *is* what the U.S. labor force will look like in 2000.

The concise presentation of the projection within *Workforce 2000* may contribute to this sense of inevitability. The report presents just one projection of labor force composition, rather than the more conventional set of high, middle, and low projections; and it says little about the assumptions used in the projection. This contrasts with the projection of "high" and "low" figures for the overall *size* of the labor force in 2000 (p. 78).[7] Presenting *one* projection for labor force composition can suggest that variation from the projected composition is unlikely.

Specific wording reinforces the sense of inevitability. *Workforce 2000* presents a list of statements based on the projection as five demographic "facts" (quotation marks are theirs, p. 75), and it includes headings such as "Demographics As Destiny."

Certainly characteristics of the 1985 population set limits on the scope of change likely, even possible, by 2000. This is a short time period, and, as the authors note, everyone who will be in the official labor force in 2000 was alive in 1985. Labor force participation can begin officially at age sixteen, so labor force projections going only fifteen years into the future do not directly incorporate assumptions about changes in the number born each year. This is just one source of variability, however. An unknown number of those who will be in the U.S. labor force of 2000 lived outside the U.S. in 1985, and labor force participation rates can change.

Demography has impact, but demography is _not_ destiny. Other factors, including public policy and corporate practice, will have substantial impact on the future labor force of the U.S.

We are concerned about this sense of inevitability because it can direct attention away from the public and corporate policies that will partially shape U.S. labor force composition in 2000 and thereafter. Consider the range of policies that can affect the labor force participation of people over age fifty. What will happen to their labor force participation if the U.S. develops effective training programs for those employed (or formerly employed) in declining industries? Training programs for those considering early retirement in part because they lack the physical strength to continue in a physically demanding job? If corporations change pensions in ways that provide workers with incentives to delay retirement? If the U.S. adopts guaranteed health care?

Projections

Our emphasis on assumptions and policies may be clearer if we describe the nature of projections. Any projection starts with information for the base year (here 1985) and then works out the consequences of a set of assumptions about processes that will operate between the base year and the final projected year (here 2000).

In labor force projections, base year labor force characteristics plus the size and composition of those just below labor force age set limits on change. The shorter the projected time period, the more important these limits will be. At the same time, the size and composition of a future national workforce will depend, in part, upon immigration policy (and policies about illegal immigration) plus the numbers who want to move in, upon emigration, upon the number and type of jobs available within the economy (and hence the extent to which native and immigrant adults enter or stay in the labor force), and upon a wide range of other factors that affect labor force participation rates.

Thus labor force projections have three parts: (1) base year figures for categories of the labor force, (2) the assumptions used to project these base year figures into the future, and (3) the projected figures for specific future years. With all three, the reader sees the connection between the projected numbers and a set of assumptions, and the reader can estimate the implications of somewhat different assumptions, such as higher immigration.

Because the Department of Labor presents its labor force projections in detail, each part of the projection is clear in the *Monthly Labor Review* articles that present these biannual projections. Two of these projections end with the year 2000 (Fullerton 1987, 1989). Each projection includes (1) labor force size and composition in the base year and (2) assumptions about (a) changes in the number within selected categories who *could* be in the labor force in the final year (e.g., the number of white males age 20-24 in the U.S. in 2000), and (b) assumptions about the labor force participation rate of those in each category. Projections for the number who could be in each category include assumptions about immigration. Different combinations of assumptions lead to the high, medium, and low projections. Articles presenting these projections describe the major assumptions used to project each category. They also show the percent of the projected labor force expected to be in selected categories, e.g., the percent male age 16-24 in 2000, or the percent Hispanic.

The important factor here is the *emphasis*, not the detail. The reader is constantly made aware that projections depend on assumptions, and hence upon a set of factors that can change. These assumptions include assumptions about public and corporate policies.

When a projection must be presented concisely, references to a source that provides a more complete description of the projection might be useful. References to a more complete discussion of the labor force projections summarized in *Workforce 2000* might have reduced the extent to which the national media reinforced common misunderstandings of the figures for "net new workers."[8]

ASSUMPTIONS USED IN THE PROJECTION

Workforce 2000 cites factors that could affect immigration, factors that could affect retirement, and factors that could affect women's labor force participation rates, but it says little about the specific assumptions that were used in this projection. We do not think that reasonable changes in any of the assumptions used in this projection will produce wildly different numbers for 2000. At the same time, a discussion of selected assumptions, some explicit in *Workforce 2000* and some implied, will illustrate possible variations in the composition of the U.S. labor force in 2000 and beyond.

We organize this discussion around the labor force participation rates of people in three overlapping categories, men, women, and immigrants; and we cite policies that can affect the labor force participation of people within each category.

Men

Workforce 2000 says little about the assumptions used to project the labor force participation rates of native white and nonwhite men. The participation rate for men age 55 to 64 declined slowly from the end of World War II to the mid-1980s. A Department of Labor article refers to the expansion of private pension coverage as one reason for this change (Fullerton 1985, 22). Department of Labor projections to 1995 and to 2000 assumed that this decline would continue (Fullerton 1985, 1987). Presumably the authors of *Workforce 2000* also used this assumption. They do refer to "the traditional process of 'creative destruction,' by which a company uses new hires to start a new division, while laying off older workers in slowly growing sectors" (p. 83). Plant closures also have meant early retirements, especially among men. The slow decline in the labor force participation rate for older men reversed after 1985 (Fullerton 1989, 6). Projections to 2005 (Fullerton 1991, 37-38) assume that the participation rate of men age 55 or more will increase. The primary reason for the increase is compositional; men age 55-64 have a higher labor force participation rate than men age 65 or older, and a larger proportion of men age fifty-five or more will be in the category "55-64" in 2000.

What other assumptions could we make?

As the "creative destruction" example points out, decisions about retirement involve prospects for continuing to work. Strong local economies could mean that a larger percentage of the men over age fifty-five remain in the labor force, and some who have retired return. When a plant closes, perhaps more of the men would remain in the labor force if they got more effective assistance in finding new jobs, or if their communities got more effective assistance in increasing local jobs. As for other retirements, what would happen if corporations developed pension plans that incorporated financial incentives for *delaying* retirement? If the U.S. developed public policies that facilitated moves to new companies or to new jobs after age forty?

A range of situations and policies affect the labor force participation rates of younger men. Economic slowdowns can increase the number who remain in school full time. Cutbacks in federal and state financial aid programs for college students can increase the proportion who work while they are in school. Perhaps more important, prospects for employment and the state of the U.S. public education system affect the proportion of young men who are neither in school nor in the "official" labor force. Males with no more than a high school education find it increasingly difficult to locate a stable job that provides benefits such as health insurance and pays much above minimum wage (Commission 1988; Mishel and Bernstein 1993).

Women

Workforce 2000 assumes a continued, but slowing, increase in women's labor force participation rates (pp. 85-87). The authors acknowledge the extent to which economic conditions influence women's participation, noting, for example, that two earners have become a necessity for many families (p. 87). As this suggests, the continued increase in women's (and specifically mothers') labor force participation rates involves (a) stagnant and declining male wages and (b) increases in the costs of basic items such as housing. Together, these trends reduce "choice" about whether or not both husband and wife work. *Workforce 2000* cites a Gallup Poll (p. 87) that found only 13% of the employed mothers wanted to work full time, regular hours. While the specific wording may have contributed to this low percent, it is still intriguing. Changes in families also have impact, for the labor force participation rates of married women living with their husband differ from the participation rates of single, divorced, or widowed women.

We no longer hear much discussion of the "family wage," a wage set at a level that can support a family. What would happen to the labor force participation rates of women (and men) over the next fifteen years if the U.S. economy added a large number of jobs for young workers which paid enough that one worker could support a family at a middle-class level? What would happen if the United States developed a national housing policy that meant a family could be well-housed while spending no more than 25 percent of its income on housing? Or, alternately, if real estate prices collapsed? The implications for labor force participation are, we think, *not* obvious. Some mothers (and some fathers) might leave the labor force, but the change in jobs could attract others. Further, such economic changes can affect labor force participation indirectly, through their effects on family formation and dissolution and on fertility.

The authors of *Workforce 2000* concentrate on other employment-related problems that two-earner and female-headed families confront. They advocate government and corporate policies that make it easier for parents to remain in the labor force: better daycare, family leaves, flexible hours, and so forth. In places, the authors seem to assume that these changes will occur. We would like to share their optimism. Inflexible hours and problems finding adequate child care certainly complicate parents' lives.

While problems with child care and inflexible hours may also somewhat reduce women's labor force participation, the continued move of mothers with young children into the labor force suggests that families are somehow coping. In 1991, 56 percent of the mothers with a husband present and with a child under age *one* were in the labor force (U.S. Bureau 1992). Problems with day care and with inflexible hours have existed for many years now without stimulating large-scale change in corporate practices or in the provision of public services. We do not see convincing evidence—within *Workforce 2000* or anywhere else—that there will be a *sizable* improvement. Indeed, employers may reduce overall fringe benefits if the cost of benefits such as health insurance continues to rise.

If labor force participation rates change in ways that mean the number of women in the labor force of 2000 is *smaller* than that projected, the proportion of the 2000 labor force that is native white male would increase through some combination of two processes. First, if some jobs assumed to be held by women in this projection do not exist in 2000 or exist but go unfilled, the total number in the labor force would decrease, without changing the number of native white males in the labor force. Second, the jobs might exist, and their existence might attract a larger proportion of native white males into the labor force. This pattern also could have implications for occupational sex segregation.

Immigrants

Workforce 2000 cites a range of factors that can affect the size of future immigration streams, both legal and illegal. These factors include international unrest, the strength of the U.S. economy, policies about illegal and legal immigration, conditions in other countries that affect the numbers who want to leave, and so forth.

The impact of changes in immigration is complex. On the one hand, immigration can create jobs that otherwise would not exist. On the other hand, immigrants can compete with native workers for other jobs, and such competition can lower labor force participation rates. These effects are difficult to measure. In their study of Mexican immigration to southern California during the 1970s, Muller and Espenshade (1985) found immigration expanded the total number of jobs, and competition for jobs was largely restricted to workers with low skills. *Workforce 2000* refers to evidence suggesting that direct competition is minor and to evidence suggesting that immigration has benefited local economies (pp. 94-95). This suggests the authors assumed that the level of immigration would have little impact on the labor force participation rates of the native-born. The authors do *not* present these studies of competition as conclusive evidence. This is just one example of a place in which *Workforce 2000* identifies areas for further research.

It is interesting to work out the impact that various hypothetical changes in the number of immigrants would have on the percent native white male in the total labor force for 2000. Suppose immigration declines to the point that there are *no* immigrant net new workers in 2000 and that jobs assumed to be held by immigrant net new workers in this projection simply do not exist. If both conditions occur, the *total* labor force in 2000 drops by 5.5 million, and the percent of this lower total who are native white males increases from 41 percent to 43 percent. If the jobs exist and those projected for "net" male immigrants are filled by native white males who otherwise would not be in the labor force, the percent native white male increases by another percent. Under either set of assumptions, it remains under 47 percent. (For simplicity, we equate labor force participation with employment here.)

PUBLIC AND CORPORATE POLICIES AND
LABOR FORCE PARTICIPATION

Throughout this discussion of assumptions we have pointed out ways in which labor force participation rates respond to political decisions, to corporate decisions, and to economic trends not easily traced to specific decisions. We can see the same connections by focusing on particular policies, such as policies affecting health insurance and pensions.

The United States has a rather unusual way of providing benefits such as health insurance: they are tied to jobs, rather than provided through public agencies. Private pensions may supplement social security. Benefits such as health insurance and pensions vary widely from employer to employer, and not every employer offers these benefits. Leaving a specific job can mean the individual and the family loses these benefits. The proportion of "medium-to-large" companies offering these benefits declined between 1979 and 1991 (Uchitelle 1993). This decline ties workers even more tightly to those jobs that do provide such benefits.

When the authors of *Workforce 2000* discuss the relative rigidity of older workers—that is, their seeming reluctance to change jobs—they note that older workers can be putting in the final years needed to qualify for a company pension (pp. 110-111). Rules about the years of work needed to qualify for lifetime health insurance can have the same effect. Johnston and Packer (1987) also note that pensions can discourage the hiring of older workers, and they suggest changes in federal laws that could promote greater flexibility in private pension systems.

Possibly this way of providing benefits also affects corporate decisions about *how* to get work done. In a period of high demand, employers can require overtime, contract out the work (possibly to a subcontractor who keeps labor costs down by providing few benefits), or hire additional employees, with their wages and fringe benefits. The choice of overtime is common. Overtime further complicates parents' lives, and it lowers the total number of jobs. Subcontracting also is common, and it contributes to the proportion of the U.S. labor force in jobs that provide low incomes and benefits. A basic change in the way U.S. residents get benefits such as health insurance and pensions could have substantial ramifications for the labor force.

IMPLICATIONS OF THE PROJECTED CHANGES IN LABOR FORCE COMPOSITION

Corporate and media response to *Workforce 2000* includes extensive discussions of the advantages of increasing labor force diversity and of the need to prepare for this increasing diversity. The title of a Conference Board report, "In Diversity is Strength: Capitalizing on the New Workforce" (1991) summarizes a common approach. Numerous corporations have developed programs designed to identify and remove blocks to the promotion of minority managers (for examples, see Nesbitt 1991).

Media discussions of increased labor force diversity include the idea that if corporations find it difficult to hire managers from the traditional pool of native white men, they will open management positions to native nonwhite men, to native non-white and white women, and to immigrants. (This argument about management jobs does not appear in *Workforce 2000*.)

"White male jobs" have gone to women or to black men during wars. After World War II, the number of "female" jobs, such as jobs in clerical work, expanded faster than the number of young, unmarried, white women. Eventually employers began to hire married women, older women, and minority women for such jobs (Oppenheimer 1970). Despite such examples, we suspect that changes in the composition of the U.S. labor force *alone* are unlikely to mean that middle and top level management becomes "diverse." One reason for skepticism is the number of middle-management jobs. They have been a rather small proportion of all jobs, and corporations have been streamlining middle management for entirely different reasons (Drucker 1988; Kanter 1989). Newspaper articles on corporate recruitment of recent college graduates emphasize the lack of job offers.

Again, demographics are not destiny. Native white males have been less than half the U.S. adult population, but they have long held the majority of good jobs. *If* a shortage of native white males for management positions should develop, this shortage could mean more opportunities for other people. Alternately, it *could* mean more intense competition among employers for native-born white males, and a bidding-up of their wages. Equality and equity do not naturally flow from short-term change in labor force composition. Greater equality and greater equity require directed attention.

Further, as we have shown, common misunderstandings of the labor force projection in *Workforce 2000* have exaggerated the change in labor force composition that is likely to occur by 2000. In fact, "new" native white men will replace those leaving the labor force, and the projection for 2000 shows "native white men" remains the single largest category. Native white women are expected to constitute about 37 percent of the labor force in 2000, leaving about 22 percent native non-white or foreign-born. All this suggests that corporations will be able to continue practices of exclusion and discrimination.

There are, of course, many *other* reasons for corporations to hire and promote "minority" managers. These reasons would be just as convincing if labor force projections predicted an *increase* in the percent native white male. One of these reasons is that if a corporation does not hire and promote blacks, Asians, or Hispanics (and white women), that corporation misses the contributions of talented people. If a shortage of native white males is the sole, or even a major, motivation for making corporate management more diverse, the likely availability of native white males and females can mean that corporate programs to increase diversity fade away. Loss of effective programs means a distinct loss for the corporations and for the country.

PROJECTED ECONOMIC TRENDS

Other parts of *Workforce 2000*, including the discussion of projected economic trends, also are influencing policy makers. Johnston and Packer use a neoclassical economic paradigm to analyze economic trends and to make recommendation. The future economic trends predicted in *Workforce 2000* are only some of many possible future trends. Here, too, the report does *not* describe destiny.

Because *Workforce 2000* is brief, data sources, major assumptions, and the evidence behind major assumptions are not always explicit.[9] Nonetheless, it is possible to question some presumed assumptions. As the following examples illustrate, sociologists need to become an integral part of economic policy development.

The authors of *Workforce 2000* identify four "key trends" in the U.S. economy, and they make six policy recommendations. One key economic trend summarizes their labor force projection (p. xiii):

1. "The workforce will grow slowly, becoming older, more female, and more disadvantaged."

The other three key economic trends are:

2. "The American economy should grow at a relatively healthy pace,"
3. "U.S. manufacturing will be a much smaller share of the economy in the year 2000," and
4. "The new jobs in service industries will demand much higher skill levels than the jobs of today."

From these trends, the authors develop six recommendations, or "challenges" (pp. xxi-xxii):

1. "Stimulate Balanced World Growth" by helping other economies grow rather than concentrating on protecting U.S. market share.
2. "Accelerate Productivity Increases in Service Industries" by methods such as increasing competition and increasing use of technology.
3. "Maintain the Dynamics of an Aging Workforce."
4. "Reconcile the Conflicting Needs of Women, Work, and Families."
5. "Integrate Black and Hispanic Workers Fully into the Economy."
6. "Improve the Educational Preparation of all Workers."

In this brief section, we raise questions about three topics central to the report's overall argument: (a) the relative importance of manufacturing versus services in the U.S. economy; (b) the implications of increasing service sector productivity; and (c) the value of policies designed to increase competition, and hence productivity.

Manufacturing versus Service Industries

The authors note that manufacturing is a declining proportion of the U.S. economy, while service industries are an increasing proportion. One of the difficulties with U.S. competitiveness, they argue, is the persistence of policies and attitudes that assume manufacturing is the base of the U.S. economy. Thus, they recommended that U.S. policy makers concentrate on the service sector. Here, they believe, the U.S. needs to remove barriers to competition and to invest in technologies that will increase service-sector productivity.

We want to point out, first, that the projected decline in manufacturing involves manufacturing employment and manufacturing as a percent of GNP, not manufacturing output. As the report makes clear, manufacturing productivity has increased. The U.S. continues to produce a substantial amount of manufactured goods, despite declining employment classified as manufacturing. Understanding the role of manufacturing in the U.S. economy requires consideration of output. Further, the distinction between employment and output reminds us that people make decisions about *how* to produce goods, and these decisions affect employment.

There are reasoned arguments for increased investment in manufacturing, including the arguments in work that advocates a new industrial policy (Piore and Sabel 1984; Bluestone and Harrison 1982). Such investment probably should emphasize manufacturing technologies that provide flexibility and customization in production (Piore and Sabel 1984). *Workforce 2000* does not acknowledge these arguments, and the authors do not discuss the human costs of plant closings. "Letting the market work" frequently means dislocations for individuals, families, companies, and communities. These dislocations should be an important consideration for any government.

Productivity as the Key to Economic Growth

The authors of *Workforce 2000* see increased productivity as the key to economic growth and therefore to the quality of life in a country. Expecting the service sector to grow most rapidly, they argue that increasing productivity within service industries will be the most important source of competitiveness for the U.S. economy. Measuring productivity is not a straightforward exercise, however, even for a goods-producing industry. Do we measure output in physical amount? In dollar value? What of changes in quality that are not captured by price changes? Serving more students with a given person-hour of input can mean each student gets less education, but measures of productivity can miss this decline in quality. Thus apparent increases in efficiency can be misleading.

Many discussions of service industries (including that in *Workforce 2000*) propose substituting machines for labor. Johnston and Packer chastise professional groups (tenured professors among them) for acting as obstacles to productivity increases. It is consumers, as much as providers, however, who resist substituting machines for people in fields such as education which require interactive information exchange. Further, the utility of specific substitutions, such as the extensive use of computers in education, has yet to be determined. Effective software requires substantial labor for production, and we suspect that *effective* classroom use is labor intensive.

Because it is so difficult to measure service output, companies trying to measure service productivity are likely to count clients served. This shifts attention from the quality of service to quantity. Classic organizational studies in sociology find that when departments and managers are evaluated on number of clients served, creaming takes place (Blau 1951), i.e., service workers concentrate on the clients who are easiest to serve.

Improved services and, perhaps, increased service productivity are desirable. In trying to reach these goals, however, it is important to consider what might be *lost* if a certain change is made, and to be sure that anticipated gains actually follow.

Further, increased productivity in the service sector means that fewer service workers produce the same total service output. If service output remains about the same, fewer workers are employed providing these services. This, in turn, means fewer jobs overall and greater unemployment. Avoiding unemployment, then, requires combining greater productivity with greater output of services (or goods). It is easy to list places in which the U.S. could expand services, particularly public sector services, but *will* this expansion of public and private services occur? Alternately, workers can have reduced hours. There are few signs of a move toward a shorter work week for "full-time" workers who receive benefits.

Public Monopolies Versus Private Competition

In their discussion of service-sector productivity, Johnston and Packer recommend policies that increase the privatization of public sector services. Privatizing introduces competition, they argue, and thus it increases innovation and productivity.

Again, quality is a critical consideration. How is it that privatization increases productivity? In some cases privatization decreases the *cost* of labor because employees of the private company get lower wages and fewer fringe benefits than the public-sector workers who did the work before privatization. Here privatization becomes part of the reason for concern about the *quality* of jobs within the U.S. economy.

Lower salaries for teachers are one way some private schools keep costs down. Presumably they can still find teachers because they provide a "privileged" atmosphere in which to work. If the U.S. encourages competition among public schools, will school systems allow schools to reject disruptive children? If so, where will these children go? Will teachers accept lower salaries? If not, where will the savings come from?

Creaming is a concern whenever a service is privatized. Private schools, private hospitals, private recreation services, can be selective. A potential patient with an expensive condition and no health insurance can be turned away. A disruptive child can be dropped from a recreation program. Public-sector service organizations do not have this option, and the higher proportion of students or patients who require intensive care raises costs per person served. With privatization of a public service, the private sector would have to serve all clients (thus raising costs), undesirable clients would remain unserved, or public sector organizations would have to continue to serve clients turned down by the private sector.

These points about privatization are not new. The frequency with which they have been mentioned makes it curious that they are not acknowledged in *Workforce 2000*.

We also question *how* the private sector uses competition to be more efficient. It is not just by technological and administrative innovations. Despite the often noted inefficiencies of public bureaucracies and occasional notorious scandals, by and large public bureaucracies run rather lean compared to large private companies. The perquisites which go with office are much less lavish in the public sector than in the private sector. Salaries are much more moderate at the top of public bureaucracies that at the top of private bureaucracies (Ballen 1990), while public salaries can be more generous at lower and middle levels (DiTomaso 1979). The public sector, then, has more equality in compensation, and perhaps this is as it should be.

We assume that there is room for greater efficiency in the public sector, but we see no reason to assume high efficiency in the private sector.[10] Perhaps those who support deregulation and privatization should think about why public monopolies were created. Perhaps certain services should be public monopolies in order to preserve access as well as quality.

Again, these are *open* questions which need to be considered.

CONCLUSION

Workforce 2000 is a valuable and timely contribution to public debate about the changes in the U.S. labor force and economy. It identifies many issues that need public debate. It is important to recognize, however, that this report—as any report—interprets data and projections using unacknowledged assumptions about how the world works. These assumptions involve matters central to sociology, and sociologists need to take part in such discussions.

NOTES

1. This chapter began as a paper presented at the 1990 meetings of the American Sociological Association.

2. We see a similar potential for confusion in the Executive Summary discussion of new jobs (p. xiii). The statement that "service industries will create all of the new jobs" must refer to "net new jobs," for new factories will open between 1985 and 2000.

3. We wish to thank Robert Althauser for the idea of developing such an example.

4. Mishel and Teixeira (1991, 87) examined the figures in detail, and they decided that the *Workforce 2000* projection included native white Hispanics in the native white categories.

5. Roughly 95% of all Hispanics in the U.S. labor force (native and immigrant) are counted as white (Fullerton 1989, 9).

6. A syndicated columnist, Claude Lewis (1991), suggests that some members of the black community have drawn quite different implications from the projected changes in labor force composition. He notes that if the percentage of white males within the labor force declines, Caucasian males may "feel threatened by the darkening of America."

7. For their high estimate of the number in the labor force, the authors combine the highest Census Bureau projections of immigration with the highest Bureau of Labor Statistics projections of labor force participation rates. For their low projection, they combine the lowest estimates of immigration and labor force participation. *Workforce 2000* presents high, middle, and low projections of total economic activity. The authors present an extended discussion of the assumptions behind those projections of total economic activity, and they connect these assumptions to public policies and to corporate practices.

8. *Workforce 2000* mentions a technical appendix available from the Hudson Institute (Jaffe 1987), but this appendix does not describe the labor force projection.

9. The authors note that they rely on Wharton Econometrics, Inc.'s long-term model of the U.S. economy for their description of likely scenarios of the future.

10. Consider what happens when your community organization needs to get 500 fliers run off. Is it a member who works for the public sector or one who works for the private sector who says: "Only 500? No problem. I'll run them off at work tomorrow."

REFERENCES

Ballen, Kate. 1990. "Let them eat bread." *Fortune*, 122 (24):9.

Blau, Peter M. 1951. *The Dynamics of Bureaucracy*. Chicago: University of Chicago Press.

Bluestone, Barry and B. Harrison. 1982. *The Deindustrialization of America*. New York: Basic Books.

Castro, Janice. 1990. "Get Set: Here They Come." *Time*, (fall):50-52.

Commission on Work. 1988. *Pathways to Success for America's Youth and Young Families*. Washington, D.C.: William T. Grant Foundation.

Conference Board. 1991. "In Diversity is Strength: Capitalizing on the New Workforce." Report No. 994. New York: Conference Board.

DiTomaso, Nancy. 1979. "A Comparison of the compensation in public and private employment and the effects of unionization in the public sector." *Journal of Political and Military Sociology*, 7 (spring):53-69.

Drucker, Peter F. 1988. "The Coming of the New Organization." *Harvard Business Review*, 66 (January-February):45-54.

Ehrlich, Elizabeth and Susan B. Garland. 1988. "For American Business, A New World of Workers." *Business Week* (September 19):112-120.

Fullerton, Howard N., Jr. 1985. "The 1995 labor force projections." *Monthly Labor Review* 108 (November):17-26.

———. 1987. "Labor force projections: 1986 to 2000." *Monthly Labor Review* 110 (September):19-29.

———. 1989. "New labor force projections, spanning 1988 to 2000," *Monthly Labor Review* 112 (November):3-12.

————. 1991. "New labor force projections: the baby boom moves on." *Monthly Labor Review* 114 (November):31-44.

Fuchsberg, Gilbert. 1990. "Many Businesses Responding Too Slowly to Rapid Work Force Shifts, Study Says." *Wall Street Journal* (July 20):B.

Jaffe, Matthew P. 1987. "Workforce 2000: Forecast of Occupational Change, Technical Appendix." Indianapolis: Hudson Institute (December).

Johnston, William B. and Arnold H. Packer. 1987. *Workforce 2000: Work and Workers for the 21st Century*. Indianapolis: Hudson Institute.

Kanter, Rosabeth. 1989. *When Giants Learn to Dance*. New York: Simon and Schuster.

Lewis, Claude. 1991. "Genocide or Paranoia?" *New York Times* (January 22):A9.

Mishel, Lawrence and Ruy A. Teixeira. 1991. "The Myth of the Coming Labor Shortage: Jobs, Skills, and Income of America's Workforce 2000." Washington, D.C.: Economic Policy Institute.

Mishel, Lawrence and Jared Bernstein. 1993. *The State of Working America, 1992-93*. Economic Policy Institute Series. Armonk: M.E. Sharpe.

Muller, Thomas and Thomas J. Espenshade. 1985. *The Fourth Wave*. Washington, D.C.: The Urban Institute.

Nesbitt, Jim. 1991. "Diversity Reaching the Top." *The Sunday Star-Ledger*, (November 25): Sec. 3, 1, 7.

Nussbaum, Bruce. 1988. "Needed: Human Capital." Business Week (September 19): 110-103.

Oppenheimer, Valerie. 1970. *The Female Labor Force in the United States: Demographic and Economic Factors Governing Its Growth and Changing Composition*. Westport: Greenwood Press.

Piore, Michael J. and Charles F. Sabel. 1984. *The Second Industrial Divide*. New York: Basic Books.

U.S. Bureau of the Census. 1987. *1988 Statistical Abstract of the United States*. Washington, D.C.: U.S. Government Printing Office, Table 608.

U.S. Bureau of the Census. 1992. *1992 Statistical Abstract of the United States*. Washington, D.C.: U.S. Government Printing Office, Table 621.

Uchitelle, Louis. 1993. "Stanching the Loss of Good Jobs." *The New York Times* (January 31): S. 3, 1, 6.

Wall Street Journal. 1989. "Labor Force Change is Greatly Exaggerated." (September 22): B1.

8

Potential Effects of Increasing the Number of Women in the Scientific and Technological Workforce

Sue V. Rosser

Demographic projections attempting to predict the composition of the workforce at the turn of the century suggest that women and minorities will comprise a much larger portion of paid employees than they have in previous decades. Men of color and women will make up 90% of the workforce growth, with 23% of the new employees being immigrants. The specific breakdown is predicted to divide as follows:

> 23% more Blacks, 70% more Asians and other races (American Indians, Alaska natives and Pacific Islanders), 74% more Hispanics and 25% more women adding 3.6 million, 2.4 million, 6.0 million and 13.0 million more workers respectively (Thomas 1989, 30).

In past decades women and men of color have not been the groups that have been attracted to the scientific and technological workforce in large numbers. Depending upon the scientific or technological field, the percentage of women scientists ranged from a low of 3.7% of employed in engineering to a high of 29.79% employed in the life sciences in 1988 (NSF 1990). These data for the science and engineering workforce compare unfavorably with the overall workforce composition which consists of 45% women and with employment in professional and related occupations where women constitute 50% of the workforce (NSF 1990).

Awareness of the data predicting the changing demographic composition of the workforce coupled with predictions from the Office of Technology Assessment (1987) and other groups (Atkinson 1990) of a shortage of American born and trained scientists, led the government and professional societies to support and encourage programs to attract women and men of color to science and technology. Although questions may be raised about the size of the anticipated shortage of scientists and engineers, particularly in the light of the downsizing and restructuring currently being undertaken by most American corporations, and about the xenophobia implied by the focus on a shortage of *American born* scientists, few question the need to attract more women and minorities (Congressional Task Force on Women, Minorities, and the Handicapped in Science and Technology 1989).

Despite controversy surrounding the accuracy and politics of prediction of a shortage of scientists and engineers, the federal government under the auspices of the National Science Foundation, the Department of Education, and the National Institutes of Health, has poured considerable resources into programs to attract women and minorities to careers in science, engineering, and technology (Congressional Task Force on Women, Minorities, and the Handicapped in Science and Technology 1989). Private foundations and scientific and professional societies have also supported such programs (AAUW 1992).

Many programs have centered on changing men of color and women to fit into science and technology as they are now taught and practiced in the United States. Some programs (Rosser 1993; Tobias 1990) have sought to explore what might be wrong with science and science teaching that it fails to attract men of color and women in percentages proportional to their numbers in the population. From these explorations, some interesting information has been accumulating regarding why many men and women who are capable of doing science, are not attracted to science and engineering because of the way that they are currently taught and practiced.Using this information, some individuals have developed programs which change the teaching of science to include methods and curricular content which are likely to be more attractive to women and men of color (Rosser 1993). Placing the emphasis upon changing the curriculum and approaches to fit the diversity of people to attract them to science represents a substantially different approach from changing diverse people to fit science as it is now taught and practiced. Attention to diversity with the intent of understanding and maintaining the value and difference of perspectives which such diversity within the pool of scientists is likely to yield, increases the possibilities for new and creative approaches to scientific research and practice. As more men of color and women enter the workforce in the twenty-first century, positive benefits and new methods may result from the diverse experiences and perspectives that individuals from these groups hold compared to the white males that have traditionally constituted the overwhelming majority of scientists and engineers.

A considerable body of literature has explored the different effects that having more women and men of color might have on the everyday life and practice of science. Some of these explorations suggest that women may prefer more cooperative (Kahle 1985; Hoffman 1972, 1974) rather than competitive models for the practice of science, might place more emphasis upon the role of scientist as only one facet which must be smoothly integrated with other aspects of their lives (Arnold 1987; Baker 1983; Kahle 1983), and might place increased efforts into teaching and communicating with nonscientists to break down the barriers between science and the lay person.

These effects that women might have on the practice of science are significant and hold the potential to alter significantly the social structure of science. Although several investigators, including the author (Rosser 1990) have written extensively about these effects which might result from the changing demographics in the scientific workforce, that will not be the primary focus of this chapter. The rest of this chapter will center on an exploration of the potential benefits of a more diverse scientific workforce upon the choice and definition of problems for study, approaches used, and theories and conclusions drawn from research, based upon the limited data gathered from research undertaken by men of color and women in science.

CHOICE AND DEFINITION OF PROBLEMS FOR STUDY

Different perspectives may result in new data. Because of their differing experiences and perspectives, men of color and women may perceive new phenomena or different observations when undertaking experiments or examining questions previously explored by the traditional scientists. These new data or phenomena may provide more

than additional information which supports hypotheses and theories and conclusions drawn from the data gathered previously. With
the more complete picture of the phenomenon under investigation,
former hypotheses or theories may have to be revised substantially
now that a more comprehensive picture of reality has been developed
in concordance with the new data.

An example of such new data observation occurred when substantial numbers of female primatologists began observing behaviors of lower primates in the field. Many of these female primatologists (Hrdy 1977, 1979, 1984; Goodall 1971; Fossey 1983) focused
particularly on female-female interaction, in addition to the other
observations of primate behavior. Until this time, male primatologists had centered their observations primarily on other types of
interactions—male-male, male-female, maternal-infant—and had
drawn their hypotheses and conclusions based on those observations.

Although nothing prevented the male primatologists from
observing female-female interaction in lower primates, in fact it had
not served as a focus of their studies. Perhaps female primatologists
were particularly drawn to observing female-female interactions
because their own experience as females made them aware of the
considerable time they spent interacting with other females. The
data they gathered from female-female interaction indicated that
some of the theories surrounding dominance hierarchies and group
interactions did not accurately describe the behavior of the group.
Since these theories had been drawn from information lacking data
about crucial interactions (female-female), they did not represent
the best hypotheses to explain group behavior when a more complete
picture was available. These additional data, collected from a perspective not previously explored, did not simply provide more of
the same kind of information. It caused a rethinking and shift in
the theories and conclusions that could be drawn from the total data
set.

Men of color and women have noted instances where data have
been collected on a restricted sample, often of males only or of
whites only, which is then inappropriately generalized to the entire
population. The use of male animal models and white male humans
to test drugs in clinical trials represents the most dramatic recent
examples of this phenomenon. Considerable publicity generated
from a congressional committee led the General Accounting Office
(GAO) to investigate the extent to which the National Institutes of
Health followed its own protocols (NIH 1986) which required that

both male and female animals and humans be included in investigations of drugs to treat diseases which affect both sexes. When the investigations revealed that not only were women excluded from substantial numbers of clinical trials but also that research investigating diseases of women had been understudied and underfunded, new compliance procedures were instituted (Healy 1991).

Exclusion of individuals affected by diseases from clinical trials has been common outside of the National Institutes of Health. A 1992 article (Gurwitz, Nananda, and Avorn 1992) in the *Journal of the American Medical Association* surveyed the literature from 1960 to 1991 of studies of clinical trials of medications used to treat acute myocardial infarction. Women were included in only about 20% of those studies; elderly people (over 75 years of age) were included in only 40% of such studies. As the authors of the article (Gurwitz, Nananda, and Avorn 1992) concluded, exclusion of women from 80% of the trials and the elderly from 60% of the trials for medication for myocardial infarction limits the ability to generalize study findings to the patient population that experiences the most morbidity and mortality from acute myocardial infarction.

Women researchers and politicians (Narrigan 1991; Pinn and LaRosa 1992) brought the problems of testing on limited populations and then generalizing those test results to the general population to the attention of the public as well as researchers. Perhaps larger numbers of women and men of color designing research protocols and formulating policy will eliminate such biases in research design and inappropriate extrapolation beyond the limits of the data in future studies.

Different perspectives may lead to a re-evaluation of old data and/or testing the hypotheses based on that data in different environments, in different species, or under different time constraints. Because they have a series of life experiences that differ from that of the white male who has traditionally undertaken much of the scientific research, men of color and women may be more likely to search for flaws and biases in data collection when theories and conclusions drawn from the data seem discordant with their experiences.

Recognizing that theories of dominance hierarchies for primate species were drawn from extensive research in only two species, female primatologists (Lancaster 1975; Leavitt 1975; Leibowitz 1975; Rowell 1974) re-examined the early work of Yerkes (1943). Yerkes indicated clearly in his early papers that he had elected to study the baboon and chimpanzee because they exhibited a social organization in which the male was dominant. He saw this as an appropriate animal model for study because it mimicked human social organization in which males dominate. Subsequent researchers forgot the "obvious" limitations imposed by such selection of species and proceeded to generalize the data to universal behavior patterns for all primates.

Rediscovering the reasons for his selection of primate species led female primatologists to study behavior in a wide variety of primate species. Expanding the number of species led to the recognition that male leadership of dominance hierarchies among primate species represented the exception, rather than the norm, for many primate species. Some women scientists (Bleier 1984) have questioned the difficulties involved with studying non-human primates in an attempt to discover what the true nature of humans would be without the overlay of culture.

In addition to expanding the number of species, female primatologists also expanded the environments and time periods during which they studied the primates. Although male primatologists did occasionally intersperse field observation with their observations of primates in the laboratory or in captive environments, Jane Goodall (1971) and Dian Fossey (1983) represented the first primatologists to spend years studying the chimps and gorillas in their natural habitats by actually living in the respective environments of the species they studied. The information they gleaned from lengthy, constant observations of the animals in their natural environments substantially increased the amount, as well as the quality, of data which led to new hypotheses and theories regarding the behavior of these species.

Historical examples from the field of astronomy also support the idea that women spend increased time in observation. Because of sexist attitudes, women astronomers in the past were often relegated to calculating the positions and analyzing other information from photographic plates (Rubin 1986). The calculating was considered tedious and menial, therefore worthy of women's work; planning and directing the projects were men's work. While relegated to this menial role and forbidden to use the giant telescopes until the mid-1960s (Rubin 1986), women astronomers helped develop systems and discoveries that laid the groundwork for modern astronomy. For example, in the early twentieth century Annie Jump Cannon established the classification spectrum for arranging spectral stars in order of decreasing temperature. Henrietta Swan Leavitt's discovery of the Cepheids in 1910 led to the most fundamental method of calculating distances in the universe (Rubin 1986). Based on her own calculations, Caroline Herschel discovered light comets and planned the next day's research, including the direction in which her brother, Sir William Herschel, should point the telescope for his observations. This led to his designation as the "pioneer of modern physical astronomy" (Mozans 1974, 182).

Many women (Chodorow 1978; Gilligan 1982) as well as men from some racial/ethnic backgrounds have been socialized to consider relationship and interdependence in their definition and conception of problems. Because of this, women and some men of color may show an interest in exploring problems of more holistic, global scope. For example, the work female environmentalist Rachel Carson emphasized was the extreme extent to which pesticides were likely to damage all aspects of the environment. Although she turned out to be correct, she extrapolated beyond the available data to underline the fact that pesticides might be carcinogenic and cause chromosomal damage. In her book *Silent Spring* (1962), she painted a picture of contamination, mutation, and possible death for all forms of life—from nitrogen-fixing bacteria up to people—from contamination of ground water due to insecticide runoff from forests and crops into nearby lakes and streams (Hynes 1989). Carson's definition of the problem on a global level contrasts with that of many male quantitative ecologists who seek to demonstrate harmful effects by a quantitative examination of change in the microenvironment.

Perhaps the emphasis upon a holistic definition of problems and consideration of interdependence and relationship leads many women to be unwilling to separate basic research from the social consequences and potential practical applications of that research. Many women scientists (Bleier 1986; Hubbard 1990; Birke 1986) question the sharp distinction male scientists have drawn between the work they do as scientists and the uses society makes of that work. Bleier (1986, 16) calls for a consideration of changing science to consider the effects of its application on a global scale:

> it would aim to eliminate research that leads to the exploitation and destruction of nature, the destruction of the human race and other species, and that justifies the oppression of people because of race, gender, class, sexuality, or nationality.

Women's desire to make the connection between basic research and its practical application may explain the growing body of research (Harding 1983; Lie and Bryhni 1983; Kahle 1985) documenting the attraction and interest of girls and women to science when they can see its beneficial social applications. Limited data from programs to attract minority students to science also suggest that they become particularly interested in science and technology when they can see its practical social benefits, particularly for the community from which they come. Increasing numbers of men of color and women in the scientific workforce might thus result in emphasis upon choosing research problems which might be socially beneficial.

RESEARCH APPROACHES AND METHODS

Women's interest in more holistic, global scope problems in which relationships and interdependencies are explored may lead to the use of a combination of qualitative and quantitative methods for solving the problems. Many of the problems in human health are best approached using both quantitative and qualitative methods. For example, studies of stress typically include such a combination of approaches. Direct quantitative methods may be used to measure prostaglandin levels and other physical stressors; however, psychological sources of stress must be determined in part by qualitative measures since what is stressful to one person may not be equally stressful to another.

More holistic, global scope problems may also require interdisciplinary approaches or methods from a variety of disciplines for their successful solution. Using only the methods traditional to a particular discipline may result in limited approaches that fail to reveal sufficient information about the problem being explored. This may be a particular difficulty for research surrounding medical problems of pregnancy, childbirth, menstruation, and menopause, for which the methods of one discipline are clearly inadequate. Methods which cross disciplinary boundaries or include combinations of methods traditionally used in separate fields may provide more appropriate approaches. For example, if the topic of research is occupational exposures that present a risk to the pregnant women working in a plant where toxic chemicals are manufactured, a combination of methods frequently used in social science research with methods frequently used in biology and chemistry might be the best approach. Checking the chromosomes of any miscarried fetuses, chemical analyses of placenta after birth, Apgar Scores of the babies at birth, and blood samples of the newborns to determine trace amounts of the toxic chemicals would be appropriate biological and chemical methods used to gather data about the problem. In-depth interviews with women to discuss how they are feeling and any irregularities they detect during each month of the pregnancy, or evaluation using weekly written questionnaires regarding the pregnancy progress, are methods more traditionally used in the social sciences for problems of this sort (Rosser 1993).

In addition to insuring that women and men of color are included in research designs that incorporate qualitative and interdisciplinary measures, women researchers may be more open to interactive research designs which shorten the distance between the researcher and the subject of study. "Particularly for understanding human, gender-related health, we need more interactive and contextual models that address the actual complexity of the phenomenon that is the subject of explanation" (Hamilton 1985).

Elizabeth Fee (1982, 24) demonstrates that active participation of subjects using qualitative methods may provide different, but equally useful, information compared to the double blind study, in testing drugs.

> Prior to 1969, occupational health research was done by specialists who would be asked by management to investigate a potential problem in the factory . . . The procedure was rigorously objective, the results were submitted to management. The workers were the individualized and passive objects of this kind of research. In 1969, however, when workers' committees were established in the factories, they refused to allow this type of investigation . . . Occupational health specialists had to discuss the ideas and procedures of research with workers' assemblies and see their "objective" expertise measured against the "subjective" experience of the workers. The mutual validation of data took place by testing in terms of the workers' experience of reality and not simply by statistical methods; the subjectivity of the workers' experience was involved at each level in the definition of the problem, the method of research, and the evaluation of solutions. Their collective experience was understood to be much more than the statistical combination of individual data; the workers had become the active subjects of research involved in the production, evaluation, and uses of the knowledge relating to their own experience.

The interactive approach used in this research design yields different data than those yielded from double-blind studies in which neither the researcher nor the subject knows who has received the drug and who has received the placebo. Has the privileging of the double-blind study to the exclusion of more interactive approaches led to the loss of valuable information? Women researchers suggest that expanding the battery of approaches might increase the quality as well as the quantity of information.

THEORIES AND CONCLUSIONS DRAWN FROM THE DATA

Scholarship produced by female linguists and other individuals studying gender, race, and language (Lakoff 1975; Kramarae and Treichler 1986) reveals that sexism and racism in language may do more than exclude and offend women and men of color. Language shapes conceptualizations and provides frameworks through which ideas are expressed.

As more women have entered primate research, they have begun to challenge the language used to describe primate behavior and the patriarchal assumptions inherent in searches for dominance hierarchies in primates. Jane Lancaster (1975, 34) describes a single-male troop of animals as follows:

> For a female, males are a resource in her environment which she may use to further the survival of herself and her offspring. If environmental conditions are such that the male role can be minimal, a one-male group is likely. Only one male is necessary for a group of females if his only role is to impregnate them.

Her work points out the androcentric bias of primate behavior theories which would describe the above group as a "harem" and consider dominance and subordination in the description of behavior. One might imagine a gynocentric bias in which the male in the group would be called a "stud."

Approximately eighteen months after I had used this example in a talk I had given at a major university, I received a call from a researcher in animal behavior. She informed me that hearing my talk had revolutionized her research. Before the talk she had used the term "harem" for years in describing the interactions she had observed among the sharks she was studying. After the talk, she attempted to use the more gender neutral language of one male and several females. To her surprise, when she conceptualized the interactions this way, she actually began to observe new behaviors which had not previously been visible to her. As she suggested, what had changed was not the way the sharks were behaving but the language she used to describe and think about their behaviors. When she changed her language, she saw new behaviors which then led her to draw new theories and conclusions from her observations.

Similarly, the limited research on AIDS in women focuses on women as prostitutes or mothers. Describing the woman as a vector for transmission to men (prostitute) or the fetus (mother) has produced little information on the progress of the AIDS disease in women themselves (Rosser 1991). Once the bias in the terminology is exposed, the next step is to ask whether that terminology leads to a constraint or bias in the theory itself.

An androcentric perspective may lead to formulating theories and conclusions drawn from medical research to support the status quo of inequality for men of color and women. Because they are more aware of the potential for such biases, men of color and women who are scientists hold a significant perspective from which they may examine when theories and conclusions drawn from data may be permeated with sexist, racist, classist, sexual orientation, or other biases which may lead to inferior diagnosis and treatment for women and men of color.

Androcentric bias in AIDS research (Marte and Anastos 1990; Rosser 1991) may also lead to underdiagnosis and higher death rates for women. Because the progress of AIDS in women has not been adequately studied and since the Centers of Disease Control (CDC) Case Definition for AIDS failed until January 1993 to include any gynecologic conditions, most health care workers are unable to diagnose AIDS in women until the disease has advanced significantly. The average death after diagnosis in men is thirty months; for women it is fifteen weeks (Rosser 1991). The representation of more women and men of color in the ranks of individuals designing and undertaking research will help to uncover the extent to which sexism, racism, classism, and homophobia have biased the theories and conclusions drawn from AIDS research which results in the differential earlier death of women and men of color compared to white men after diagnosis with AIDS.

CONCLUSION

Scientific and technological research represent explorations by human beings to uncover knowledge and information about the physical and natural world. All human beings bring experiences and perspectives to their search for knowledge that may be biased in part by their gender, race, class, sexual orientation and a myriad of other attributes they hold as human beings. For decades in the United States, an overwhelming majority of the individuals undertaking research in science, engineering, and technology have been male, white, and middle- to upper-class. Although there is nothing wrong with being male, white and middle-class, any biases that might result from such attributes were unlikely to be eliminated from research since most scientists searching for bias shared the homogeneity of those attributes.

To eliminate bias, the community of scientists undertaking research needs to include individuals from backgrounds of as much variety and diversity as possible with regard to race, class, gender, and sexual orientation (Rosser 1988). Only then is it less likely that the perspective of one group will bias research designs, approaches, subjects, and interpretations.

The changing demographics of the United States which predict that most of the workforce growth by the year 2000 will be men of color and women plus the current programs to attract more individuals from those groups to careers in science and technology should increase substantially the diversity in the pool of research scientists. Increasing diversity is likely to help eliminate racial, gender, and other biases that have sometimes flawed scientific research. This elimination demonstrates one of the positive aspects of the changing composition of the workforce in modern times.

REFERENCES

American Association of University Women Educational Foundation. 1992. *How Schools Shortchange Girls*. Washington, D.C.: AAUW Educational Foundation.

Arnold, Karen. 1987. *Retaining high achieving women in science and engineering*. Paper presented at Women in Science and Engineering: Changing Vision to Reality conference, University of Michigan, Ann Arbor. Sponsored by the American Association for the Advancement of Science.

Atkinson, Richard C. 1990. *Supply and demand for scientists and engineers: A national crisis in the making*. Presidential Address, AAAS National Meeting, New Orleans, February 18.

Baker, D. 1983. "Can the difference between male and female science majors account for the low number of women at the doctoral level in science?" *Journal of College Science Teaching*, Nov.:102-107.

Birke, Lynda. 1986. *Women, feminism, and biology: The feminist challenge*. New York: Methuen.

Bleier, Ruth. 1984. *Science and Gender: A critique of biology and its theories on women*. Elmsford, NY: Pergamon Press.

———. 1986. "Sex differences research: Science or belief?" In Ruth Bleier (Ed.), *Feminist approaches to science*. Elmsford, NY: Pergamon Press, 147-164.

Carson, Rachel. 1962. *Silent spring*. New York: Fawcett Press.

Chodorow, Nancy. 1978. *The reproduction of mothering: Psychoanalysis and the sociology of gender*. Berkeley and Los Angeles: The University of California Press.

Congressional Task Force on Women, Minorities, and the Handicapped in Science and Technology. 1989. *Changing America: The new face of science and engineering*. Final Report of the Congressional Task Force on Women, Minorities, and the Handicapped in Science and Technology.

Fee, Elizabeth. 1982. "A feminist critique of scientific objectivity." *Science for the People* 14 (4):8.

Fossey, Dian. 1983. *Gorillas in the mist*. Boston: Houghton Mifflin.

Gilligan, Carol. 1982. *In a different voice: Psychological theory and women's development*. Cambridge, MA: Harvard University Press.

Goodall, Jane. 1971. *In the shadow of man*. Boston: Houghton Mifflin.

Gurwitz, Jerry H., Col. F. Nananda, and Jerry Avorn. 1992. "The exclusion of the elderly and women from clinical trials in acute myocardial infarction." *Journal of the American Medical Association* 268 (11):1417-1422.

Hamilton, Jean. 1985. "Avoiding methodological biases in gender related research. In *Women's health report of the Public Health Service Task Force on Women's Health Issues*. Washington, D.C.: US Department of Health and Human Services Public Service.

Harding, Jan. 1983. *Switched off: The science education of girls*. Schools Council programme 3, York, England: Longman Resources Unit.

Healy, Bernadine. 1991. "Women's health, public welfare." *Journal of the American Medical Association* 264 (4):566-568.

Hoffman, Lois W. 1972. "Early childhood experiences and women's achievement motives." *Journal of Social Issues*, 28 (2):129-155.

Hoffman, Lois W. 1974. "Fear of success in males and females: 1965 and 1971." *Journal of Consulting and Clinical Psychology*, 42:353-358.

Hrdy, Sarah. B. 1977. *The langurs of Abu: Female and male strategies of reproduction.* Cambridge: Harvard University Press.

———. 1979. "Infanticide among animals: A review, classification and examination of the implications for the reproductive strategies of females." *Ethology and Sociobiology* 1:3-40.

———. 1984. "Introduction: Female reproductive strategies." In M. Small (Ed.), *Female primates: Studies by women primatologists.* New York: Alan Liss.

Hubbard, Ruth. 1990. *The politics of women's biology.* New Brunswick, NJ: Rutgers University Press.

Hynes, Patricia. 1989. *The recurring silent spring.* Elmsford, NY: Pergamon Press.

Kahle, Jane B. 1983. *The disadvantaged majority: Science education for women.* Burlington, NC: Carolina Biological Supply Company. AETS Outstanding Paper for 1983.

———. 1985. *Women in science.* Philadelphia, PA: Falmer Press.

Kramarae, Cheris and Paula Treichler. 1986. *A feminist dictionary.* London: Pandora Press.

Lakoff, Robin. 1975. *Language and woman's place.* New York: Harper and Row.

Lancaster, Jane. 1975. *Primate behavior and the emergence of human culture.* New York: Holt, Rinehart and Winston.

Leavitt, Ruth. 1975. *Peaceable primates and gentle people: Anthropological approaches to women's studies.* New York: Harper and Row.

Leibowitz, Lila. 1975. "Perspectives in the evolution of sex differences. In Rayna Reiter (Ed.), *Toward an anthropology of women.* New York: Monthly Review Press, 20-35.

Lie, Svein, and Eva Bryhni. 1983. "Girls and physics; Attitudes, experiences and underachievement." *Contributions to the Second Girls and Science and Technology Conference.* Oslo, Norway: University of Oslo, Institute of Physics, 202-211.

Marte, Christine and Karen Anastos. 1990. "Women—the missing persons in the AIDS epidemic, Part II." *Health/PAC Bulletin* 20 (1):11-23.

Mozans, H.J. 1974. *Women in science—1913*. Cambridge, MA: The MIT Press.

Narrigan, Deborah. 1991. "Research to improve women's health: An agenda for equity." *The Network News: National Women's Health network*. March/April/May, 3, 9.

National Science Foundation. 1990. *Report on women and minorities in science and engineering*. NSF 90-301. Washington, D.C.: author.

"NIH urges inclusion of women in clinical study populations." 1986. *National News and Development* 16 (2):3.

Office of Technology Assessment. 1987. *New developments in biotechnology background paper: Public perceptions of biotechnology*. OTA-BP-BA-45. Washington, DC: OTA.

Pinn, Vivian and Judith LaRosa. 1992. "Overview: office of research on women's health." *National Institutes of Health*, 1-10.

Rosser, Sue V. 1990. *Female friendly science*. Elmsford, NY: Pergamon Press.

———. 1988. "Women in science and health care: A gender at risk." In S.V. Rosser (Ed.), *Feminism within the science and health care professions; Overcoming resistance*. Elmsford, NY: Pergamon Press.

———. 1991. "AIDS and women." *AIDS Education and Prevention*, 3 (3):230-240.

Rosser, Sue V. and Bonnie Kelly. 1994. "From hostile exclusion to friendly inclusion." *Journal of Women and Minorities in Science and Engineering*, 1:29-44.

Rowell, Thelma. 1974. "The concept of social dominance." *Behavioral Biology* 11:131-154.

Rubin, Vera. 1986. "Women's work: For women in science, a fair shake is still elusive." *Science* 86:58-65.

Thomas, Valerie. 1989. "Black women engineers and technologists." *Sage* VI (2): 24-32.

Tobias, Sheila. 1990. *They're not dumb, They're different*. Tucson, AZ: Research Corporation.

Yerkes, R.M. 1943. *Chimpanzees*. New Haven: Yale University Press.

III

Future Directions

9

The Worker as Active Subject:
Enlivening the "New Sociology of Work"

Randy Hodson

The theory and practice of workplace relations was dominated until recently by industrial psychologists, human relations sociologists, organizational theorists, and management consultants (see Walton and Hackman 1986). The theories and goals of these researchers led them to an analysis of individual and small group phenomena in the workplace. When problems occurred at work, individuals and group processes were identified as the cause. The proposed solutions to workplace problems typically involved changes in management style, in payment systems, in the socialization and values of workers, in the socio-technical organization of work, and in small group structure (see Mayo 1945).

Recent decades have seen the emergence of a sustained critique of this individual and small group approach to the workplace. Those who have participated in this critique have argued that individualistic and small group approaches miss the "big structures" that mold work and the workplace. These critiques have come from several different sources including the dual economy and dual labor market literatures (Averitt 1968; Gordon 1972; Bonacich 1976), the labor process literature (Braverman 1974), and the "new industrial sociology" centered in Great Britain (Edwards 1986; Edwards and Scullion 1982; Friedman 1977; Thompson 1983). The large scale structures these critics feel have been overlooked include those of exploitation, deskilling, and labor market segmentation.

The structuralist critique has generated new energy and insight in fields that had grown increasingly stagnant. It has not, however, been without its costs (see Simpson 1989). The earlier management-inspired view of the worker as an object to be either cajoled or encouraged into cooperation, has been replaced by a view of workers as manipulated by forces even further removed from workers' immediate control. Rather than theoretically liberating the worker from control by management, such theories have replaced supervisory and management control with control emanating from system imperatives. In such accounts, the worker is allowed even less of a theoretical role as active participant in the workplace. These earlier theories explicitly recognized that workers had at least a limited role as active subjects in the workplace and recognized this role through studies of soldiering and other types of output restriction in work groups (Roy 1954).

This theoretical shortcoming in the structural critique of industrial sociology, organizational behavior research, and social stratification research has led to difficulties in explaining and interpreting current changes in the workplace. These changes include management practices entailing an increased focus on quality circles and worker participation and changing technologies based on the application of microprocessor related technologies to the workplace. The structural analysis of the workplace has generated few insights that inform us about these processes, their implications and limitations, or their probable future directions.

While the structural critique has produced many valuable concepts, including those of economic segmentation, deskilling, and core-periphery relations, we need to extend this critique by incorporating a vision of the worker as active agent in organizing the nature of work. This new sociology of work, which includes both structural elements and an image of the worker as an active agent in determining the nature of work, can be used to inform related literatures on human relations, complex organizations, working-class culture, workplace democracy, and collective action. A new sociology of work that includes both structure and agency has the potential to reestablish for industrial sociology a leading role in addressing questions at the mainstream of sociology (Hodson and Sullivan 1990).

A Typology of Worker Behaviors

In this section I develop a typology of worker behaviors that incorporates the worker as active agent. Worker behavior can be conceptualized around three central dimensions: behavior oriented toward the individual's goals, behavior oriented toward group goals, and behavior oriented toward the organization's goals. A typology based on these three goals of worker behavior is presented in Figure 3. In this typology each dimension is divided between positive and negative poles. Thus, behavior may meet or fail to meet individual, group, or organizational goals.

Eight cells depicting possible worker behaviors are created by cross-classifying individual, group, and organizational goals. The group may be defined as a small shop floor group or as a broader group, such as an occupational community or a social class. Behaviors that are oriented toward small group goals are much more common than behaviors that are oriented toward social class goals. As the literature on social movements informs us, revolutionary class behaviors, or even genuinely reformist class-oriented behaviors, are relatively uncommon. Instead, workers generally struggle to "get by," or to "make out" (Burawoy 1979). The literature on strikes and collective bargaining tells us that class-oriented behaviors are unlikely unless workers have power, based on their position in the division of labor or in the labor market, and they possess a strong organization and a strong organizing ideology (Cornfield 1989). Class-oriented behaviors are, however, a possibility. The literature on workplace democracy argues that such behaviors are capable of overcoming schisms between various factions of workers and that organized workers are capable of carrying out the functions of management. The dimension depicting group goals can thus be interpreted either in terms of shop floor groups or in terms of larger social groups such as classes or occupational communities.

In the left hand table in Figure 3, four cells depict possible behaviors that meet group goals. Workers who meet personal, organizational, *and* group goals can be labeled "pros." At some level,

Figure 3. A Typology of Worker Behaviors

| | | Group Goals (+) Individual Goals | | Group Goals (-) Individual Goals | |
		(+)	(-)		(+)	(-)
Organiza-tional Goals	(+)	pro	sucker	(+)	brown noser	company man
	(-)	regular guy/ union man	saboteur	(-)	smooth operator	wimp

this is what we all want to be. Those who meet personal and group goals but resist organizational goals are labeled "regular guys," or they might be called a "union man" in a unionized context. Such workers use the power based on their position in the division of labor to attain both individual and group goals and to resist the imposition of organizational goals. Those who fail to meet individual goals but who act to meet group and organizational goals might be labeled "suckers." We all feel like we have acted like this at times, that we have been taken advantage of, that we have not looked out for ourselves. The final cell in this table is defined by meeting group goals but not meeting individual and organizational goals. I hesitatingly label such behaviors "sabotage" in recognition of their antithesis to organizational goals, their generally collective character, and their non-constructive nature for the individual (Taylor and Walton 1971). However, there are forms of sabotage that do not fit in this cell. Some acts of sabotage may be purely for the release of individual frustrations (Molstad 1988; Westwood 1984). Such behaviors would fall into the "regular guy" cell. Other acts of sabotage may be for the purpose of pressuring management to change objectional job conditions (Jermier 1988). Such acts are oriented toward the attainment of individual and group goals and would thus also fall in the "regular guy" cell (Hodson 1991; Weinstein 1979). I label this behavioral cell saboteur with an awareness that not all acts of sabotage are counterproductive for the individual.

The right hand table in Figure 3 depicts behaviors that do *not* meet group goals. Individuals engaging in these sorts of behaviors may meet their own needs or organizational needs but rarely meet group needs. Thus, they will tend to be social isolates to some degree. Most of us try to avoid being identified with these types of behaviors. Those who meet organizational and personal goals but not group goals can be labeled "brown nosers." We have all encountered this type. The literature on human resource management is full of suggestions on how to set up organizational rewards so that individuals experience an overlap between their own interests and those of the organization and so that the attraction of alternative group goals is minimized. It is perhaps surprising that this cell does not include even a larger share of behavior at the workplace given the potential rewards of such behaviors. Those who meet individual goals but neither group nor organizational goals can be labeled "smooth operators." Such behaviors feather the individual's own nest. These behaviors may be at the expense of organizational and group goals. Or, they may facilitate organizational and group goals.

Indeed, a good smooth operator often selects behaviors that both facilitate their own goals and group and organizational goals. Such behaviors would be identical with those of the "pro." However, for the smooth operator, the leading motivation is personal gain, not group or organizational gain. When these goals come into conflict, the behaviors of smooth operators and pros become differentiated. Those who do not meet individual or group goals, but who act to meet organizational goals are labeled "company men." Their behavior recognizes only the goals of the formal organization as valid and ignores both individual and work group goals. The final type of behavior is that which fails to meet individual, group, or organizational goals. Such behaviors are anemic and the individuals who engage in them are often labeled "wimps" or some equally pejorative term. Such behaviors are unsuccessful at meeting any goals and are counterproductive for all concerned.

It will perhaps be illuminating for the reader to review again the behavioral categories we have just discussed but in a different order. This can be done by first considering the four types of behavior that meet individual goals and the four types of behavior that do not meet individual goals. Next, review the four types of behavior that meet organizational goals and the four types of behavior that to not meet organizational goals. Finally, review the four types of behavior that meet group goals and the four types of behavior that do not meet group goals.

A MODEL OF WORKER BEHAVIORS

At this point we turn to the task of modeling the behaviors outlined above. This model includes a central role for the worker as active participant. A schematic version of this model is presented in Figure 4. On the left side of Figure 4 are measures of objective job and workplace characteristics. These factors create motivations and provide resources that eventually become translated into behaviors. Thus, organizational structure and technology allow certain types of behaviors, but prohibit others, or make them more difficult. For example, the use of a new technology, the output potential of which is understood only by workers, empowers workers with greater control over their work. Similarly, the opportunities for advancement in a job create motivations in workers to engage in certain types of behavior if these are available. High pay and opportunities for advancement reduce quits, even if the work is onerous. These job

Figure 4. A Model of Worker Behaviors

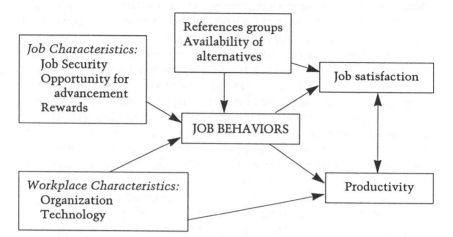

and workplace characteristics, which create the motivations and opportunities for action, play a similar conceptual role to the concepts of grievances and resources for action identified by the sociological analysis of collective action. Small group processes, cultural factors, organized worker power, and ideology enter this model as mediating factors that facilitate or discourage the selection and utilization of specific behaviors.

The job behaviors positioned in the center of Figure 4 are diverse and impossible to reduce to a single dimension of positive versus negative, constructive versus destructive, or rational versus irrational. Figure 3 offers a tentative model of these behaviors based on how the behaviors reflect individual, group, and organizational goals. The behavior selected by a worker in turn gives rise to both job satisfaction and productivity. The job satisfaction and productivity of workers depend on the behavioral strategy they select and on their success in implementing those strategies. In this model, job satisfaction is influenced by working conditions but only after these conditions are mediated by workers' selection of behavioral strategies.

Job satisfaction also depends on the reference groups that workers use to evaluate their situation and on the availability of alternative employment opportunities (Hodson 1985). If a worker's friends and relatives are doing better than the worker, then he or she will be dissatisfied. However, if few opportunities for improving his or her condition exist, then expectations will be downgraded and job dissatisfaction will be repressed in the interests of reducing cognitive dissonance that might arise from being stuck in a dissatisfying job. Workers' reference groups and the availability of alternatives may also influence their selection of behaviors at work. Job satisfaction is thus a result of workers' behaviors and their expectations and options; it is a result of job and workplace conditions only as these are mediated by the behavioral options workers select.

Productivity in this model results from workers' behavioral strategies and from the organizational structure and technology used in production. Note that productivity and job satisfaction are not causally related in this model. Thus, any relationship between them results from their common roots in workers' behavioral strategies. For instance, a successful strategy of being a pro will increase both productivity and job satisfaction, giving rise to the appearance of a relationship between productivity and job satisfaction. Being a sucker, however, will increase productivity but not necessarily satisfaction.

The model of worker behaviors outlined in Figures 3 and 4 has important implications for how we approach the study of the workplace. These implications are developed in the following sections by analyzing recent development in the major subfields of industrial sociology.

IMPLICATIONS OF CONCEPTUALIZING THE WORKER AS AN ACTIVE SUBJECT

In this section I will explore some of the implications that can be derived from a model of the active worker for current research in industrial sociology. The literatures reviewed include those on organizational behavior, working-class culture, workplace democracy, strike behavior, collective action and resource mobilization, and technology and work.

Organizational Behavior

Much of the early organizational behavior literature was motivated by a desire to increase worker productivity and to reduce worker resistance to work through soldiering, working to rule, sabotage, striking, or forming unions. Not all early studies in industrial sociology, however, were motivated by these goals (see for example, Nosow and Form 1962). Nor should the findings of these studies be completely discounted because of their motivating question. Serendipitous findings abound in this field: recall for a moment the discovery of the Hawthorne effect (Roethlisberger and Dickson 1939). Even though increasing productivity was the common orienting goal of these studies, the existence and importance of small group processes among workers was the most important and lasting finding.

Much of this literature was organized and presented to a generation (or more) of sociologists in Miller and Form's seminal text, *Industrial Sociology* (1951, 1964, 1980). The materials covered in this text include small group processes, informal work behavior, cliques, ceremonies, rituals, and beliefs and myths. Informal processes and emergent cultures in small groups have continued as favored topics in the human relations literature and in several related literatures influenced by its traditions, including urban anthropology (Bensman and Gerver 1963; Mars 1982) and the sociology of occupations (Abbott 1988; Haas 1987; Pavalko 1988). It is important not to lose these insights about small group processes and workplace cultures as we develop theories that also take larger scale structures into account.

Contemporary theories of human relations in industry continue to be dominated by concerns for productivity. Yet such theories sometimes also include an active view of the worker. The new theories that have emerged are often referred to collectively as Theory Z (Ouchi 1981). These theories view productivity as embedded in workers, in their skills, in their attitudes, and, most centrally, in the small group structure of work, rather than as embedded in specific bureaucratic procedures or in particular management styles. Indeed, much of the new theorizing about human relations at work has been motivated by the inefficiencies and rigidities associated with bureaucratic means of motivating workers and allocating rewards. In Europe, these theories have helped motivate and legitimate the widespread use of work groups in the labor process. Under the group organization of work, teams of workers have at least a limited degree of control over decision making about their day-to-day operations and activities (Gyllenhammar 1977; see also Dohse, Jurgens and Malsch 1985; Grenier 1988; Parker 1985).

Such theories of productivity have been implemented in Japan through the concept of "life-time employment" (Abegglen and Stalk 1985). Guaranteeing life-time employment to workers insures their job security and thus their trust in the organization and their enthusiasm for work. It also retains workers' presence in the organization as a repository of skills and knowledge (Cole 1989). These benefits are amplified by having workers rotate through a variety of jobs during their careers, thus building their reservoirs of knowledge. This accumulated knowledge is invaluable for coordinating activities between different parts of the organization and is a more efficient mechanism for coordinating and integrating production than more bureaucratic structures.

Potential tensions between the worker as active agent and the labor process as worker control are highlighted by Burawoy's analysis of "making out" on the shop floor. Burawoy (1979) argues that workers devise a variety of ways to "make out" on their jobs. Often this entails maneuvering to keep piece rates up and to keep time allocations for work high. Burawoy argues that organized and individual acts of resistance are the everyday stuff of workplace life and he observes that workers take great pride in devising creative ways to make out.

Burawoy also notes, however, that workplace struggles are often displaced from management onto relations between co-workers. Thus, in the factory Burawoy studied, struggles over making out were often translated into struggles between production workers and tool crib attendants or struggles between production workers and fork lift drivers. Such conflicts between workers are also noted by Sabel (1982, 16): "Each group's defense of its own niche in the division of labor can isolate it from its most likely allies against management, the other groups in the plant." Such conflicts are labeled "lateral displacements" by Thompson (1983).

In *The Politics of Production*, Burawoy (1985) takes an even more pessimistic view of worker struggle on the shop floor. He refers to the new shop floor relations as "hegemonic despotism." He argues that the despotism of early factory regimes is replaced by a hegemonic despotism in contemporary capitalism in which workers' patterns of making out become part of the system that reproduces exploitation. That is, capitalists have organized the production process so that the available means of making out serve to displace conflict from the management-worker relationship to relationships between different groups of workers or to make the only available solutions ones in which workers participate in their own heightened exploitation. Thus, workers' solutions (ways of making out) serve to reproduce the system of exploitation rather than to change it. This view seems overly negative and may overlook important ways in which workers' activities of resistance limit and condition the labor process and structure the nature of worklife (Tucker 1993).

The analysis of small group processes and effort bargaining at the workplace need to be incorporated into the new sociology of work. These insights and observations are frequently either treated with disdain by critical theorists because of their association with the management goal of increased productivity or relegated to the theoretical dustbin of obscurity by considering them "displacements" that serve only to reproduce the existing system. However, the insights that workers are social animals, work best in small groups, help each other to learn, and can be controlled by peer pressure need to be taken seriously, rather than jettisoned as excess baggage or rejected as theoretically trivial. These insights provide essential building blocks toward a more active vision of the role of workers in structuring the nature of work.

Working-Class Culture

There is a vast literature on working-class culture both on and off the shop floor that has often been poorly integrated into the sociology of work (Fantasia 1988). Paul Willis' *Learning to Labour* (1977) is one of the more widely read contributions to this literature. Willis focuses on the culture of working-class youth as they encounter the educational system. Willis argues that working-class kids experience school in much the same way that their parents experience work and that they themselves will experience work: as an alien imposition. They resist this imposition: "Opposition to the school is principally manifested in the struggle to win symbolic and physical space from the institution and its rules and to defeat its main perceived purpose: to make you 'work'" (Willis 1977, 26).

Forms of oppression, first experienced in the school and later in the workplace, provide the basis for a working-class culture of resistance to regimes of enforced labor. The pace and timing of work in modern industrial nations is based on periods of forced intense labor alternating with periods of forced inactivity when no work is available (for example, during "leisure time" or during periods of unemployment). Workers often resist this pattern, preferring to establish cycles of intense labor and periodic idleness under their own control through working ahead, soldiering, and so on (Cavendish 1982; Juravich 1985; Thompson 1967). Craft workers also frequently follow a norm of refusing to work while being watched by a supervisor in order to preserve their skills from interference and to preserve specified time allocations (Hamper 1991; Montgomery 1979, 42).

Working-class culture prescribes pride work, particularly for skilled craft workers. In a discussion of machinists, Shaiken (1984, 28) lists four elements in this cultural matrix: "pride of craftsmanship, independence on the job, a sensitivity to changes in skill and job content, and a strong sense of collective action." Working-class cultural norms for workplace behavior are thus not restricted to resistance but also include positive agendas for taking charge of how work is to be performed and for the content of workplace relations (Wardell 1990).

Although the analysis of working-class culture and shop floor practices is generally looked upon favorably by advocates of the new sociology of work because it takes the "worker's viewpoint," little has been done to incorporate its insights into new structural models of the workplace. The insights of working-class resistance, pride, group solidarity, and intergroup competition and conflict thus have had only a limited role in the new sociology of work.

Workplace Democracy

Researchers on workplace democracy argue that workplace democracy provides an alternative to bureaucratic organizations and a solution to some of their inefficiencies (Cooke 1990; Rothschild-Whitt 1979). Workplace democracy and worker ownership are also seen as partial solutions to the problem of plant closings (Lindenfeld 1982), as a way to get needed work done in society (Pearson and Baker 1982), as a way to provide work for marginal groups in society (Zwerdling 1980), as a way to foster alternative value systems (Schlesinger and Bart 1982; Schrank 1983), and, potentially, as a way to transform society (Gorz 1973; Schuster 1984).

The ways in which greater worker participation can be incorporated into the workplace are extremely diverse (Greenberg 1987). One important form of worker participation occurs through small work groups of 8 to 12 that are given collective responsibility for a task (Lillrank and Kano 1989). Such groups can be an important source of innovation. Worker participation can also occur through consultation with workers at various levels of the organization from the shop floor to the board room. Such participation can include consultation with union leaders, consultation with elected bodies of workers, as in Germany's workers' councils, or worker representation on boards of directors or on national economic planning boards, as in Sweden (Russell and Rus 1991).

Worker participation programs have had a difficult birth in North America. No broad policy agenda guides their development and no systematic social theory lights their way (Sirianni 1987; Woodworth, Meek and Whyte 1985). One relatively common type of worker participation in North America, however, is based on worker ownership through Employee Stock Ownership Plans (ESOPs). In 1987, 8.6 million workers, or about 7 percent of the labor force, participated in ESOPs (*New York Times* 1987). These ESOPs include both employer-initiated plans and union-initiated plans. Union initiated ESOPs have become of increasing importance in rescuing failing companies in order to save jobs. Worker buy-outs have also provided an important counterbalance to the tendency of conglomerate companies to shut down operations in one city or region and move elsewhere in the search for cheaper labor, lower taxes, or less stringent environmental regulations. In 1987, for instance, the Air Line Pilots Association bid $4.5 billion for United Air Lines. Although the bid was not successful, it did force the company to reorganize its activities in ways favored by the Pilots Association, such as selling off several recently purchased companies outside the airline industry (Moberg 1987).

Broader forms of worker participation occur in worker-owned cooperatives in which workers not only own the firm but actively manage its day-to-day affairs (Rothschild and Russell 1986). Also important are joint union-management quality of work life programs which primarily focus on more limited issues concerning working conditions. Even management-initiated quality circles offer a role for worker participation, although here the topic is generally limited to product quality. In Western Europe several other forms of worker participation are also widespread. These include workers' councils in Germany, in which an elected council of workers acts as an autonomous board to review management policy, and the development of technology stewards in Norway who review and advise on technological change.

Different forms of worker participation vary greatly in the level at which workers are incorporated in an active role in decision-making (Thomas 1988). At one extreme, workers are involved only in decisions about how to improve product quality or efficiency. At the other extreme, workers are involved in investment decisions about when and where to build new factories and what new lines of endeavor to pursue. Workers have shown themselves able to participate effectively in decisions about the production process, in decisions about their own working conditions, and in decisions about investment (Schervish and Herman 1986). All of these forms of worker participation are important; all have been proven to be effective in some circumstances; and all have problems. No one form or level of participation is appropriate in all circumstances. In industries with rapidly changing technologies, worker participation in job design appears to be most important. In industries with a rapidly changing market situation, worker participation in investment decisions may be more important (Greenberg 1987).

An important foundation for increased worker participation is job security (Cornfield 1987). Without job security guarantees, both on paper and in terms of a proven history of commitment, workers are often suspicious of participatory arrangements (Grenier 1988). This is especially true in areas of active technological change where the possibility of displacement for large numbers of workers is very real. Only where there is a strong commitment by the organization to maintain employment levels will workers give their full support to programs entailing increased participation and effort (Kochan, Katz and McKersie 1986).

What *preconditions* underlie the expansion of worker participation at this particular point in history? One important factor is the more sophisticated technologies and more elaborate organizational structures of today's economy that demand greater worker involvement for their effective operation. In addition, workers in industrially advanced nations are more highly educated today than ever before in history. They are also more interested in safety and health issues and in other aspects of their employment situation. They have come to have high expectations about the satisfactions and rewards that work can provide. These realities and expectations are important preconditions motivating the expansion of worker participation.

The persistence of enthusiasm for worker participation and job redesign during the slowed economic growth of the 1980s and 1990s demonstrates that these programs are here to stay. Economic miracles should not be expected from worker participation (Fantasia, Clawson and Graham 1988). However, greater worker participation can make an important contribution to productivity and such programs may indeed be precursors to a new system of industrial relations that will become increasingly dominant in the twenty-first century (Cordova 1982).

The rapidly expanding literature on workplace democracy and worker ownership has been neglected by the new sociology of work. Few, if any, of its insights have been incorporated into this literature. The dynamics of work groups, elected workers' councils, ESOPs, cooperatives, and the possibilities and dilemmas of these various forms of worker participation provide fertile soil for a new sociology of work based on an active view of the worker. This literature demonstrates that forms of collective worker activity are possible that are capable of overcoming divisions between various groups of workers and effectively carrying out the functions of management.

Collective Bargaining and Strikes

There is a vast literature on collective bargaining and strike behavior. (See Cornfield 1989 and Lewin and Feuille 1983 for recent reviews of this literature.) A central finding in this literature is that workers with power tend to strike in response to job related problems, while workers without power tend to quit their jobs (Cornfield 1985). "Power" can be derived from an effective union, location in an industry that is sheltered by a product market monopoly, or employment in a growing industry. Workers without power are forced to respond to unsatisfactory job conditions by quitting the job rather than by taking collective action to improve conditions. As Bluestone (1970) writes, "for such workers, losing a job is not much worse than keeping it." Besides power, the most important factor facilitating collective action among workers is the availability of ideologies that support such action (Snyder 1975). Without ideological support, few workers are willing to accept the individual sacrifices that may accompany strike activity (Hodson 1987).

There is also a large literature on how the individual characteristics of workers influence strike behavior (Leicht 1989). A principal finding from this literature is that a wide variety of types of workers are potentially available for collective action (Batstone, Boraston and Frankel 1978). Many fewer workers, however, are interested in the types of action that involve direct violent confrontations with management (Grant and Wallace 1991).

The analysis of workers' responses at the workplace has been conceptualized by Hirschman (1971) as a three category typology: exit, voice, and loyalty. Voice refers to a variety of individual and collective behaviors (including union activity, professional association lobbying, and individual acts of bargaining and resistance) through which workers can express their complaints at the workplace and push for redress. Exit refers primarily to quitting, but also includes more subtle and partial forms of withdrawal such as absenteeism, apathy, and carelessness. Loyalty refers to commitment to the organization and to working to achieve individual goals within the parameters laid out by the organization, its rules, and goals. The model of workplace behaviors suggested in this chapter shares common terrain with Hirschman's three category model but it covers a more comprehensive range of behaviors. This range of behaviors is especially important for extending Hirschman's model to include collective responses.

Resource Mobilization and Collective Action

The literature on collective action, and particularly on resource mobilization, offers a fertile terrain for the development of a more integrated model of the workplace incorporating a more active view of workers. Areas in which the collective action literature has successfully incorporated an activist model of worker behavior include the analysis of peasant rebellions, folk resistance and unionization (Cornfield 1989; Tilly and Shorter 1974).

Scott (1986) traces peasant resistance in northern Malaysia to dislocations caused by the extension of irrigation and green revolution "miracle grains." These agricultural innovations bring with them a polarization between rich and poor peasants as agricultural productivity becomes increasingly dependent on capital intensive technologies. Scott finds a variety of subtle forms of resistance among poor and middle-status peasants including minor sabotage, foot dragging, chicanery, petty pilferage, deception, character assassination, ridicule, and low-key recalcitrance in the fulfillment of paid labor and other obligations to the upper echelon of peasant landlords. Most of these acts of resistance are oriented toward securing minor improvements in the lives of the peasants rather than toward attempting to overthrow the existing social or political system. Scott argues, however, that peasants have little trouble seeing through the mystifying ideologies put forward by those in power to legitimate the status quo and that even low level resistance can have profound long term consequences.

Theories of resource mobilization stress the roles of resources, opportunities, and other facilitators in determining the likelihood and nature of collective action (McCarthy and Zald 1977). Resources for action include organization as well as material and financial resources and labor. Opportunities for action include spatial and timing factors that make collective action a possibility. Facilitators of action include precipitating events and the existence of effective leadership (Tilly 1978). In addition, culture is seen as providing a matrix that may facilitate or retard collective action (Gamson, Fireman and Rytina 1982; Schutt 1986).

The literature on collective action and resource mobilization notes that collective action occurs across a variety of spheres in society and includes a wide range of behaviors from mass demonstrations to subtle non-compliance. The goals of collective action are only rarely revolutionary. More typically, the goals are reformist at most, or, even more likely, they are oriented to securing relatively minor benefits and redresses that may be of fleeting and temporary consequence. An important contribution of the resource mobilization literature is its explicit theorization of the roles of resources, opportunities, facilitators, and culture in the emergence of collective action.

Technology: Control versus Empowerment

A final research area to be considered for developing the implications of a model of the worker as active agent is the rapidly growing literature on technology and work. Two areas are of particular interest: the effects of new technology on skills and the consequences of new technology for the organization of work.

Deskilling or Skill Upgrading? Blauner's (1964) classic study of continuous process automation in the chemical industry is among the most widely cited empirical studies on the relationship between advanced technology and skill. Blauner finds that continuous process automation requires a greater proportion of skilled maintenance workers than mass production and that operators in automated settings have greater responsibility for the care and functioning of expensive capital equipment. Riche (1982), in a review of technological change in four industries, and Adler (1984), in a study of banks and bank tellers, arrive at similar conclusions. Both emphasize the increasing level of skill required by advanced technology. These studies can be interpreted as providing support for Bell's (1973) thesis that new, knowledge-based industries are creating a "post-industrial society" typified by increased skill and autonomy.

Research on the computerized numeric control (CNC) in the machine tool industry supports Blauner's contention that automation produces increased demands for skill.

> CNC operators are likely to have to deal with a greater and more frequently changing range of jobs; part of this is related to the increased sophistication of the machine control-system through which more flexible change-overs and improvements of programmes can be achieved (Hartmann, Nicholas, Sorge and Warner 1983, 226).

Increased skills were also needed in settings such as those described above to prevent bottle-necks in production that result from system components with highly differential levels of flexibility and efficiency.

Advanced technologies may thus demand greater skills from workers, allowing them greater power. Hirschhorn (1984, 58) quotes a management consultant in a high technology power plant in this regard: "The operator can achieve better results than the engineer. This can probably be put down to his ability, derived from intimate experience of the plant, to take into account the many ill-understood factors which affect the plant's running but which he cannot communicate to the engineer." Hirschhorn (1984, 73) argues for an historical progression in which the worker moves "from being the controlled element in the production process to operating the controls to controlling the controls."

Other researchers argue that *deskilling* is the most likely consequence of advanced technology. Bright (1966) argues that, as mechanization progresses, initial changes demanding increased skill levels yield to a progressive loss of skill, resulting in an inverted "U-shaped" skill curve. Bright's thesis has been popularized by Braverman (1974) who coined the phrase "deskilling" to typify the progressive loss of skill.

Boddy and Buchanan (1983), basing their analysis on a series of case studies, illustrate how new technologies are creating a growing proportion of deskilled occupations. One of the cases documented by Boddy and Buchanan involved the introduction of automated mixing equipment at a biscuit factory. The major effect of advanced technology on work in the biscuit factory was to transform the "doughman" into a mixer operator. Previously, the position of doughman was held by a master baker. However, once automated equipment was introduced into the mixing process, the doughman suffered a substantial loss of craft skills. In addition, as control of the operation was moved further up the organizational hierarchy, the doughman was left with less discretion over other aspects of work as well. (See also Finlay 1987, and Francis et al. 1981.)

The literature on advanced technology and skills suggests that the tasks required of workers in high technology settings may involve both skill upgrading and deskilling. Workers may experience skill upgrading through an increased role in decision-making and through an increased range of skills required on the job. Deskilling may occur as craft skills are lost to increasing automation and as previous elements of worker autonomy are captured

by the organizational hierarchy or incorporated into new computerized "management information systems."

Job Quality and Quality Control. A second theme in the literature on technology and work is that the introduction of advanced
technologies alters the organizational structure of enterprises. For
example, Burawoy (1979) argues that technological advances have
improved the experience of work because quality control functions
are increasingly reintegrated into production. Proponents of this
vision also argue that "participative management" schemes, char-
acteristic of many automated environments, reduce the level of
alienation experienced by workers (Zisman 1978).

Other researchers see a strong connection between advanced
technology and the centralization of authority (Mowshowitz 1976).
Proponents of this view argue that the natural tendency of automation is to centralize the functions of control and decision-making
in the upper levels of management. In support of this position,
research in the United States has indicated that workers in high-
technology industries are less satisfied than other manufacturing
workers as a result of more rigid rules and closer supervision and
monitoring (Robinson and McIlwee 1989).

Some observers have suggested that the effects of advanced
technology on organizational structure are contingent on the circumstances in which the technology is introduced. Hartmann et al.
(1983) find that the effect of CNC machine tools on workers is contingent on national differences between their two cases studies
(Germany and Great Britain) and on differences between large and
small enterprises. In Germany and in smaller British companies,
CNC increased the integration of engineers and machinists in the
production process. In larger and more formalized British factories,
such integration of functions was preempted by the removal of programming from the shop floor. In the United States, regional differences may generate similar differentiations. The anti-labor climate of
the "Sunbelt" may provide a harsher setting for the implementation of technological advances than the more unionized Northeast
and Midwest (Robinson and McIlwee 1989).

Two major insights from the literature on work in high technology settings are suggested by focusing on the worker as active
subject: 1) Advanced technologies both disrupt old skills and create
new skills. This tendency is better conceived of as "skill disruption" than as a clear deskilling or skill upgrading. In this process,
workers may have important new opportunities to exercise power

and discretion at work; 2) Workers often like new technology itself and the power it gives them (Form and McMillen 1983). Job satisfaction and commitment to work, however, tend to decrease following the introduction of advanced technologies, especially for production workers. This occurs because of demands for increased pace and because of tighter systems of management control. In sum, the rapid introduction of advanced technologies based on the application of microprocessors to the workplace creates a wealth of new opportunities and vulnerabilities for workers as they struggle to develop behavioral strategies at the workplace.

Hypotheses Emerging from the Study of the Active Worker

The model of the active worker developed in this chapter is capable of producing a variety of new hypotheses about the nature of work in the 1990s and beyond. The generation of such hypotheses is an important first step in further developing and refining a model of the worker as an active partner in defining the nature of work. Five such hypotheses are listed below:

> Hypothesis 1: A culture of solidarity is necessary for transforming grievances into behaviors that further class goals.

> Hypothesis 2: A supportive small group structure is necessary for transforming grievances into behaviors that further group goals.

> Hypothesis 3: The absence of class solidarity and supportive group structures will result in the selection of individualistic behaviors which may or may not be supportive of organizational goals.

> Hypothesis 4: Bureaucratic organizational structures move behavioral strategies toward resistance to rules rather than individuals.

> Hypothesis 5: After controlling for behavioral strategies, productivity and job satisfaction have no net relationship.

The systematic investigation of these and other hypotheses derived from the model of the active worker developed in this chapter has the potential to yield new insights that could enliven the study of workplace conditions, behaviors and attitudes. From such research we may be able to develop models of the conditions giving rise to various workplace behaviors analogous to those suggested by Tilly (1978) for larger scale collective action.

Conclusions

The typology of workplace behaviors and the causal model of how these behaviors emerge and operate in the workplace proposed in this chapter are compatible with insights drawn from recent work in a variety of fields, including industrial sociology, the study of complex organizations, class culture, and workplace democracy, and the study of strikes and other forms of collective behavior. This unifying model has the potential to yield significant new insights into the relationships between workplace conditions, worker behaviors and workplace outcomes.

The proposed model also has the potential to reframe existing questions and resolve old debates in the study of the workplace. For instance, the lack of a relationship between job satisfaction and productivity has troubled the study of organizational behavior for decades. A model based on the worker as active subject suggests that this is not because of measurement problems or mediating factors. Rather, it is because job satisfaction and productivity share a common cause but no causal relationship beyond that.

Further development and refinement of a model of the worker as active agent is obviously possible. The conditions leading to various behaviors can be more precisely specified. The model can also be further developed by incorporating insights from additional literatures. For instance, contemporary work on game theory specifies that the behaviors of actors are contingent on the behaviors of other actors in the system (Elster 1982). This insight might be useful in further specifying the conditions that lead to the selection of one or another behavioral strategy. Similarly, a consideration of the ethnographic literature on various forms of resistance and consent both inside and outside the workplace might yield additional insights leading to further extensions or specifications of the model (see de Certeau 1984; Halle 1984; Haraszti 1978; Hodson et al. 1993; Jackall 1978; Mars 1982; Tucker 1993).

Several additional avenues of research are also suggested by the model presented here. The typology of behaviors we have outlined is a logical construction based on cross classifying individual, group, and organizational goals. It would be instructive to know to what extent workers' cognitive maps of workplace behaviors correspond to this model. Are all cells represented in workers' cognitive maps? Are some missing? What is the distribution of workers across cells? Do workers in different occupations use different cognitive maps of possible workplace behaviors? These question can be answered by empirical research. The simple procedure of asking a sample of workers from a variety of occupations, "Do you ever give less than (or more than) 100 percent effort at work, why, and under conditions?" could provide the beginnings of an empirical base for answering these and related questions. Similarly, it would be informative to know the changes that occur over workers' careers in their behavioral responses to the situations they encounter at work. It is hoped that the model of the worker as an active agent proposed in this chapter can serve as a starting framework for the pursuit of these and other research questions which incorporate a fuller role for the worker as active subject in the new sociology of work.

REFERENCES

Abbott, Andrew. 1988. *The System of Professions*. Chicago: University of Chicago.

Abegglen, James and George Stalk. 1985. *The Japanese Corporation*. New York: Basic.

Adler, Paul. 1984. "Tools for Resistance: Workers Can Make Automation Their Ally." *Dollars and Sense* 100 (October):7-8.

Averitt, Robert T. 1968. *The Dual Economy*. New York: W. W. Norton.

Batstone, E, I. Boraston and S. Frankel. 1978. *The Social Organization of Strikes*. Oxford: Basil Blackwell.

Bell, Daniel. 1973. *The Coming of Post-Industrial Society*. New York: Basic.

Bensman, Joseph and Israel Gerver. 1963. "Crime and Punishment in the Factory." *American Sociological Review* 28 (4):588-98.

Blauner, Robert. 1964. *Alienation and Freedom*. Chicago: University of Chicago.

Bluestone, Barry. 1970. "The Tripartite Economy: Labor Markets and the Working Poor." *Poverty and Human Resources* 5:15-35.

Boddy, D. and D. Buchanan. 1983. "Advanced Technology and the Quality of Working Life: The Effects of Computerized Controls on Biscuit-Making Operators." *Journal of Occupational Psychology* 56 (2):109-19.

Bonacich, Edna. 1976. "Advanced Capitalism and Black/White Race Relations in the United States: A Split Labor Market Interpretation." *American Sociological Review* 41:34-51.

Braverman, Harry. 1974. *Labor and Monopoly Capital.* New York: Monthly Review.

Bright, James R. 1966. "The Relationship of Increasing Automation and Skill Requirements." In *The Employment Impact of Technological Change, Volume 2: Technology and the American Economy,* National Commission on Technology, Automation and Economic Progress. Washington, D.C.: U.S. Government Printing Office, 203-221.

Burawoy, Michael. 1985. *The Politics of Production.* London: New Left Books.

———. 1979. *Manufacturing Consent.* Chicago: University of Chicago.

Cavendish, Ruth. 1982. *Women on the Line.* London: Routledge and Kegan Paul.

Cole, Robert E. 1989. *Strategies for Learning: Small-Group Activities in American, Japanese, and Swedish Industry.* Berkeley: University of California Press.

Cooke, William N. 1990. "Factors Influencing the Effect of Joint Union-Management Programs on Employee-Supervisor Relations." *Industrial and Labor Relations Review* 43 (5):587-603.

Cordova, E. 1982. "Workers' Participation within Enterprises: Recent Trends and Problems." *International Labour Review* 121 (2):125-40.

Cornfield, Daniel B. 1989. *Becoming a Mighty Voice: Conflict and Change in the United Furniture Workers of America.* New York: Russell Sage Foundation.

Cornfield, Daniel B. (editor). 1987. *Workers, Managers, and Technological Change.* New York: Plenum.

Cornfield, Daniel B. 1985. "Economic Segmentation and the Expression of Labor Unrest." *Social Science Quarterly* 66 (2):247-65.

de Certeau, Michel. 1984. *The Practice of Everyday Life* (translated by Steven F. Rendall). Berkeley: University of California Press.

Dohse, Knuth, Ulrich Jurgens and Thomas Malsch. 1985. "From 'Fordism' to 'Toyotism'? The Social Organization of the Labor Process in the Japanese Automobile Factory." *Politics and Society* 14 (2):115-45.

Edwards, P. K. 1986. *Conflict at Work.* London: Basil Blackwell.

Edwards, P. K. and Hugh Scullion. 1982. *The Social Organization of Industrial Conflict.* London: Basil Blackwell.

Edwards, Richard. 1979. *Contested Terrain*. New York: Basic.

Elster, Jon. 1982. "Marxism, Functionalism, and Game Theory." *Theory and Society* 11 (4):453-82.

Fantasia, Rick. 1988. *Cultures of Solidarity*. Berkeley: University of California Press.

Fantasia, Rick, Dan Clawson and Gregory Graham. 1988. "A Critical View of Worker Participation in American Industry." *Work and Occupations* 15 (4):468-88.

Finlay, William. 1987. "Commitment and Control in the High-tech Workplace." Paper presented at the Annual Meetings of the American Sociological Association.

Form, William and David Byron McMillen. 1983. "Women, Men, and Machines." *Work and Occupations* 10 (2):147-78.

Francis, Arthus, Mandy Snell, Paul Willman, and Graham Winch. 1981. "The Impact of Information Technology at Work: The Case of CAD/CAM and MIS in Engineering Plants." In *Information Technology: Impact on the Way of Life*. Dublin, Ireland: Tycooly, 182-193.

Friedman, Andrew L. 1977. *Industry and Labor: Class Struggle at Work and Monopoly Capitalism*. London: MacMillan.

Gamson, William A., Bruce Fireman and Steven Rytina. 1982. *Encounters with Unjust Authority*. Homewood, Illinois: Dorsey.

Gordon, David M. 1972. *Theories of Poverty and Underemployment*. Lexington, Massachusetts: Heath.

Gorz, Andre. 1973. "Workers' Control is More Than Just That." In Gerry G. Hunnius (Ed.), *Participatory Democracy in Canada*. Black Rose.

Grant, Don Sherman, II, and Michael Wallace. 1991. "Why Do Strikes Turn Violent?" *American Journal of Sociology* 96 (5):1117-50.

Greenberg, Edward S. 1987. *Workplace Democracy*. Ithaca, New York: Cornell University.

Grenier, G. J. 1988. *Inhuman Relations: Quality Circles and Anti-unionism in American Industry*. Philadelphia: Temple University Press.

Gyllenhammar, Pehr G. 1977. "How Volvo Adapts Work to People." In Richard M. Steers and Lyman W. Porter (Eds.), *Motivation and Work Behavior, Third Edition*. New York: McGraw-Hill, 564-576.

Haas, J. 1987. *Becoming Doctors: The Adoption of a Cloak of Competence.* Greenwich, Connecticut: JAI Press.

Halle, David. 1984. *America's Working Man.* Chicago: University of Chicago.

Hamper, Ben. 1991. *Rivethead: Tales from the Assembly Line.* New York: Warner.

Haraszti, Miklos. 1978. *A Worker in a Worker's State.* New York: Universe Books.

Hartmann, Gert, Ian Nicholas, Arndt Sorge and Malcolm Warner. 1983. "Computerized Machine Tools, Manpower Consequences and Skill Utilization." *British Journal of Industrial Relations* 21 (2):221-31.

Hirschhorn, Larry. 1984. *Beyond Mechanization.* Cambridge: MIT.

Hirschman, Albert O. 1971. *Exit, Voice, and Loyalty.* Cambridge, Massachusetts: Harvard University.

Hodson, Randy. 1991. "Good Soldiers, Smooth Operators, and Saboteurs: A Model of Workplace Behaviors." *Work and Occupations* 18 (3):271-90.

———. 1987. "Who Crosses the Picket Line? An Analysis of the CWA Strike of 1983." *Labor Studies Journal* 12 (2):19-37.

———. 1985. "Workers' Comparisons and Job Satisfaction." *Social Science Quarterly* 66 (2):266-80.

Hodson, Randy, Sandy Welsh, Sabine Rieble, Cheryl Sorenson Jamison and Sean Creighton. 1993. "Is Worker Solidarity Undermined by Autonomy and Participation?" *American Sociological Review* 58 (3):398-416.

Hodson, Randy and Teresa A. Sullivan. 1990. *The Social Organization of Work.* Belmont, California: Wadsworth.

Jackall, Robert. 1978. *Workers in a Labyrinth: Jobs and Survival in a Bank Bureaucracy.* Montclair, New Jersey: Allanheld and Osmun.

Jermier, John M. 1988. "Sabotage at Work." In Nancy DiTomaso (Ed.), *Research in the Sociology of Organizations*, Volume 6. Greenwich, Connecticut: JAI Press, 101-135.

Juravich, Tom. 1985. *Chaos on the Shop Floor.* Philadelphia: Temple University.

Kochan, Thomas A., Harry C. Katz and Robert B. McKersie. 1986. *The Transformation of American Industrial Relations.* New York: Basic.

Leicht, Kevin. 1989. "Unions, Plants, Jobs and Workers: An Analysis of Union Satisfaction and Participation." *Sociological Quarterly* 30 (2):331-62.

Lewin, David and Peter Feuille. 1983. "Behavioral Research in Industrial Relations." *Industrial and Labor Relations Review* 36 (3):341-60.

Lillrank, Paul and Noriaki Kano. 1989. *Continuous Improvement: Quality Circles in Japanese Industry*. Ann Arbor: University of Michigan Center for Japanese Studies.

Lindenfeld, Frank. 1982. "Workers' Cooperatives: Remedy for Plant Closings?" In Frank Lindenfeld and Joyce Rothschild-Whitt (Eds.), *Workplace Democracy and Social Change*. Boston, Massachusetts: Horizons, 337-352.

McCarthy, John D. and Mayer N. Zald. 1977. "Resource Mobilization and Social Movements." *American Journal of Sociology* 82 (6):1212-41.

Mars, Gerald. 1982. *Cheats at Work*. London: Unwin.

Mayo, Elton. 1945. *The Social Problems of an Industrial Civilization*. Cambridge, Massachusetts: Harvard University.

Miller, Delbert C. and William H. Form. 1951, 1964, 1980. *Industrial Sociology*, 1st, 2nd, and 3rd editions. New York: Harper and Row.

Moberg, David. 1987. "Will United Airlines Pilots' Takeover Bid Fly?" *In These Times* (April 29):6.

Molstad, Clark. 1988. "Control Strategies Used by Industrial Brewery Workers: Work Avoidance, Impression Management and Solidarity." *Human Organization* 47 (4):354-60.

Montgomery, David. 1979. *Workers' Control in America*. Cambridge, England: Cambridge University.

Mowshowitz, Abbe. 1976. *The Conquest of Will: Information Processing in Human Affairs*. Reading, Massachusetts: Addison-Wesley.

New York Times. 1987. "ESOPs Edge Up." *New York Times* (July 5):Section 3,1.

Nosow, Sigmund and William H. Form (Eds.). 1962. *Man, Work, and Society*. New York: Basic.

Ouchi, William G. 1981. *Theory Z*. Reading, Massachusetts: Addison-Wesley.

Parker, Mike. 1985. *Inside the Circle: A Union Guide to QWL*. Boston: South End Press.

Pavalko, Ronald M. 1988. *Sociology of Occupations and Professions*, 2nd Edition. Itasca, Illinois: Peacock.

Pearson, Peg and Jake Baker. 1982. "Seattle Workers' Brigade." In Frank Lindenfeld and Joyce Rothschild-Whitt (Eds.), *Workplace Democracy and Social Change*. Boston, Massachusetts: Horizons, 279-289.

Riche, Richard W. 1982. "Impact of New Electronic Technology." *Monthly Labor Review* 105 (3):37-9.

Robinson, J. Gregg and Judith S. McIlwee. 1989. "Obstacles to Unionization in High-Tech Industries." *Work and Occupations* 16 (2):115-36.

Roethlisberger, F. J. and William J. Dickson. 1939. *Management and the Worker*. Cambridge, Massachusetts: Harvard University.

Rothschild, Joyce and Raymond Russell. 1986. "Alternatives to Bureaucracy: Democratic Participation in the Economy." In Ralph H. Turner and James F. Short, Jr. (Eds.), *The Annual Review of Sociology*, Volume 12. Palo Alto, California: Annual Reviews, 307-328.

Rothschild-Whitt, Joyce. 1979. "The Collectivist Organization: An Alternative to Bureaucratic Models." *American Sociological Review* 44:509-27.

Roy, Donald. 1954. "Efficiency and 'The Fix': Informal Intergroup Relations in a Piecework Machine Shop." *American Journal of Sociology* 60:255-66.

Russell, Raymond and Veljko Rus (editors). 1991. *International Handbook of Participation in Organizations, Volume 2, Ownership and Participation*. Oxford: Oxford University.

Sabel, Charles F. 1982. *Work and Politics*. Cambridge, England: Cambridge University.

Schervish, Paul G. and Andrew Herman. 1986. "Conceptualizing Class Structure in the Transition to Socialism." *Work and Occupations* 13 (2):264-91.

Schlesinger, Melinda Bart and Pauline B. Bart. 1982. "Collective Work and Self-identity: Working in a Feminist Illegal Abortion Collective." In Frank Lindenfeld and Joyce Rothschild-Whitt (Eds.), *Workplace Democracy and Social Change*. Boston, Massachusetts: Horizons, 139-153.

Schrank, Robert (Ed.). 1983. *Industrial Democracy at Sea*. Cambridge, Massachusetts: MIT.

Schuster, Michael H. 1984. *Union-Management Cooperation*. Kalamazoo, Michigan: W.E. Upjohn Institute for Employment Research.

Schutt, Russell K. 1986. *Organization in a Changing Environment: Unionization of Welfare Employees*. Albany: State University of New York Press.

Scott, James C. 1986. *Weapons of the Weak: Everyday Forms of Peasant Resistance*. New Haven, Connecticut: Yale University.

Shaiken, Harley. 1984. *Work Transformed*. New York: Holt, Rinehart, and Winston.

Simpson, Ida Harper. 1989. "The Sociology of Work: Where Have All the Workers Gone?" *Social Forces* 67 (3):563-81.

Sirianni, Carmen. 1987. *Worker Participation and the Politics of Reform*. Philadelphia: Temple University.

Snyder, David. 1975. "Institutional Setting and Industrial Conflict: Comparative Analyses of France, Italy and the United States." *American Sociological Review* 40:259-78.

Taylor, Laurie and Paul Walton. 1971. "Industrial Sabotage: Motives and Meanings." In Stanley Cohen (Ed.) *Images of Deviance*. London: Penguin, 219-245.

Thomas, Robert J. 1988. "Quality and Quantity? Worker Participation in the U.S. and Japanese Automobile Industries." In Melvyn Dubofsky (Ed.), *Technological Change and Workers' Movements*. Beverly Hills, California: Sage, 162-188.

Thompson, E. P. 1967. "Time, Work-discipline, and Industrial Capitalism." *Past and Present* 38 (December):56-97.

Thompson, Paul. 1983. *The Nature of Work*. London: MacMillan.

Tilly, Charles. 1978. *From Mobilization to Revolution*. Reading, Massachusetts: Addison-Wesley.

Tilly, Charles and Edward Shorter. 1974. *Strikes in France, 1830-1968*. London: Cambridge University.

Tucker, James. 1993. "Everyday Forms of Employee Resistance." *Sociological Forum* 8 (1):25-45.

Walton, Richard E. and J. Richard Hackman. 1986. "Groups under Contrasting Management Strategies." In Paul S. Goodman and Associates (Eds.), *Designing Effective Work Groups*. San Francisco: Jossey Bass, 168-201.

Wardell, Mark. 1990. "Organizations: A Bottom-up Approach." In Michael L. Reed and Michael Hughes (Eds.), *Rethinking Organizations.* London: Sage.

Weinstein, Deena. 1979. *Bureaucratic Opposition.* New York: Pergamon.

Westwood, Sallie. 1984. *All Day Every Day: Factory and Family in the Making of Women's Lives.* London: Pluto.

Willis, Paul. 1977. *Learning to Labour.* New York: Columbia University.

Woodworth, Warner, Christopher Meek and William Foote Whyte. 1985. *Industrial Democracy.* Beverly Hills, California: Sage.

Zisman, Michael. 1978. "Office Automation: Revolution or Evolution?" *Sloan Management Review* 19 (spring):1-16.

Zwerdling, Daniel. 1980. *Workplace Democracy.* New York: Harper and Row.

10

Employers, Employees, and Work: A Research Program

Arne L. Kalleberg
Richard C. Rockwell

INTRODUCTION

A number of important challenges related to work and industry will increasingly occupy the attention of social scientists and policy makers in the coming decades. Among these are: designing policies and programs attuned to structural changes in the economy; enhancing product quality; restructuring work in light of computerization, automation, and other forms of technological change; increasing productivity and American economic competitiveness in response to foreign challenges in product and labor markets; dealing with the employment, training, and other emerging needs of a changing labor force; enabling the growing number of employees in dual career families to obtain the flexibility of employment they require; and improving the workings of industrial relations in a changing labor market.

Despite the importance of these issues, researchers and policy analysts still lack a nationally representative body of information on which to base generalizable inferences and conclusions. Several elements of the needed research effort are already in place. Examples include: the 1991 National Organizations Study (NOS), which has collected information on the human resource practices and policies of the organizations in which respondents to the 1991 General Social Survey (GSS) were employed; the University of Michigan's Panel Survey of Income Dynamics (PSID) (the NOS, GSS, and PSID have all been supported by the National Science Foundation); the National Longitudinal Surveys of Labor Market Experience and the Quality of Employment Surveys (sponsored by the Department of Labor); and the Census Bureau's Survey of Income and Program Participation. While these surveys are significant tools for addressing national economic and social problems, only one (the 1991 NOS-GSS) permits even a limited analysis of the impacts of different *organizational* conditions of work on outcomes such as: worker productivity, well-being and satisfaction; labor force behaviors such as absenteeism and quitting work; and labor-management and industrial relations.

It is imperative to study the organizational contexts of work and employment since organizations—small or large—are today the central structures in American society through which changes in the nature of work and industry occur and where policies are enacted. It is organizations that, among other things, sign union contracts, adopt automated equipment, relocate to communities or nations with lower wage rates, make capital investments, create supervisory structures, provide fringe benefits, set salary scales, and create or eliminate jobs. The concept of "employment" implies a relationship between the worker and the employer, and in modern societies, organizations are the employers of the vast majority of the labor force.

Recognition of the importance of organizational and other ecological contexts in shaping outcomes of the employment relationship is reflected in recent theoretical advances in economics, sociology, psychology, industrial relations, organizational behavior, and related social sciences. New theories and models are emerging in each of these fields to explain or interpret the responses of firms, unions, workers and government policy makers to current challenges. Labor economists as well as human resource management and industrial relations specialists have recently begun to develop theoretical models in a variety of areas related to workplace organization, including: the quality of worker-employer matches; duality in labor market outcomes; the importance, scope, and nature of long-term implicit "contracts" between workers and employers; wage rigidity and aggregate unemployment; and decisions regarding unionization. Similarly, recent sociological explanations of economic stratification have underscored the need to understand the organizational bases of inequality and how the socioeconomic achievements of individuals are conditioned by differences in the social and economic organization of production. The convergence of these often disparate theoretical paradigms persuades us that a properly designed research program that addresses these issues would attract the attention and interest of a large body of researchers from many disciplines.

Embedding information on employees in their organizational and ecological contexts is equally essential for guiding public and private decision-makers as they seek to achieve a balance in prevailing and newly emerging policies between organizations' competitive needs and workers' values and expectations. Such data would also help to establish a basis for evaluating employment, training, health and safety, and labor policies affecting productivity, the workings of labor markets, and the standard of living of the work force. For example, the changing composition of the labor force calls for informed policy decisions related to working parents, such as the need for day care services and parental leaves. Moreover, since public policy efforts must be complemented by initiatives on the part of the private sector, employers and unions need such information in order to devise and assess emerging strategies for achieving their aims. Managers, for example, need to know how organizational policies and structures—such as those related to experiments with employee involvement and/or total quality management—are related both to the variety of styles of organizational philosophies now in place as well as the morale and motivation of their employees. Managers would also benefit from the development of national norms in a variety of employment-related areas so that they can better evaluate the attitudes and behaviors of their own employees. Hence, the informational needs of government agencies as well as management and union leaders are best met by research focused on both sides of the employment picture—employees and their organizations.

In this chapter, we outline a research program that links characteristics of employers to attributes of their employees, and thereby permits the investigation of how organizational structures affect the people who work in them. Our description of this research program is based on the recommendations of the Advisory Group on a 1986 Quality of Employment Survey, an ad hoc committee convened by the Social Science Research Council at the request of the U.S. Department of Labor's Bureau of Labor-Management Relations and Cooperative Programs.[1] We first summarize the research designs that constitute the key elements of the proposed research program; these designs are complementary, each having particular advantages and disadvantages. We then discuss some of the major issues—related to both employers and employees—that need to be investigated in this research program.

COLLECTING DATA ON EMPLOYERS AND EMPLOYEES:
TWO RESEARCH DESIGNS

A research program designed to meet the informational needs of sociologists and economists concerned with work and employment should have several key features.

1. Information should be collected from a broadly representative sample of the employed labor force. This would preserve continuity with many former studies of the U.S. labor force, and enable analysts to examine important changes in the nature of work and workers.

2. Information should also be collected from a diverse group of employers, in both the private and public sectors. Data on organizational structures would enable researchers to test hypotheses in which the independent and dependent variables are both measured at the organizational level of analysis. Examples include: do cooperative labor-management relations result in lower quit rates, lower turnover, and/or less absenteeism?; how is organizational performance related to its hierarchical structure?; are firms that face foreign competition more likely to adopt advanced production technology?; and, are unionized companies more likely to experience layoffs than nonunionized companies?

3. Information obtained from particular companies should be *linked* to the data collected from their employees. This would enable policy makers and analysts to examine the "contextual effects" of different kinds of organizational arrangements on workers' attitudes and behaviors.[2] Examples of questions that require the use of contextual data include: Does participation in decentralized decision-making structures such as "quality circles" enhance organizational commitment and job satisfaction (Lincoln and Kalleberg 1990)?; What is the role of networks in employers' recruitment and potential employees' job search (Bridges and Villemez 1986)?; Do technological advances such as the introduction of computers increase or decrease the number of job dangers to which employees are exposed?; Are the commitments of younger employees to their organizations increased most by high earnings, by nonwage fringe benefits, or by opportunities for advancement?; And, do internal labor markets and

job ladders increase the chances that employees will be able to utilize their skills and abilities on their jobs?

4. Information should be obtained from many employees within particular companies. Collecting data from employees at different levels and positions within the same organization permits the analysis of issues such as: how an employee's relative standing within an organization affects his or her levels of commitment, satisfaction, and productivity; the extent to which individuals within the same organization differ in their degree of commitment; and, how individuals differ in their perceptions of organizational structures, such as whether they think that the distribution of authority is more or less centralized. In addition, it is necessary to obtain data from a sufficiently large group of employees within an organization to permit aggregation for statistical description in order to study how the "climate" of organizations affects individuals (see Note 2).

5. The information on individuals and organizations will be most valuable if it is longitudinal, collected at more than one point in time, since this would allow some processes of change to be examined more directly. Longitudinal observation is needed to answer questions such as the impacts of business and product life cycles on the human resource policies of firms and on workers' attitudes and labor market behaviors.

6. This research program should be cross-national, in order to study how the political, cultural, historical, and economic characteristics of different nations affect the work-related experiences of their citizens. This is essential, since there is ample reason to suspect that organizational structures shape individuals' experiences and attitudes in different ways in different countries (e.g., Lincoln and Kalleberg 1990). Moreover, cultural differences help to define what is considered expected or unacceptable behavior in otherwise similar organizational forms.[3] By examining these differences across nations, we will be able to draw stronger conclusions than is possible from research on a single country. And, since many nations are facing the same challenges with respect to work and employment as the United States, there is good reason to believe that their national scientific and policy agencies also have the same needs for better information.

In the terminology of Allen H. Barton's typology of designs for organizational studies in the *International Encyclopedia of the Social Sciences* (1968), this research program can be described as a "multistratum relational panel survey of a large sample of workers in a large sample of organizations": "multistratum" because several levels of workers and managers should be interviewed; "relational" because ecological data on organizations and other work structures need to be collected; "panel" because it is hoped that both employees and employers can be followed over time; and "large samples" so that analytically useful samples can be secured for both employees and employers. Barton provides no examples of such studies in his 1968 article, and there is no reason to believe that this empty cell has been filled since then: while the social science literature provides ample examples of less ambitious organizational studies, none has attempted to accomplish all of these goals in a single design. Indeed, it may not be practical to try to accomplish these goals in a single survey. The costs of trying to do so would probably be prohibitive, and it is by no means clear that a research design that satisfies one criterion would not undermine another. For example, a broadly representative sample of employees would be very unlikely to generate sizable samples of employees within particular organizations; and a heterogeneous sample of organizations is not likely to provide a representative sample of the employed labor force.

In order to collect the needed information from both employees and employers, a research program should include at least two complementary surveys. In the first survey, information would be obtained from a representative sample of employees and limited information would be collected from their employing organizations. In the second survey, data would be gathered from key informants in a diverse sample of companies as well as from samples of employees within these organizations. These two research designs are complementary and, taken together, are capable of satisfying the criteria outlined above. We describe each of these designs in turn.

Survey of Employees

A survey of employees involves two steps. In the first stage, a representative sample of the labor force is obtained using a household/labor force sampling frame. Such samples are widely available, their properties are well-known, and they enable comparisons to be made with previous surveys of the employed labor force. Moreover, this sampling strategy ensures the inclusion in the sample of those individuals who are self-employed, who work in new or very small establishments, who are marginal to the labor force in terms of part-time and temporary employment, and who are members of diverse segments of the labor force (e.g., minorities, women, labor union members, new migrants, and so on). The chosen individuals would then be interviewed regarding the topics mentioned below (see the section on "Information on Employees and their Work"). However, we can obtain only a very limited amount of information on organizational characteristics from these employees, since they are usually not knowledgeable about these things; what they can provide, though, are the names and addresses of their employers.

In a second stage, a key informant(s) in each employing company thus identified would be interviewed (probably by telephone) about the characteristics of the organization. Information on organizational structures would thus be collected from persons—such as plant managers—who are likely to be able to provide complete and accurate information. This design was used in the 1991 National Organizations Study. Employed persons in the 1991 General Social Survey were asked the names, addresses, and telephone numbers of their employers. These employers were then surveyed by telephone, and information was gathered about their organization's human resource policies and practices. This approach has also been used in: Sweden, where employed respondents in the 1991 Level of Living Survey were asked the names of their employers, who were then interviewed (le Grand et al. 1990); a study comparing employees' and their managers' perceptions of the hiring process in the Chicago SMSA by Bridges and Villemez (1986); and a study of employees and their organizations in Columbus, Ohio (Parcel, Kaufman, and Jolly 1991).

While useful in many respects, the information that is collected through such surveys of employees and their managers is limited in several respects. For example, only a modest amount of information on the employing organization can be collected in a relatively short interview with a single key informant. Addressing many research questions requires information that can best be obtained from interviews with several management personnel at different levels in the company as well as from employers' records and computerized data bases containing financial information. In addition, this research design does not permit the investigator to examine differences in work-related outcomes among individuals within the same organization, since it is unlikely that more than one or two employees will be sampled from a particular organization.[4] The second research design overcomes in part these limitations.

Survey of Employers

A survey of employers also involves two steps. In the first stage, a sample of organizations is selected. This sample could be a simple random sample of private and public sector organizations in the U.S., but more realistically, it would be stratified according to certain criteria. For example, the sample might be comprised largely of organizations of particular policy interest (e.g., those who have introduced advanced automation and computerization, or those experiencing high levels of turnover or unemployment), or of companies in particular industries or regions. In each of the sampled organizations, extensive information on organizational structures and objective conditions of work could then be collected from key persons (managers and, where applicable, union leaders) as well as from documents and public sources.

In the second stage, information would be collected from a sample of employees within each organization, either by telephone or personal interviews, questionnaires, or another method. These interviews or questionnaires could include a large subset of the questions asked in the first stage of the previous research design; this would permit some comparisons to be made between the results for the two employee samples—the first obtained through population sampling and the second by establishment sampling.

This strategy is illustrated by Lincoln and Kalleberg's (1990) study of manufacturing plants and their employees in the comparable regions in the United States and Japan, and by the Norwegian Study of Organizations and their Employees. In the latter study, over a thousand establishments were sampled from complete lists of all public and private sector establishments maintained by the Norwegian Central Bureau of Statistics; these establishments were stratified by size and industry sectors. Plant managers, personnel managers (in larger organizations), and union leaders in these establishments were interviewed. Then, a sample of employees of these establishments was selected and interviewed (see Mastekaasa 1992).

Methodological Issues

These research designs raise a number of methodological issues related to the collection of data at multiple levels of analysis. Some of these—how to define the "organization"—are common to both research designs; others—how to sample organizations—are unique to the second, organizational-based approach. We briefly note some of the issues that need to be resolved in order to implement the surveys that we have just described (see also Kalleberg 1990).

1. Defining the "organization." The two most commonly discussed organizational units are the "firm" and the "establishment" (for a discussion, see Granovetter 1984). The salience of these organizational units may differ for different kinds of occupations: for example, the "establishment" may be most relevant for blue-collar and other production workers, while the "firm" or "corporation" may be most salient for professionals, managers, and other white-collar workers. Hence, it is desirable to collect certain information on *both* the establishment and the firm.

Given the mammoth size of many firms, a considerable number of which have establishments at different sites, the "establishment" appears to be the most tractable unit for data collection, since it refers to a specific physical site within which respondents are actually employed. It is also often the most easily defined and recognized organizational unit, and aggregation and disaggregation into larger and smaller units, such as firm and department, can proceed from there. However, information also needs to be obtained on any larger organizational entity (e.g., the firm) of which the establishment is a part, such as: whether or not the establishment is an independent company, and if not, whether it is a profit/cost center; the kinds of decisions local managers have the authority to make on their own; and whether the establishment's products or services are intermediate parts of a flow process within the firm or are delivered to consumers without further processing.

2. Sampling establishments and firms. The success of surveys of employers depends in large degree on the availability and quality of lists of the relevant populations of employing organizations. These lists will generally be more complete for larger organizations than smaller ones; indeed, in view of the problems of locating very small organizations, it may be necessary to restrict a survey of employers to companies above a certain size, say twenty employees.

The Norwegian study cited above illustrates the utility of a list-based approach, which can be implemented in countries that maintain lists of all businesses and make these publicly available to researchers. This is not done in the United States, and thus researchers must rely on partial lists with their own particular inclusion criteria.

Lists of establishments and firms in the United States are available from two major sources: agencies of the federal government, and commercial companies. In the case of the federal government, the most comprehensive lists are compiled by the Bureau of the Census and the U.S. Department of Labor. The Census Bureau's best list appears to be its Standard Statistical Establishment List (SSEL), which covers business organizations in all industries (by contrast, the Census' Longitudinal Establishment File covers only manufacturing establishments). An even better list of organizations appears to be the Department of Labor's Unemployment/Insurance (UI) sampling frame, which is under the control of the Bureau of Labor Statistics. This list provides good coverage across all industries, though it may underrepresent firms that are less than one year old and does not include sole proprietorships and family workers. Unfortunately, confidentiality restrictions and other bureaucratic constraints are likely to limit the availability of the lists generated by the federal government. Hence, commercial lists may be the most viable sources of organizational sampling frames. Possibilities include the very large business data bases maintained by Dun and Bradstreet (the Dun's Market Indicator, or DMI, which is based largely on the credit applications of firms) and the business samples available from Trinet, Inc., or Survey Sampling, Inc. The latter source, for example, lists telephone numbers for 8.8 million different businesses; 6.7 million of these listings include the name of the company and its address. These various sources of lists differ in their representativeness, practicality, and costs, as was demonstrated by the study of organizational sampling frames in Durham, North Carolina, by Kalleberg, Marsden, Aldrich, and Cassell (1990). They found that, on balance, the DMI and UI files were probably the most useful sampling frames among the five they studied.

3. Sampling employees. Within each establishment, a list of employees needs to be obtained. These lists should contain information on the employee's position within the organization (such as his or her occupation, department, supervisory level, and union membership status) and identifying information such as his or her address and/or telephone number. Then, it is necessary to draw a sample of employees that is representative of the various occupations and authority levels found in the organization. The relative sizes of the employee samples will probably differ among organizations, due to factors such as the number, complexity and size of the companies, as well as the importance placed on analyzing differences among the employees of given establishments or firms.

In the Norwegian study cited above, researchers were able to sample systematically employees within each establishment since the Central Bureau of Statistics also maintained a separate list of persons who worked in each of the sampled organizations.

4. Key informants. It is desirable to collect information on organizational correlates from *several* key informants, since some persons are better able than others to provide particular kinds of information. The head of an establishment, such as the general plant manager, for example, is probably the best person to provide information about the overall structure of the organization. On the other hand, the personnel manager might be a more appropriate person to supply information on the nature of the organization's compensation system and promotion patterns. The use of multiple informants is highly desirable, though this is more necessary when seeking to collect some kinds of information (e.g., on corporate culture) than others (e.g., structural information such as size) (see Knoke, Reynolds, Marsden, Miller, and Kaufman 1991). It would also be useful from the viewpoints of both error reduction and efficiency to draw as much information as possible from administrative records.

CONTENT OF THE EMPLOYEE AND EMPLOYER SURVEYS

We have broadly categorized the contents of the proposed surveys of employees and employers as: (1) information on the nature of the labor force and of work; and (2) information on organizations and workplaces. It is important to note that both sides of the employment picture—employees and the organizations in which they work—would be examined in each of these complementary surveys. We now turn to a brief discussion of the specific kinds of concepts that need to be investigated in each of these surveys. Our emphasis will be on breadth of content, not because we are uncertain about what to study, but because we want to accommodate a range of interests in a variety of policy and scientific arenas.

Information on Employees and their Work

This information should be obtained from employees representing a range of authority positions (for example, managers, supervisors and workers), as well as from members of diverse occupations and industries. The topics enumerated below are not listed in any order of priority; such decisions must be made by the sponsors of the research and by those directly responsible for the survey, as must decisions regarding the exact wording of each of these measures.

1. Job rewards. Information needs to be obtained on the various benefits and utilities that people derive from their work. These include both economic rewards (such as hourly wages, annual earnings, and fringe benefits), and non-economic rewards (such as having challenging work, good co-workers, a pleasant locale, and a safe work environment). Information should also be obtained on the "trade-offs" among economic and non-economic rewards that employees and unions are often called upon to make. For example, to what extent are workers willing to exchange earnings or fringe benefits for benefits such as profit-sharing plans, flexible work schedules, more interesting work, or more extensive insurance coverage? Information should also be collected on how equitable (or inequitable) employees perceive the distribution of job rewards within their organizations to be. Finally, the issue of "comparability of work" needs to be addressed; this issue is growing in importance and could significantly affect existing wage structures and union contracts.

2. Task and work organization characteristics. Information should be collected on the nature of the actual task(s) employees perform and on the organization of work as it relates to the job and the work group. These characteristics include: the level and types of skills required; the tools employed; the degree of contact with people and/or with things; the nature and extent of supervision, autonomy, substantive complexity, and other "structural imperatives of work"; the nature of decision-making within the organization; the way in which the organization handles feedback from customers and employees; and on whether rewards are given to individuals or to teams. Questions that might be addressed include: Are employees able to participate (through quality circles, quality of work life programs, or other employee involvement programs) in decisions about organizing their work, in exercising quality control, and in making other decisions that affect them?; Is work divided into narrow, specialized, and closely monitored or technologically controlled tasks and jobs, or are broader, more flexible, and team-oriented work patterns present in the company?; Are employees exposed to technological changes such as manufacturing robots and personal computers?; And, how does the introduction of new technology affect the organization of work?

3. Part-time and temporary employment. Workers holding part-time jobs should be asked about their motivations for working part-time, what other responsibilities they have (such as household maintenance and/or other employment), and whether they wish to work more hours and/or to hold full-time jobs. Workers holding jobs designated as temporary should be asked a similar set of questions, and management could be asked about its intentions of converting such jobs to permanent positions. This information would permit an examination of the correlates and consequences of the recent increases in part-time and temporary work, and in employment of mothers of young children. Moreover, those who are employed full-time might be asked about their degree of control over the number of hours they work, and whether they would like to work fewer hours. We also need to determine what portion, if any, of work is typically done off-site, particularly in the home; this will permit an analysis of telecommuting, a practice that is growing in importance in many organizations.

4. Subjective perceptions of work and job attitudes. This category includes concepts such as job satisfaction, commitment to work and to the employing organization, and ratings of the relative importance of various conditions of employment. It would also be useful to include "standard" life satisfaction and self-esteem measures in order to provide a baseline for comparisons with other surveys such as the General Social Survey. The survey instrument should offer both employees and management an opportunity to identify and discuss specific areas of dispute or concern. These could include the adequacy of income and fringe benefits, job pressures arising from the pace or content of work, and unsatisfactory working conditions. Measurements are also needed of employees' sense of "distributive justice"—are rewards of work fairly apportioned on the basis of job qualifications and responsibilities? Finally, particular effort is required to elicit information on any special problems faced by blacks, Hispanics, working parents, persons in poverty, and other minorities, in such areas as compensation, recruitment, interaction with fellow workers, and promotion.

5. Household economics. This topic has become increasingly important in recent years due to the growing number of women workers and dual career couples. Questions that need to be investigated include: How do employers respond to the needs of workers for flexible work time?; for day care?; for job sharing?; for extended leaves of absence?; And, what trade-offs are workers willing to make in order to receive some of these benefits?

6. Occupational health and safety. The current significance of issues related to health and safety hazards in the workplace warrants a detailed and extensive examination of these problems, especially since available data on job safety tend to be collected only in aggregated form and are often inadequate. Research has shown that workers' subjective perceptions about health and safety are crucial to whether changes in the work environment are sought; at the same time, the "Hazard Communication Rule" potentially provides workers with a great deal of information about the hazardous substances with which they are working. Examples of issues that need to be studied include: What are the types of job dangers or hazards to which the employee is exposed?; Are safety procedures taught to workers and do they use them in performing their task?; What is the perceived probability of being injured on the job?; What kinds of job pressures does the employee experience?; And, what kinds of physical conditions (heat, unpleasant odors) are associated with the job?

7. Employment stability and job change. Both employees and their employers should be asked about absenteeism and their feelings about job security and mobility. Also, information should be collected on employees' recent employment histories—including recent quits or layoffs and the reasons for any quits—and their intentions to quit their jobs. In addition, information should be collected (from interviews with key informants) on employers' recent experiences with the creation of new jobs, layoffs, or the abolition of jobs, and their intentions to create new jobs (or to abolish jobs).

8. Union membership and worker representation. It is, of course, essential to determine an employee's membership and role in a union. Beyond that, it would be useful to obtain information on the attitudes and expectations that union members have towards their unions. How would union members vote on the continuation of union representation on their current jobs? What are the roles that union members see for their unions in collective bargaining, at the workplace, and in strategic decisions that affect the future of the enterprise? What are the priority issues that members would like their unions to address? Should job safety, for example, be a union issue? How do union members evaluate the performance of their unions and union leaders? What are the attitudes of union members with respect to union representation on corporate boards? What are their attitudes with regard to union "give backs"? Would non-union members vote for or against union representation on their current jobs? Such data could be important in interpreting patterns of responses in other areas, such as worker satisfaction and intentions to quit, acceptance of or resistance to work restructuring, technological change, and changes in compensation and employment practices. The "networks" of which an employee is a part, including but not limited to the union, should be ascertained, because they have been shown to be of considerable importance both for getting a job and for promotion and productivity within the company. Finally, the ability of both union and non-union workers to have their interests and concerns represented in organizational decision-making should be assessed. How widespread, and how effective, are the various employee involvement and participatory processes that have gained attention in recent years? What kinds of issues and what groups of workers do they cover?

9. Job/employment histories. Information should be collected on: the employee's current job and occupation as well as other jobs and occupations he or she has held with the present company; past employment/labor force statuses and occupations the person has held prior to joining the present company; and the kinds and amount of training the person has received in the organization. Information should also be obtained on the employee's starting wage with the company; this would permit an analysis of changes in earnings during the organizational career.

Information on Employers and Workplaces

We have already suggested that some information on the organization of work, as it pertains to the job or work group, can be usefully collected from individual employees. However, most employees are not in a position to know about many of the more macrostructural aspects of the organizations in which they work, and what they do know may be shaped by their own often idiosyncratic perspectives. Rather, many of the things that one needs to know about a company requires direct knowledge of organization-wide personnel policy, finances, and markets—matters of concern to managers but not matters of which workers are necessarily aware. Hence, this information needs to be collected from key informants in the organization.

In addition, information should be collected from public sources whenever possible, including financial information available in annual reports or in the Dun and Bradstreet data bases, market concentration data provided by the Census Bureau's Surveys of Manufacturers and other industries, and similar publicly available information. Moreover, information on individuals and organizations should be supplemented by ecological information such as the local unemployment rate, population size, age and sex distributions, and racial composition; much of this information can also be collected from public data sources. The 1991 National Organizations

Survey included such ecological data on the organization's industry and on the county in which the employee resided.

The kinds of information on organizations that need to be collected include, again listed in no particular order of priority:

1. Basic business characteristics. These include the types of products made or services provided, how large a geographic area the business serves, how many other companies are in competition with the organization, whether the firm faces significant foreign competition, whether it does substantial business with the government, and whether it exports a considerable amount of its goods.

2. Demographic characteristics of the organization's labor force. Interviews with managers are needed to provide a description of the demographic composition of the entire organizational labor force (e.g., race, sex, age, and education). Included here are basic measures of an organization's size (in terms of number of employees as well as assets). It would be desirable to obtain this information for the current year as well as five years ago, in order to provide a sense of whether the organization is growing or declining. Also needed is information on the technologies employed in the organization (see below), in sufficient detail to be able to determine the skill levels required to use these technologies.

3. Employment patterns. This includes characteristics of the organization's labor force such as quit rates, rates of new hires, and rates of job creation. Information also needs to be obtained on layoffs, job security and related issues. For example, have any of the firm's plants closed in the past several years? How are reductions in force accomplished?

4. Compensation structure and job families. Measurements are needed of the entire pay structure, including wage and salary scales, the distribution of employees within brackets, and the rate and extent of movement between pay brackets. If any portion of salaries or wages is tied to profitability, this should also be determined. Moreover, measurements are needed of the system of job classification and personnel management in use, including job qualifications, job descriptions, the presence of job ladders and internal labor markets, expected trajectories for career advancement, and the associations of particular jobs with power, prestige, and privilege. These data will allow the analyst to place the employee in the internal labor market contexts of the organization of which he or she is a member.

5. Benefits. The personnel office should be able to provide information on employee benefits. This information should go beyond that on pension and insurance plans to include data on child care, maternal and paternal leave, stock purchase plans, provision for education and training, exercise facilities, subsidized lunchrooms, discount purchase arrangements, and similar in-kind contributions to employee welfare. The relative contributions of employers and employees to these benefits should be ascertained. In addition, personnel brochures could be collected from the companies that have them.

6. Employment scheduling. This topic is of particular importance in view of the changing composition of the labor force: for example, working parents and dual career couples have special needs regarding the scheduling of their working hours. Issues on which information needs to be gathered include the degree of flexibility of hours of work (for example, the availability of "flextime" and other alternative work schedules), and the degree to which employees have some choice in determining the hours they work.

7. Employment training. In a changing industrial context, organizations may put greater emphasis either on upgrading employee skill levels or on redirecting employees towards entirely new skills. It would be useful to determine the types of training programs that exist within the organization; whether the organization tends to recruit people based on their ability to acquire new skills or on their present skill levels; whether employees are encouraged to acquire training outside the organization; and whether nearby institutions can provide such training. A particularly important issue from the standpoint of public policy is whether employers use public training programs (such as the Job Training Partnership Act) as sources of entry-level employees.

8. Technology. The process(es) in use at the workplace should be identified, with full descriptions of all the technologies employed, giving particular emphasis to automation. What are the consequences of new technologies, particularly computerization, for the match of employees' skill levels with the skill requirements of their jobs (e.g., with respect to blurring the distinction between skilled and unskilled, and between blue-collar and white-collar occupations)? Similarly, what are the consequences of new technologies for the organization of work and for such work-related problems as eyestrain and exposure to toxic chemicals? The need for such information is emphasized by a study sponsored by the Panel on Technology and Women's Employment of the National Academy of Sciences, which suggested that there are no good data on the correlates and consequences of technological change. And, as this report noted (p. 43): ". . . These data [on the employment effects of technological change] must be collected from the firm; there is no other feasible approach."

9. Work restructuring. In the last several years, there has been considerable and growing interest among American managers in restructuring the organization of work, including the sharing of decision-making authority (or even of ownership) with employees. Other innovations include quality control circles, the organization of production in teams, reduction of the routinization of tasks, and profit sharing. The adoption of any such form of work restructuring in an organization needs to be identified, and the extent of employee participation needs to be ascertained. The organization's philosophy and culture with regard to various forms of employee involvement and total quality management should also be assessed.

10. Labor relations. Among the aspects of labor relations that should be described at the organizational level are: the history of an organization's relations with its employees (and with unions, if appropriate); how disputes have been resolved; whether there have been recent union certification or decertification elections; the percentage of employees in the establishment and firm that are unionized; the nature and status of any issues currently in negotiation or under litigation; the formal policies and contracts that govern labor relations; and strategies and informal practices of labor relations. These data will be useful in evaluating which kinds of organizational policies lead to good and bad industrial relations climates and labor-management relations.

11. Formal structural and economic characteristics. These include the organization's span of control, its number of ranks, number of sections and departments, formalization, centralization or decentralization of authority (both formal and actual), and administrative intensity. Also included here is information on the ownership structure of the organization, such as whether or not it is an independent company.

12. Organizational performance. If the organization is a profit center, does it make a profit? What is its market share? What priorities does it give to different competitive strategies such as cost minimization, product or service quality, innovation, etc.? What is its productivity, its rate of growth or decline? How do these rates compare to similar organizations? What is its record on quality? What is its record on safety and how does this compare with similar organizations? Has it been responsible for innovations? Some of the information on performance should also be available from secondary sources, such as the Dun and Bradstreet credit ratings, the COMPUSTAT data base, and the Census Bureau's surveys of manufacturers and other industries.

CONCLUSIONS

Meeting the informational needs of social scientists and policy makers in the area of work and employment requires a research program that links employers and their employees. In this chapter, we have outlined two complementary types of surveys—based on samples of employees and organizations—that constitute key elements of such a research program. Taken together, these surveys would contribute greatly to our understanding of the connections between organizations and the people who work in them.

Some progress has been made toward the development of such a program since this chapter was originally written in 1986. In the United States, the 1991 National Organizations Study has produced data on the human resource practices and policies of a representative national sample of work organizations. While limited in various ways (e.g., only one employee per organization was interviewed), this data set permits the initial examination of many of the issues described above. Moreover, similar studies have been (and are being) carried out in Norway, Sweden, the Netherlands, and other countries, increasing the possibilities for much needed comparative research on these issues.

As enthusiasm and support for such a research program builds, the need to resolve several important conceptual and methodological issues related to these research designs—particularly the organizationally-based surveys—becomes more pressing. For example, it is necessary to define more precisely what we mean by a "population" of organizations. There are advantages to broad, "national" samples of work organizations; such samples provide researchers with data sets that exhibit a great deal of variation in organizational structures. On the other hand, considerable theoretical mileage can often be gained by restricting the organizations studied to those sharing industrial and product market environments, those that are similar in their relations with unions, and so on. Moreover, the need to sample employees and informants within given organizations raises a number of questions about the intersections among organizations, occupations and jobs that are yet to be satisfactorily addressed. We hope that these and related problems will shortly be resolved and that the research program we have described will soon become a reality.

NOTES

1. This chapter is based on the committee's final report, "America at Work: National Surveys of Employees and Employers". We thank the other members of the committee for their contributions to the final report: Clifford C. Clogg; Philip E. Converse; Henry S. Farber; Martin R. Frankel; Robert L. Kahn; Thomas A. Kochan; Robert Kraut; Stanley Lebergott; Roberta Balstad Miller; and Phyllis Moen. We also thank Richard P. Shore, then a member of the Department of Labor's Bureau of Labor-Management Relations and Cooperative Programs, for his efforts in undertaking this project.

2. "Contextual analysis" was Paul F. Lazarsfeld's term for the study of how ecological contexts affect individuals. Lipset, Trow, and Coleman's classic study of the International Typographical Union, *Union Democracy* (1956), and Lazarsfeld and Thielens' *The Academic Mind: Social Scientists in a Time of Crisis* (1958) are early exemplars of this methodology. In the latter study, Mr. Lazarsfeld and his associates—Wagner Thielens, Jr. and David Riesman—interviewed 2,451 social science faculty members in 165 colleges and universities (at least half of the social science faculty members in each institution were interviewed). Their analyses examined variations in faculty opinion and behavior in relation to: (1) individual characteristics, such as age and scholarly productivity; (2) "the climate of opinion" on the campus—characteristics of the local campus that are aggregates of individual characteristics, such as a school's political "permissiveness" measured as an average of attitudes of the local faculty in the sample; and (3) "global characteristics"—collective properties of the school itself, such as its student body size, quality, and public or private control. (See David L. Sills' biography of Lazarsfeld in Vol. 18 of the *International Encyclopedia of the Social Sciences.*)

3. There are, of course, also cultural differences within a country such as the United States: the way things are run in New York City differs from Los Angeles; and the corporate cultures of IBM or Xerox are distinctive in many ways.

4. For example, Hodson (1983) reports that the 6602 persons in his sample of Wisconsin high school graduates were employed by 4200 different companies. In the 1991 National Organizations Survey, only 33 out of 727 persons worked in the same organization as another person in the sample.

REFERENCES

Barton, Allen H. 1968. "Organizations: Methods of Research." In David L. Sills (Ed.) *International Encylopedia of the Social Sciences*, V. II. New York: MacMillan Co. and The Free Press, 334-343.

Bridges, William P. and Wayne J. Villemez. 1986. "Informal Hiring and Income in the Labor Market," *American Sociological Review* 51:574-582.

Granovetter, Mark. 1984. "Small is Bountiful: Labor Markets and Establishment Size." *American Sociological Review* 49:323-334.

Hodson, Randy. 1983. *Workers' Earnings and Corporate Economic Structure*. New York: Academic Press.

Kalleberg, Arne L. 1990. "The Comparative Study of Business Organizations and their Employees: Conceptual and Methodological Issues." *Comparative Social Research* 12:153-175.

Kalleberg, Arne L., Peter V. Marsden, Howard E. Aldrich, and James W. Cassell. 1990. "Comparing Organizational Sampling Frames." *Administrative Science Quarterly* 35:658-688.

Knoke, David, Paul D. Reynolds, Peter V. Marsden, Brenda Miller and Naomi Kaufman. 1991. "The Reliability of Organizational Measures from Multiple-Informant Reports." Unpublished manuscript, Department of Sociology, University of Minnesota.

Lazarsfeld, Paul and Wagner Thielens. 1958. *The Academic Mind: Social Scientists in a Time of Crisis*. Glencoe, IL: Free Press.

le Grand, Carl, Peter Hedström, Ryszard Szulkin and Michael Tåhlin. 1990. "Samspelet Mellan Individ och Struktur på den Svenska Arbetsmarknaden." Paper presented at the NAUT conference, Oslo, 19-21, March.

Lincoln, James R. and Arne L. Kalleberg. 1990. *Culture, Control, and Commitment: A Study of Work Organization and Work Attitudes in the United States and Japan*. Cambridge: Cambridge University Press.

Lipset, Seymour M., Martin A. Trow, and James S. Coleman. 1956. *Union Democracy: The Internal Politics of the International Union.* Glencoe, IL: Free Press.

Mastekaasa, Arne. 1992. "Organizational Contexts and Individual Behavior: Potential and Limitations of the Norwegian Study of Organizations." *Acta Sociologica* 35:141-150.

Panel on Technology and Women's Employment, Committee on Women's Employment and Related Social Issues, Commission on Behavioral and Social Sciences and Education, National Research Council. 1985. *Technology and Employment Effects* [Interim Report]. Washington, D.C.: National Academy Press.

Parcel, Toby L., Robert L. Kaufman, and Leeann Jolly. 1991. "Going Up the Ladder: Multiplicity Sampling to Create Linked Macro-to-Micro Organizational Samples." *Sociological Methodology* 21:43-79.

Contributors

Robert Asher is Professor of History at the University of Connecticut. He is the coeditor of *Autowork*, an anthology on the relations of production in assembly line work in the United States in the twentieth century, to be published in 1995 by the State University of New York Press, and is coeditor of the SUNY Series in American Labor History.

David B. Bills is Associate Professor and Chair of the Department of Planning, Policy, and Leadership Studies at the University of Iowa. In addition to his interests in the changing nature of work, he is conducting research on the response of high schools to teenage employment, employer hiring and promotion practices, and the school-to-work transition. His recent publications include "Educators' Perspectives on Student Employment" (with Lelia Helms and Mustafa Ozcan), *Educational Policy*, forthcoming; "A Survey of Employer Surveys: What We Know about Labor Markets from Talking with Bosses," *Research in Social Stratification and Mobility*, 1992, Vol. 11: 3-31; and "The Mutability of Educational Credentials as Hiring Criteria: How Employers Evaluate Atypically Highly Credentialed Candidates," *Work and Occupations* 1992, 19: 79-95.

Bills currently serves as Director of the Honors Program of the American Sociological Association.

Sandra L. P. Boutelle is a doctoral student in Higher Education Administration at the University of Iowa. She anticipates receiving her Ph.D. in 1995. Her current research is in the area of cardiovascular disease. She presently works as a research assistant in the Department of Pharmacology at the University of Iowa.

303

Nancy DiTomaso is Professor and Chair of the Department of Organization Management on the Faculty of Management at Rutgers, the State University of New Jersey. Her research interests include the management of diversity and change, the management of scientists and engineers, and organizational culture. She has coauthored and coedited four books and has recently published articles in *Leadership Quarterly*, *The Journal of Engineering-Technology Management*, *Research-Technology Management*, and *Journal of Management Studies*.

Judy J. Friedman is an Associate Professor in the Rutgers University Department of Sociology, New Brunswick, NJ. Much of her research focuses on the ways that international economic changes affect U.S. communities, and on the different ways that communities respond to resulting problems.

A current project, one of several that link concentrations of specific resources within a community to specific economic change or to a community action, identifies reasons that U.S. urbanized areas generated different numbers of small, fast-growing businesses through the 1980s. She also investigates reasons for differences among suburbs in residents' opposition to further growth, and the reasons that suburbs with populations 10 percent or more Black have greater fiscal problems than other suburbs.

Friedman's recent publications include "Suburban Variation within Highly Urbanized Regions: The Case of New Jersey," in Mark Baldassare (Ed.) *Suburban Communities*, 1994; "Suburban Landscape: Views of New Jersey Artists," *Visual Sociology*, 8 Fall 1993: 28-39; and "The Importance of Specific Resources to Community Actions; The Case of Foreign Trade Zones," *Social Science Quarterly*, 71, September 1990: 602-618.

Doug Gustafson is Associate Professor of Industrial Technologies at Kirkwood Community College in Cedar Rapids, Iowa. For over ten years, he has taught electronics engineering technology, applied math and physics, and computer programming courses. Before teaching at Kirkwood, he designed Air Force cockpit avionics test stations as an engineer at Rockwell International.

Mr. Gustafson is very involved politically for community colleges in Iowa and is currently serving on the Iowa Department of Education's Community College Strategic Planning Committee. He has served on a statewide committee to articulate crosswalk agreements for all community college electronics programs, and is currently gathering data for researching the optimum electronics curriculum for Iowa's Tech Prep grant program.

Randy Hodson is Professor of Sociology at Indiana University. His research interests are in social stratification and the sociology of work. He is currently studying the maintenance of dignity, autonomy, and power by workers through survey techniques and through analyzing the descriptions provided in workplace ethnographies. He is also investigating ethnic relations and changing patterns of social organization in the former Yugoslavia. His recent publications include "Is Worker Solidarity Undermined by Autonomy and Participation?" *American Sociological Review*, June 1993, 398-416; "Good Soldiers, Smooth Operators, and Saboteurs: A Model of Workplace Behaviors," *Work and Occupations*, August 1991, 271-90; "National Tolerance in the Former Yugoslavia" (with Dusko Sekulic and Garth Massey), *American Journal of Sociology*, March 1994; and "Who Were the Yugoslavs? Failed Sources of a Common Identity in the Former Yugoslavia" (with Dusko Sekulic and Garth Massey), *American Sociological Review*, February 1994. He is co-author with Teresa A. Sullivan of *The Social Organization of Work*, 2nd edition (1995).

Arne L. Kalleberg is a Professor and Chair of Sociology at the University of North Carolina at Chapel Hill. Kalleberg's research specialities are in the Sociology of Work, Labor Force, and the study of Organizations, Occupations and Industries. He has published over fifty scholarly articles and has co-authored or edited three books in these areas. His most recent books are: *Work and Industry: Structures, Markets and Processes* (with Ivar Berg, 1987) and *Culture, Control, and Commitment: A Study of Work Organization and Work Attitudes in the United States and Japan* (with James Lincoln, 1990).

Donald Mayall has done occupational and labor market research for the State of California, Stanford Research Institute, University of California, Berkeley, and other institutions. He has published articles on his research on temporary work and career information. Since retiring from his position as Institutional Research Analyst at Ohlone College, he has been engaged in making compilations of occupational data. His most recent is *The Worker Traits Data Book*, 1994.

A Professor of History at the University of Wisconsin-Parkside, **Stephen Meyer** is the author of *The Five Dollar Day: Labor Management and Social Control in the Ford Motor Company, 1908-1921* and *"Stalin over Wisconsin": The Making and Unmaking of Militant Unionism, 1900-1950*. He is also co-editor of *On the Line: Essays in the History of Auto Work*.

Lawrence Mishel is the Research Director of the Economic Policy Institute and specializes in the fields of productivity, competitiveness, income distribution, labor markets, industrial relations and training and human resource policies. He is the author of various EPI publications, including *Manufacturing Numbers, The State of Working America* (with David M. Frankel) and *Shortchanging Education* (with M. Edith Rasall). His most recent publications are *The Myth of the Coming Labor Shortage* (with Ruy Teixeira) and *The State of Working America, 1992-93* (with Jared Bernstein).

Sue Rosser, a Ph.D. in zoology, is Director of Women's Studies at the University of South Carolina at Columbia and Professor of Family and Preventive Medicine in the Medical School there. She has edited collections and written numerous journal articles on the theoretical and applied problems of women and science, and is author of the books *Teaching About Science and Health from a Feminist Perspective: A Practical Guide* (1986), *Feminism Within the Science and Health Care Professions: Overcoming Resistance* (1988), *Female-Friendly Science* (1990), *Feminism and Biology: A Dynamic Interaction* (1992), *People Friendly Medicine* (1994), and *Teaching the Majority*. She also served as the Latin and North American Co-Editor of *Women's Studies International Forum* from 1989-1993.

Chet Rzonca is an Associate Professor at the University of Iowa. He holds an appointment in the Division of Planning, Policy, and Leadership Studies and is a member of the Higher Education program faculty. His teaching and research interests lie in the area of vocational and technical education as offered in a public setting at both the secondary school and community college levels. He has served as a consultant to the Iowa Department of Education and as director of the Health Occupations Education program at the University. He is currently conducting a needs-assessment survey for the Iowa Department of Education and serves as a third-party evaluator for a federally sponsored project conducted by a local community college for special needs populations. Student selection and attrition at the community college level are among his major research interests.

Ken Spenner is a Professor of Sociology and Psychology and the Director of the Markets and Management Studies Program at Duke University. His research interests include work and personality, career dynamics, technology, and the sociology of markets. His current major research project involves a three-year panel study of organizational survival and adaptation of state-owned enterprises facing market reforms in Eastern Europe. The comparisons center on issues of adaptation versus inertia in manufacturing enterprises, and in particular, which enterprises adapt to the cataclysmic changes, how, and why, including effective uses of advanced technologies.

Ruy A. Teixeira is a sociologist at the Economic Research Service of the U.S. Department of Agriculture, where he studies U.S. labor markets, with special emphasis on the issue of skills shortages in the U.S. economy. He has published widely (with his coauthor Lawrence Mishel of the Economic Policy Institute) in the latter area, including the widely cited *Myth of the Coming Labor Shortage* (1991). He is currently concentrating on the issue of worker skill levels in the U.S. economy, using recent data from the National Assessment of Education Progress (NAEP) and the National Adult Literacy Survey (NALS).

Teixeira is also a recognized expert on American voting behavior and public opinion. In conjunction with that work, he is Director of Political Studies at the Progressive Foundation, a Washington think tank, and a staff associate at the Brookings Institution. His most recent book on American politics is *The Disappearing American Voter* (1992). He is currently working on a project relating economic change to changing attitudes toward government among the middle class.

Author Index

Subject Index